CONTENTS

Acknowledgments   vii
Inside a Unit   viii

UNIT 8   Travel   240
The Past: Part 1

LESSON 1: Simple Past of *Be*: Statements   242
  Reading: *Next Stop... A Travel Blog*   242
    8.1   Simple Past of *Be*: Statements   244
    8.2   Past Time Expressions with *Last, Yesterday,* and *Ago*   245

LESSON 2: Simple Past of *Be*: Questions   249
  Reading: *Iceland*   249
    8.3   Simple Past of *Be*: Yes/No Questions   251
    8.4   Simple Past of *Be*: Wh- Questions   252

LESSON 3: Simple Past: Affirmative Statements   256
  Reading: *Antarctic Adventure*   256
    8.5   Simple Past: Affirmative Statements with Regular Verbs   258
    8.6   Spelling Rules: *-ed* Forms   259
    8.7   Simple Past Irregular Verbs: Group 1   261

LESSON 4: Simple Past: Negative Statements   265
  Reading: *Amazon Explorer Ed Stafford*   265
    8.8   Simple Past: Negative Statements   267
    8.9   Simple Past Irregular Verbs: Group 2   267
    8.10   Simple Past Irregular Verbs: Group 3   268

Review the Grammar   272
Connect the Grammar to Writing: Write a Blog Entry about a Trip   274

UNIT 9   Achievements   276
The Past: Part 2

LESSON 1: Simple Past: Questions   278
  Reading: *Wangari Maathai*   278
    9.1   Simple Past: Yes/No Questions and Short Answers   280
    9.2   Simple Past: Wh- Questions   282
    9.3   Wh- Questions with *Who* or *What*   284

LESSON 2: Past Time Clauses   288
  Reading: *Ernest Shackleton's Expedition*   288
    9.4   Past Time Clauses with *Before* and *After*   290
    9.5   Past Time Clauses with *When*   292

LESSON 3: Past Progressive   297
  Reading: *Tenzing Norgay*   297
    9.6   Past Progressive   299
    9.7   Simple Past vs. Past Progressive   300

Review the Grammar   303
Connect the Grammar to Writing: Write a Biography   306

UNIT 10 Human and Animal Encounters 308
Adjectives and Adverbs

LESSON 1: Adjectives   310
  Reading: *Fennec Foxes*   310
    10.1 Modifying Nouns with Adjectives   312
    10.2 Adjectives with *How* and *What* Questions   314
    10.3 Using Nouns as Adjectives   316

LESSON 2: Adverbs of Manner and Adjectives   320
  Reading: *Gorilla Encounter*   320
    10.4 Adjectives vs. Adverbs of Manner   322
    10.5 Linking Verbs + Adjectives   323
    10.6 Adverbs and Adjectives with the Same Form   324

LESSON 3: Adjectives and Adverbs with *Too, Very*, and *Enough*   329
  Reading: *Save the Iberian Lynx*   329
    10.7 *Too/Very* + Adjective or Adverb   331
    10.8 Adjective or Adverb + *Enough*   332

Review the Grammar   336
Connect the Grammar to Writing: Write about an Animal   338

UNIT 11 Challenges and Abilities   340
Modals: Part 1

LESSON 1: *Can/Could*   342
  Reading: *Look! I can fly!*   342
    11.1 *Can/Could* for Ability and Possibility: Statements   344
    11.2 *Can/Could* for Ability and Possibility: Questions   346

LESSON 2: *Be Able To; Know How To*   352
  Reading: *Winter the Dolphin*   352
    11.3 *Be Able To*   354
    11.4 *Know How To*   356

LESSON 3: *And, But,* and *So*   359
  Reading: *Challenges for Athletes*   359
    11.5 *And, But, So*   361
    11.6 Contrasts after *But*   362

Review the Grammar   367
Connect the Grammar to Writing: Write about a Challenge   370

GRAMMAR EXPLORER 1B

Daphne Mackey
Series Editors: Rob Jenkins and Staci Johnson

NATIONAL GEOGRAPHIC LEARNING | CENGAGE Learning

Australia • Brazil • Japan • Korea • Mexico • Singapore • Spain • United Kingdom • United States

Grammar Explorer 1B

Daphne Mackey

Publisher: Sherrise Roehr
Executive Editor: Laura Le Dréan
Senior Development Editor: Mary Whittemore
Assistant Editor: Vanessa Richards
Senior Technology Product Manager: Scott Rule
Director of Global Marketing: Ian Martin
Marketing Manager: Lindsey Miller
Sr. Director, ELT & World Languages: Michael Burggren
Production Manager: Daisy Sosa
Content Project Manager: Andrea Bobotas
Senior Print Buyer: Mary Beth Hennebury
Cover Designer: 3CD, Chicago
Cover Image: George F. Herben/National Geographic Creative
Compositor: Cenveo® Publisher Services

Copyright © 2015 National Geographic Learning, a part of Cengage Learning

ALL RIGHTS RESERVED. No part of this work covered by the copyright herein may be reproduced, transmitted, stored, or used in any form or by any means graphic, electronic, or mechanical, including but not limited to photocopying, recording, scanning, digitizing, taping, Web distribution, information networks, or information storage and retrieval systems, except as permitted under Section 107 or 108 of the 1976 United States Copyright Act, or applicable copyright law of another jurisdiction, without the prior written permission of the publisher.

> For product information and technology assistance, contact us at
> **Cengage Learning Customer & Sales Support,**
> **1-800-354-9706**
> For permission to use material from this text or product,
> submit all requests online at **www.cengage.com/permissions.**
> Further permissions questions can be e-mailed to
> **permissionrequest@cengage.com.**

Grammar Explorer 1B: 978-1-111-35098-7

National Geographic Learning
20 Channel Center Street
Boston, MA 02210
USA

Cengage Learning is a leading provider of customized learning solutions with office locations around the globe, including Singapore, the United Kingdom, Australia, Mexico, Brazil and Japan.

Cengage Learning products are represented in Canada by Nelson Education, Ltd.

Visit National Geographic Learning online at **NGL.cengage.com**

Visit our corporate website at **www.cengage.com**

Printed in the United States of America
1 2 3 4 5 6 7 8 9 10   17 16 15 14

UNIT 12   Amazing Places   372
Comparative and Superlative Adjectives

LESSON 1: Comparative Adjectives   374
   Reading: *Two Amazing Mountains*   374
   12.1   Comparative Forms of Short Adjectives   376
   12.2   Comparative Forms of Long Adjectives   377
   12.3   Questions with Comparatives   378

LESSON 2: Superlative Adjectives   383
   Reading: *The National Museum of Anthropology*   383
   12.4   Superlative Forms of Short Adjectives   385
   12.5   Superlative Forms of Long Adjectives   386
   12.6   Questions with Superlatives   387

LESSON 3: Possessive Pronouns; *Whose*   391
   Reading: *Frank Gehry: An Unusual Architect*   391
   12.7   Possessive Pronouns   393
   12.8   *Wh-* Questions with *Whose*   394

Review the Grammar   399
Connect the Grammar to Writing: Write a Comparison between Two Places   402

UNIT 13   Customs and Traditions   404
Modals: Part 2

LESSON 1: *Should/Shouldn't*   406
   Reading: *Subject: A Business Trip to Tokyo*   406
   13.1   *Should* for Advisability: Statements   408
   13.2   *Should* for Advisability: Questions   409

LESSON 2: *May* and *Can*; *Have To/Don't Have To*   413
   Reading: *You can't do that here!*   413
   13.3   *Can/May* for Permission   415
   13.4   *Have To* for Necessity: Statements   417
   13.5   *Have To* for Necessity: Questions   418

LESSON 3: *Can/Could/Would:* Polite Requests and Offers   422
   Reading: *Disappearing Cultures*   422
   13.6   *Can You/Could You/Would You* for Polite Requests   424
   13.7   *Can I/Could I/Would You Like* for Polite Offers   425

Review the Grammar   428
Connect the Grammar to Writing: Write a Request   430

UNIT 14 Education and Learning   432
The Future

LESSON 1: Future with *Be Going To* and Present Progressive   434
　Reading: *An Unusual College Experience*   434
　　14.1 Future with *Be Going To*: Statements   436
　　14.2 Future with *Be Going To*: Questions   437
　　14.3 Future with Present Progressive   438

LESSON 2: Future with *Will;* Possibility with *May/Might*   443
　Reading: *The Internet and the Future of Education*   443
　　14.4 Future with *Will:* Statements   445
　　14.5 Future with *Will:* Questions   447
　　14.6 Possibility with *Might/May*   448

LESSON 3: *If* Clauses; Future Time Clauses   452
　Reading: *Color and Test Scores*   452
　　14.7 *If* Clauses   454
　　14.8 Future Time Clauses with *Before, After,* and *When*   455

Review the Grammar 460
Connect the Grammar to Writing: Write a Personal Statement   462

Appendices   A1
Glossary of Grammar Terms   G1
Index   I1
Credits   C1

ACKNOWLEDGMENTS

The authors and publisher would like to thank the following reviewers and contributors:

Gokhan Alkanat, Auburn University at Montgomery, Alabama; **Dorothy S. Avondstondt**, Miami Dade College, Florida; **Heather Barikmo**, The English Language Center at LaGuardia Community College, New York; **Kimberly Becker**, Nashville State Community College, Tennessee; **Lukas Bidelspack**, Corvallis, Oregon; **Grace Bishop**, Houston Community College, Texas; **Mariusz Jacek Bojarczuk**, Bunker Hill Community College, Massachusetts; **Nancy Boyer**, Golden West College, California; **Patricia Brenner**, University of Washington, Washington; **Jessica Buchsbaum**, City College of San Francisco, California; **Gabriella Cambiasso**, Harold Washington College, Illinois; **Tony Carnerie**, English Language Institute, University of California San Diego Extension, California; **Whitney Clarq-Reis**, Framingham State University; **Julia A. Correia**, Henderson State University, Arkansas; **Katie Crowder**, UNT Department of Linguistics and Technical Communication, Texas; **Lin Cui**, William Rainey Harper College, Illinois; **Nora Dawkins**, Miami Dade College, Florida; **Rachel DeSanto**, English for Academic Purposes, Hillsborough Community College, Florida; **Aurea Diab**, Dillard University, Louisiana; **Marta Dmytrenko-Ahrabian**, English Language Institute, Wayne State University, Michigan; **Susan Dorrington**, Education and Language Acquisition Department, LaGuardia Community College, New York; **Ian Dreilinger**, Center for Multilingual Multicultural Studies, University of Central Florida, Florida; **Jennifer Dujat**, Education and Language Acquisition Department, LaGuardia Community College, New York; **Dr. Jane Duke**, Language & Literature Department, State College of Florida, Florida; **Anna Eddy**, University of Michigan-Flint, Michigan; **Jenifer Edens**, University of Houston, Texas; **Karen Einstein**, Santa Rosa Junior College, California; **Cynthia Etter**, International & English Language Programs, University of Washington, Washington; **Parvanak Fassihi**, SHOWA Boston Institute for Language and Culture, Massachusetts; **Katherine Fouche**, The University of Texas at Austin, Texas; **Richard Furlong**, Education and Language Acquisition Department, LaGuardia Community College, New York; **Glenn S. Gardner**, Glendale College, California; **Sally Gearhart**, Santa Rosa Junior College, California; **Alexis Giannopolulos**, SHOWA Boston Institute for Language and Culture, Massachusetts; **Nora Gold**, Baruch College, The City University of New York, New York; **Ekaterina V. Goussakova**, Seminole State College of Florida; **Lynn Grantz**, Valparaiso University, Indiana; **Tom Griffith**, SHOWA Boston Institute for Language and Culture, Massachusetts; **Christine Guro**, Hawaii English Language Program, University of Hawaii at Manoa, Hawaii; **Jessie Hayden**, Georgia Perimeter College, Georgia; **Barbara Inerfeld**, Program in American Language Studies, Rutgers University, New Jersey; **Gail Kellersberger**, University of Houston-Downtown, Texas; **David Kelley**, SHOWA Boston Institute for Language and Culture, Massachusetts; **Kathleen Kelly**, ESL Department, Passaic County Community College, New Jersey; **Dr. Hyun-Joo Kim**, Education and Language Acquisition Department, LaGuardia Community College, New York; **Linda Koffman**, College of Marin, California; **Lisa Kovacs-Morgan**, English Language Institute, University of California San Diego Extension, California; **Jerrad Langlois**, TESL Program and Office of International Programs, Northeastern Illinois University; **Janet Langon**, Glendale College, California; **Olivia Limbu**, The English Language Center at LaGuardia Community College, New York; **Devora Manier**, Nashville State Community College, Tennessee; **Susan McAlister**, Language and Culture Center, Department of English, University of Houston, Texas; **John McCarthy**, SHOWA Boston Institute for Language and Culture, Massachusetts; **Dr. Myra Medina**, Miami Dade College, Florida; **Dr. Suzanne Medina**, California State University, Dominguez Hills, California; **Nancy Megarity**, ESL & Developmental Writing, Collin College, Texas; **Joseph Montagna**, SHOWA Boston Institute for Language and Culture, Massachusetts; **Richard Moore**, University of Washington; **Monika Mulder**, Portland State University, Oregon; **Patricia Nation**, Miami Dade College, Florida; **Susan Niemeyer**, Los Angeles City College, California; **Charl Norloff**, International English Center, University of Colorado Boulder, Colorado; **Gabriella Nuttall**, Sacramento City College, California; **Dr. Karla Odenwald**, CELOP at Boston University, Massachusetts; **Ali Olson-Pacheco**, English Language Institute, University of California San Diego Extension, California; **Fernanda Ortiz**, Center for English as a Second Language, University of Arizona, Arizona; **Chuck Passentino**, Grossmont College, California; **Stephen Peridore**, College of Southern Nevada, Nevada; **Frank Quebbemann**, Miami Dade College, Florida; **Dr. Anouchka Rachelson**, Miami Dade College, Florida; **Dr. Agnieszka Rakowicz**, Education and Language Acquisition Department, LaGuardia Community College, New York; **Wendy Ramer**, Broward College, Florida; **Esther Robbins**, Prince George's Community College, Maryland; **Helen Roland**, Miami Dade College, Florida; **Debbie Sandstrom**, Tutorium in Intensive English, University of Illinois at Chicago, Illinois; **Maria Schirta**, Hudson County Community College, New Jersey; **Dr. Jennifer Scully**, Education and Language Acquisition Department, LaGuardia Community College, New York; **Jeremy Stubbs**, Tacoma, Washington; **Adrianne Thompson**, Miami Dade College, Florida; **Evelyn Trottier**, Basic and Transitional Studies Program, Seattle Central Community College, Washington; **Karen Vallejo**, University of California, Irvine, California; **Emily Young**, Auburn University at Montgomery, Alabama.

From the Author: It has been a pleasure to work with such talented people on this project. I would like to thank Mary Whittemore for her dedication, her sense of humor, and her wonderfully diplomatic way of giving negative feedback. I have enjoyed working with Laura Le Dréan and the team at National Geographic Learning as well as fellow authors Sammi Eckstut, Amy Cooper, and Paul Carne. Lastly, I would like to thank Daria Ruzicka for her hard work and contributions on the initial stages of the project and Diane Piniaris for her outstanding work on the final stage.

Dedication: With love to George and Caroline

INSIDE A UNIT

National Geographic images introduce the unit theme—real world topics that students want to read, write, and talk about.

Units are organized in **manageable lessons**, which ensures students **explore, learn, practice**, and **apply** the grammar.

INSIDE A UNIT

LESSON 1 Simple Present: Affirmative Statements

EXPLORE

1 **READ** the article about Doctor Bugs. Notice the words in **bold**.

Doctor Bugs

Most people don't like bugs, but Doctor Mark Moffet **loves** them! In fact, his nickname is Doctor Bugs. He's a photographer and an entomologist. An entomologist **studies** bugs.

Doctor Moffett's favorite bug is the ant. He **goes** all over the world to study ants. He **watches** them as they **eat**, **work**, **rest**, **sleep**, and **fight**.

He **takes** photographs of the ants. He **lies** on the ground with his camera and **waits** for the right moment. The ants and other bugs often **bite** him, but that doesn't stop Doctor Bugs. He **has** an interesting

▲ Doctor Mark Moffett

Each lesson begins with the ***Explore*** section, featuring a captivating National Geographic article that introduces the target grammar and builds students' knowledge in a variety of academic disciplines.

LESSON 2 Simple Present: Negative Statements and Contractions

EXPLORE

1 **READ** the article about life on the International Space Station. Notice the words in **bold**.

Life on the Space Station

Astronauts on the International Space Station have a busy schedule. Every day they wake up at 7:00 GMT.[1] **From 7:00 to 8:00,** they wash up and eat breakfast. **At 8:00 in the morning,** they call Ground Control[2] in their countries. After they talk to Ground Control, their workday begins. The astronauts **don't do** the same thing every day. Their schedules change every week.

The astronauts **don't work** all the time. Each day they exercise for an hour **in the morning** and an hour **in the afternoon**. After dinner, they have free time. Then, it's time to go to sleep. Sometimes this isn't easy because the sun rises and sets 16 times each day on the space station.

The astronauts' work **doesn't end** on Friday. They work a half day **on Saturday** and all day **on Sunday**. Astronauts are very busy people.

[1] **GMT:** Greenwich Mean Time
[2] **Ground Control:** People on Earth who work with astronauts in space.

◀ The International Space Station (ISS)

80 SIMPLE PRESENT: PART 1

Verbs + Objects **LESSON 3**

elephant keepers in Kenya. Notice the words in **bold**.

They're so cute! Where are

keepers. They work at a place for orphan[1] elephants in
nts, take care of **them**, and even play **soccer** with them.
n interesting job.

eed to feed **the baby elephants** every three hours.

o. The keepers sleep in buildings with the baby
rom the article. One of the keepers says, "Every three
d pull **your blankets**[2] off. The elephants are our alarms."
ant to read **that article**.
e dead.

▼ Baby elephants and elephant keepers in Nairobi, Kenya

88 SIMPLE PRESENT: PART 1

UNIT 3 LESSON 3 97

INSIDE A UNIT ix

INSIDE A UNIT

In the **Explore** section, students discover how the grammar structures are used in the readings and in real academic textbooks.

The **Learn** section features clear grammar charts and explanations followed by controlled practice of the grammar forms.

x INSIDE A UNIT

INSIDE A UNIT

In the **Practice** section, students practice the grammar using all four skills through communicative activities that prepare them for academic work.

8 SPEAK. Work with a partner. Change the affirmative imperatives to negative imperatives. Student A reads the affirmative. Student B says the negative. Then change roles.

Student A: *Eat in the library.*
Student B: *Don't eat in the library.*

1. Eat in the library.
2. Be late for work.
3. Sit in that seat.
4. Use the elevator.
5. Call him at midnight.
6. Open the window.
7. Park your car here.
8. Feed the animals.
9. Close your book.
10. Use your phone in class.

PRACTICE

9 SPEAK & WRITE. Work with a partner. What do these signs mean? Match with the correct sign below.

a. Stop.
b. Do not use your cell phone.
c. Be careful.
d. Do not feed the animals.
e. Do not eat or drink.
f. Do not enter.
g. Drive slowly.
h. Be quiet.

1. a   2. ___   3. ___
5. ___   6. ___   7. ___

108 SIMPLE PRESENT: PART 1

10 EDIT. Read the advice. Find and correct five more errors with imperatives.

How to Be a Good Employee

1. Be on time. ~~Doesn't~~ Don't be late.
2. Be friendly and polite to customers. You say "thank you."
3. Don't rude to coworkers.
4. Don't leaves work early. Stay until five o'clock.
5. Do not you use your cell phone in meetings.
6. Doesn't play computer games at work.

11 Complete the conversations with affirmative or negative imperatives. Use the verbs in the box. You can use each verb more than once.

| call | drink | get | go | quit | save | stay | take |

1. A: I want a job at a computer company, but I also want to take a psychology course.
   B: _Don't take_ a psychology course. _____ a course in math or computer science.
2. A: I don't like my job. I want to quit.
   B: _____ your job now. _____ another job first.
3. A: I have a cold. I need to go to a hospital.
   B: _____ to a hospital. Just _____ a doctor or _____ at home and _____ hot tea.
4. A: I'm tired. I need more sleep.
   B: Well, _____ to bed early, and _____ coffee at night.
5. A: I don't have very much money, but I want to go shopping.
   B: _____ shopping. _____ home and

UNIT 3 LESSON 4 109

12 LISTEN, SPEAK & WRITE.

CD1-41

A Read the list of activities. Then listen to advice on how to be an underwater photographer. Does the speaker think each activity is a good idea or a bad idea? Check (✓) the correct column.

	Good Idea	Bad Idea
1. Swim a lot.		
2. Learn about the ocean.		
3. Try to catch fish.		
4. Choose the right camera.		
5. Practice in a swimming pool.		
6. Jump into the water with your camera.		
7. Leave your camera in the sun.		
8. Have fun.		

▼ A hawksbill turtle

B Compare your answers from exercise A with a partner.

C Complete the chart with information from exercise A. Use affirmative and negative imperatives.

| How to Be an Underwater Photographer: Advice ||
Good Ideas	Bad Ideas
Swim a lot.	

Students use their new language and critical thinking skills in the **Apply** section.

13 APPLY.

A Work with a group. Discuss ways to improve your English. Use affirmative and negative imperatives.

Read in English.
Don't miss class.

B Make a chart in your notebook. Organize your ideas from exercise **A** in a chart. Use affirmative and negative imperatives. Use the chart from exercise **12C** as a model.

C As a group, present your advice to the class.

Improve your English! Here is our advice. Read in English. . . .

110 SIMPLE PRESENT: PART 1

INSIDE A UNIT xi

INSIDE A UNIT

Review the Grammar gives students the opportunity to consolidate the grammar in their reading, writing, listening, and speaking.

xii INSIDE A UNIT

INSIDE A UNIT

Connect the Grammar to Writing

1 READ & NOTICE THE GRAMMAR.

A Read the paragraph. What is the writer's advice for new teachers? Discuss with a partner.

My Job as a Teacher

I am a teacher. I work from 8:00 a.m. to 1:30 p.m. I teach four English classes. In class, I write on the board. I ask a lot of questions. I use pictures when I teach vocabulary. I don't arrive late. At home, I plan my lessons. I correct homework and tests. My advice for new teachers – learn your students' names on the first day.

GRAMMAR FOCUS

In the paragraph in exercise **A**, the writer uses the simple present to talk about habits or routines and schedules.

I **work** from 8:00 a.m. to 1:30 p.m.
I **don't arrive** late.

B Read the paragraph in exercise **A** again. Underline the verbs in the simple present. Circle the imperative. Then compare your answers with a partner.

C Complete the chart with information from the paragraph in exercise **A**. What does a teacher do in class? At home?

The Job of a Teacher	
In Class	At Home
She asks a lot of questions.	

Advice: Learn your students' names.

114 SIMPLE PRESENT: PART 1

Connect the Grammar to Writing provides students with a clear model and a guided writing task where they first notice and then use the target grammar as it is used naturally in one of a variety of writing genres.

Write about a Job

2 BEFORE YOU WRITE. Complete the chart with information about your job as a student. What do you do in class? At home? What advice do you have for new students? Use the chart from exercise **1C** as a model.

My Job as a Student	
In Class	At Home

Advice:

3 WRITE a paragraph about your job as a student. Give advice for new students. Use the information from your chart in exercise **2** and the paragraph in exercise **1A** to help you.

WRITING FOCUS   Indenting Paragraphs

Good writers indent the first line of a paragraph. To indent, begin the first line of a paragraph five spaces to the right.

   I am a teacher. I work from 8:00 a.m. to 1:30 p.m. I teach four English classes. In class, I write on the board. I ask a lot of questions.

4 SELF ASSESS. Read your paragraph. Underline the verbs in the simple present. Then use the checklist to assess your work.

☐ I did not put *be* in front of other verbs in the simple present. [3.1, 3.3]
☐ The verbs in the simple present are spelled correctly. [3.3]
☐ I used the base form of the verb for imperatives. [3.9, 3.10]
☐ The first line of my paragraph is indented. [WRITING FOCUS]

UNIT 3   CONNECT THE GRAMMAR TO WRITING   115

INSIDE A UNIT   **xiii**

UNIT **8** Travel

The Past: Part 1

▶ Highway 101, Oregon, USA

Lesson 1
page 242

Simple Past of
Be: Statements

Lesson 2
page 249

Simple Past of
Be: Questions

Lesson 3
page 256

Simple Past:
Affirmative
Statements;
Irregular Verbs
(Group 1)

Lesson 4
page 265

Simple Past:
Negative
Statements;
Irregular Verbs
(Groups 2-3)

Review the Grammar
page 272

Connect the Grammar to Writing
page 274

LESSON 1 Simple Past of *Be:* Statements

EXPLORE

1 READ the travel blog about the Atlas Mountains. Notice the words in **bold**.

Next stop...
A Travel Blog

June 2
The Atlas Mountains

I'm on the train again. I **wasn't** online **yesterday,** so I have a lot of stories for you today. Our three days in Marrakech **were** great. The city **was** exciting, but it **was** very noisy. It **was** also very hot. **On Wednesday**, it **was** 100 degrees Fahrenheit (38 degrees Celsius)! We visited Djemaa el Fna Square. It's a huge outdoor market with food and entertainment. It **was** a very interesting place.

On Thursday, we hired a guide[1] and drove to the Atlas Mountains. The Atlas mountain range is amazing! It's more than 1200 miles (2000 kilometers) long. It crosses Morocco, Algeria, and Tunisia. The weather in the mountains **was** sunny and cool, and there **was** snow on the tops of the mountains.

Our hikes in the mountains **weren't** easy, but the views **were** incredible. Our guide, Simo, **was** great. He **was** helpful and funny. There are some small villages in the Atlas Mountains. The people there **were** very friendly. In one village, we had lunch in a family's home. We had fresh bread with honey and mint tea. It **was** delicious!

Next stop: The Sahara!

[1] **guide:** a person who shows the way and gives information, especially to tourists

Recent posts:
- **Atlas Mountains**
- Marrakech!
- Rabat
- Fez
- Tangier
- Seville

2 CHECK. Read each statement about the travel blog. Then circle **T** for *true* or **F** for *false*.

1. On Wednesday it was very hot in Marrakech.   T   F
2. It was cloudy in the Atlas Mountains.   T   F
3. The hikes in the mountains were easy.   T   F
4. Simo wasn't a helpful guide.   T   F
5. The fresh bread was delicious.   T   F

3 DISCOVER. Complete the exercises to learn about the grammar in this lesson.

A Find these sentences in the travel blog from exercise **1**. Write the missing words.

1. I'_____ on the train again.
2. I _____ online yesterday.
3. Our three days in Marrakech _____ great.
4. There _____ some small villages in the Atlas Mountains.
5. Our guide, Simo, _____ great.

B Which sentences in exercise **A** talk about the present? Which sentences talk about the past? Discuss with your classmates and teacher.

▼ The village of Ait Benhaddou, Atlas Mountains, Morocco

UNIT 8   LESSON 1   243

LEARN

8.1 Simple Past of *Be*: Statements

Affirmative

Subject	Be	
I He She It Amy	was	in Miami yesterday.
We You They Carl and Ann	were	

Negative

Subject	Be	
I He She It Amy	was not wasn't	in Miami yesterday.
We You They Carl and Ann	were not weren't	

1. The verb *be* has two forms in the past: *was* and *were*.	**I was** sick yesterday. They **were** in Hong Kong last week.
2. The contractions *wasn't* and *weren't* are usually used in conversation and informal writing.	A: Our hike yesterday was wonderful. It **wasn't** very difficult, and there **weren't** any bugs. B: Nice!

4 Complete each statement with *was* or *were*.

1. Our trip ____was____ very exciting.
2. The city _____ noisy.
3. Our guide _____ friendly.
4. The mountains _____ beautiful.
5. The weather _____ cool and sunny.
6. I _____ tired yesterday.
7. There _____ some villages in the mountains.
8. The people _____ friendly.
9. Our hikes _____ easy.
10. You _____ in the mountains yesterday.

5 SPEAK. Work with a partner. Make the sentences from exercise **4** negative.

1. *Our trip wasn't very exciting.*

8.2 Past Time Expressions with *Last*, *Yesterday*, and *Ago*

1. Time expressions with *last*, *yesterday*, and *ago* tell when an action or event happened in the past.	I was at home **last night**. They weren't in class **yesterday**. He was here ten minutes **ago**.
2. Use time expressions at the beginning or end of a sentence. Do not use time expressions in the middle of a sentence.	✓ I was in Seoul **last week**. ✓ **Last week** I was in Seoul. ✗ I was last week in Seoul.
3. Use *last* with *night*, *week*, *month*, and *year*. Do not use *the* before *last* in these time expressions.	It was cold **last night**. We were in Beijing **last week**. **Last month** she was in Colombia. There were a lot of people on the tour **last year**. ✓ I was in my hotel room **last night**. ✗ I was in my hotel room the last night.
4. Use *yesterday* alone or with times of day (except *night*).	The weather was beautiful **yesterday**. **Yesterday morning** it was very windy. They were on a tour **yesterday afternoon**. ✓ He was at home **yesterday evening**. ✗ He was at home yesterday night.
5. Use *ago* after a period of time. Do not use *before*.	✓ **Two weeks ago** they were in Madrid. ✓ We were in India **eight months ago**. ✗ We were in India before eight months.

6 Complete each sentence with *yesterday*, *last*, or *ago*.

1. I was in New York _____last_____ night.

2. Two years _____ I was in Tokyo.

3. We were on a tour _____ afternoon.

4. Many years _____ Frank was a tour guide.

5. Mike wasn't in Hong Kong four years _____.

6. They were on vacation in Turkey _____ week.

7. We were in London three weeks _____.

8. Airplane tickets weren't this expensive ten years _____.

9. I was really tired _____ night after the hike.

10. We were at a Moroccan restaurant _____ evening.

PRACTICE

7 LISTEN to each sentence. Is it past or present? Put a check (✓) in the correct column.

	Present	Past		Present	Past
1.	☐	☐	5.	☐	☐
2.	☐	☐	6.	☐	☐
3.	☐	☐	7.	☐	☐
4.	☐	☐	8.	☐	☐

8 READ, WRITE & SPEAK.

A Read the travel plan and Lila's notes about her trip to Guatemala. Then complete the sentences in her journal. Use the past of *be* and the information in Lila's notes.

Your Visit to Guatemala

Day 1
Arrive Guatemala City
Antigua by bus
lunch and dinner at the hotel

Day 2
Antigua
Tour of 18th-century ruins

Day 3
Bus to Lake Atitlan

Day 4
Boat trip around Lake Atitlan

Day 5
Bus to Chichicastenango ("Chi Chi")

Day 6
Market in Chi Chi
Bus back to Guatemala City

Day 7
Tikal by plane

Day 8
Tikal, Guatemala City Depart

Notes . . .

short bus ride
hotel—very nice;
food—not very good

ruins—beautiful!
restaurant food—delicious

scenery—amazing

villages—interesting

drive—not fun!
road—very narrow
bus driver—friendly;
bus ride—scary!

prices—very good
weather—not good,
cool and rainy

Tikal—crowded

Very tired!

Journal

Day 1
The bus ride _was short_
The hotel _____
but the food _____.

Days 2-4
The ruins of Antigua _____
The food at the restaurant _____
The scenery at Lake Atitlan _____.

The villages _____

Days 5-6
The drive _____ because the road _____
The bus driver _____,
but the bus ride _____

In Chi Chi, the prices _____.
The weather _____ because _____.

Days 7-8
Tikal _____.
On the last day, I _____,
but it was a great trip!

◀ Lake Atitlan and Toliman volcano, Guatemala, Central America

B Work with a partner. Choose two days from Lila's trip and tell your partner about them. Use the information from exercise **A** and some of your own ideas.

Day 1: The bus ride was short, and the hotel was very nice. The food wasn't very good.

C Discuss these questions with your partner.

1. What do you think? Was this a good trip?

2. Do you prefer to visit cities or small towns? Why?

9 SPEAK. Work with a partner. Say sentences with time expressions. Use the past of *be*. Talk about the weather or people using the past.

| an hour ago | yesterday | last week | last year |

Student A: *Yesterday the weather was good.*   Student B: *I wasn't in this class last year.*

10 EDIT. Read the e-mail. Find and correct five more errors with the past of *be* and time expressions.

Hi Marco,

Greetings from Italy! We were in Rome ~~before~~ two days ^ago^. Now we're in Florence. We're having a great time! Yesterday the weather is rainy, so it was a good day to visit the Uffizi. The Uffizi is a huge art museum. We was there for five hours. I was really tired yesterday night. The last week we were in Venice. There weren't many tourists, so it weren't very crowded. It's a beautiful city. Have a great summer, and please say hello to your family.

Todd

11 LISTEN & SPEAK.

A Read each statement. Then listen to the conversation about a trip. Choose the correct word(s) to complete each sentence.

1. They were on a **skiing** / **(camping)** trip.

2. Their trip was **yesterday** / **last week** / **a month ago**.

3. Selena **was** / **wasn't** happy about the trip.

4. Nick **was** / **wasn't** happy about the trip.

B Listen again. What do Selena and Nick say about each topic? Write **S** if Selena uses the word and **N** if Nick uses it.

1. The camping trip	terrible	N	fun	S
2. The weather on Friday	warm	___	wet	___
3. The weather on Saturday and Sunday	sunny	___	wet	___
4. The insects	terrible	___	not bad	___
5. The hike	easy	___	difficult	___
6. The views	amazing	___	incredible	___

C Write three sentences about Selena's ideas and three sentences about Nick's ideas. Use words from the chart in exercise **B**.

Selena 1. The camping trip was fun.

2. _____

3. _____

Nick 1. _____

2. _____

3. _____

D Work with a partner. Role-play a conversation between Selena and Nick. Use ideas from exercises **B** and **C**. Student A, take the part of Selena. Student B, take the part of Nick.

Student A: *Our trip was really fun!*   Student B: *No, it wasn't. It was terrible!*

12 APPLY.

A Talk about your own experience on a trip. Use the topics from the list to help you.

| when | the food | the weather | where | the people | the scenery |

I was in Costa Rica. The trip was last summer…

B Write six sentences about the place you visited. Use the past of *be*.

1. I was in Costa Rica.

2. _____

3. _____

4. _____

5. _____

6. _____

248 THE PAST: PART 1

Simple Past of *Be*: Questions — LESSON 2

EXPLORE

1 READ the conversation. Notice the words in **bold**.

Iceland

Ben: Hi, Andy. **How was your vacation?**
Andy: It was great.
Ben: **Were you in Denmark?**
Andy: No, I was in Iceland.
Ben: Really? I was there two years ago.
Andy: I didn't know that. **Were you on a tour?**
Ben: No, I was with my brother. It was a lot of fun.
Andy: **Were you there in the summer?**
Ben: No, we were there in March.
Andy: In March? **How was the weather?**
Ben: It was cold, but it was a good time. We saw the Northern Lights.
Andy: Wow. **Were they amazing?**
Ben: Yeah, they really were. The sky was green and yellow.
Andy: Interesting! We didn't see them.
Ben: Well, the best time to see them in Iceland is from September to April. **When were you there?**
Andy: In July, so there was daylight almost all of the time.
Ben: That's right. The sun only sets for a few hours during the summer. **Was that strange?**
Andy: Yeah, it was. It was a great trip. I want to go back sometime.
Ben: Me, too.

◀ The Northern Lights over icebergs off the black sand beach of Breiarmerkursandur, Iceland

2 CHECK. Circle the correct words to complete each statement.

1. Ben was in Iceland **two months ago** / **two years ago**.
2. He **was** / **wasn't** on a tour.
3. The weather in March was **cold** / **warm**.
4. Andy was in Iceland **in July** / **in March**.
5. Andy's trip was **great** / **terrible**.

3 DISCOVER. Complete the exercises to learn about the grammar in this lesson.

A Find these questions in the conversation from exercise **1** on page 249. Write the missing words.

1. How _____ your vacation?
2. _____ in Denmark?
3. _____ on a tour?
4. How _____ the weather?
5. When _____ there?
6. _____ that strange?

B Look at the questions from exercise **A**. Then choose the correct word to complete the statement below. Discuss your answer with your classmates and teacher.

The subject comes **before** / **after** *was* and *were* in questions.

▼ The fishing village of Djupivogur, Iceland

250 THE PAST: PART 1

LEARN

8.3 Simple Past of *Be*: *Yes/No* Questions

Yes/No Questions

Was/Were	Subject	
Was	he / she / it / the information	helpful?
Were	we / you / they / the guides	

Short Answers

	Affirmative		Negative	
Yes,	he / she / it	was.	he / she / it	wasn't.
	we / you / they	were.	we / you / they	weren't.

(No,)

Remember: The verb comes before the subject in *Yes/No* questions with *be*.

Were you in Mexico last week?
Was the weather nice?

REAL ENGLISH

People usually give more information after short answers to *Yes/No* questions.

A: *Were you in Tokyo last week?*
B: *No, I wasn't. I was in Kyoto.*

A: *Was Alice absent yesterday?*
B: *Yes, she was. She was sick.*

4 Change each statement to a *Yes/No* question. Then complete each short answer.

1. He was with a tour.
   A: ___Was he___ with a tour?
   B: No, ___he wasn't.___

2. He was in Iceland two years ago.
   A: _____ in Iceland two years ago?
   B: Yes, _____.

3. They were on vacation last week.
   A: _____ on vacation last week?
   B: No, _____.

4. The scenery was beautiful.
   A: _____ the scenery beautiful?
   B: Yes, _____.

5. There were a lot of tourists.
   A: _____ a lot of tourists?
   B: Yes, _____.

6. It was cold in Iceland.
   A: _____ cold in Iceland?
   B: Yes, _____.

7. We were there in the winter.
   A: _____ there in the winter?
   B: No, _____.

8. The Northern Lights were beautiful.
   A: _____ beautiful?
   B: Yes, _____.

8.4 Simple Past of *Be*: *Wh-* Questions

Wh- Word	Was / Were	Subject		Answers
Who	was	your guide?		Carlos.
Where	was	Barbara	yesterday?	In Rome.
What	was	your guide's name?		Erik.
When	were	you	in Norway?	Last summer.
Why	were	they	In Iceland?	Because their aunt lives there.
How	was	the weather	in Sydney?	Warm and sunny.

1. **Remember:** Use *Wh-* questions to ask for specific information.

   A: **When** were they in Venice?
   B: Last month.

   A: **Where** was your hotel?
   B: Near the airport.

2. **Remember:** When a *Who* question is about a subject, use the singular form of the verb even if the answer is plural.

   A: **Who** was on vacation last week?
   B: Margo and Fabian.

3. **Remember:** In conversation, the answers to *Why* questions often begin with *because*. In writing, use complete sentences to answer *Why* questions.

   A: Why was he in Hong Kong last week?
   B: Because he had a business meeting.

   He was in Hong Kong last week because he had a meeting.

5 Complete each of A's questions with *When, Where, What, How, Who,* or *Why*. Use each of B's answers to help you.

1. A: _____How_____ was your trip? B: It was wonderful!

2. A: _____ was your trip? B: Last summer.

3. A: _____ was the flight late? B: The weather was bad.

4. A: _____ was your hotel? B: Near the airport.

5. A: _____ were you yesterday? B: I was at the beach.

6. A: _____ was he angry? B: Because his flight was late.

7. A: _____ weren't you at work last week? B: I was on vacation.

8. A: _____ was the weather in Hawaii? B: It was great.

9. A: _____ was the temperature yesterday? B: It was 90 degrees.

10. A: _____ was your hotel? B: It was OK.

6 Put the words in the correct order to make questions.

1. When / in China / he / was When was he in China?
2. late / Why / the tour bus / was _____
3. in India / was / How / the weather _____
4. the tour / Was / interesting _____
5. your last vacation / was / When _____
6. Where / you / two hours ago / were _____
7. were / last summer / Where / you _____
8. absent / were / Why / our classmates _____
9. last / you / on vacation / week / Were _____
10. you / Where / were / born _____

7 SPEAK. Work with a partner. Ask and answer questions 5-10 from exercise **6**.

Student A: *When was your last vacation?*

Student B: *Two months ago.*

PRACTICE

8 LISTEN and choose the correct answer to each question.

1. a. In November.   b. In Canada.   c. Yes, it was.
2. a. Last year.   b. In India.   c. No, I wasn't.
3. a. I was in Montreal.   b. France.   c. Yes, it was great.
4. a. To Thailand.   b. Great!   c. Yes, it was.
5. a. They were sick.   b. In Dubai.   c. No, they weren't.
6. a. In London.   b. Yes, they were.   c. No, it wasn't.
7. a. My sister.   b. At the hotel.   c. Yes, we were.
8. a. It was expensive.   b. Near the airport.   c. No, it wasn't.
9. a. Yes, she was.   b. From Spain.   c. Maria.
10. a. Warm and sunny.   b. Yes, it was.   c. In Iceland.

UNIT 8   LESSON 2   253

9 Complete the conversation. Use *Wh-* questions, *Yes/No* questions, and answers. Then listen and check your answers.

Ann: Hi, Beth. (1) _Where were_ you last week? (2) _____ you in California again on business?

Beth: No, (3) _____. I was in Africa.

Ann: Africa? (4) _____ you in Africa?

Beth: I (5) _____ on vacation.

Ann: (6) _____ you in Africa?

Beth: I (7) _____ in South Africa, Botswana, and Zambia.

Ann: (8) _____ you on a safari¹?

Beth: Yes, (9) _____. It was amazing. We saw a lot of zebras, some giraffes, . . . and a few lions, too.

Ann: Lions? Wow! (10) _____ you afraid?

Beth: No, I (11) _____. It was fun and really interesting.

¹ A **safari** is a trip to look at wild animals.

10 READ, WRITE & SPEAK.

A Read the paragraph about David Livingstone. Then use the words in the box to write *Wh-* questions. The underlined words are the answers.

| what | when | where | who | why |

DAVID LIVINGSTONE

David Livingstone was (1) <u>a famous traveler</u>. He was from (2) <u>Scotland</u>. He was interested in (3) <u>science, medicine, and nature</u>. He was also very interested in Africa. His first trip (4) <u>to Africa</u> was in 1841. His most famous trip was (5) <u>in 1855</u>. This trip was (6) <u>to the great falls on the Zambezi River</u>. His guides were from the Makololo tribe. The name of the falls was (7) <u>Mosi oa Tunya</u>. Livingstone gave the falls an English name. The English name was Victoria (8) <u>because Victoria was the queen of England</u>.

1. _Who was David Livingstone?_
2. _____
3. _____
4. _____
5. _____
6. _____
7. _____
8. _____

254 THE PAST: PART 1

▲ Victoria Falls between Zambia and Zimbabwe

B Work with a partner. Compare your answers from exercise **A**. Then practice asking and answering your questions.

Student A: *Who was David Livingstone?* Student B: *He was a famous traveler.*

11 LISTEN & SPEAK.

A Listen to the conversation. Then match each question with the correct answer.

Column A

1. Where was Jackie all summer? _e_
2. Where was Neeta in June? ___
3. Was Neeta's summer great? ___
4. Why was Neeta in India? ___
5. Was Jackie's summer fun? ___
6. Why was Jackie's summer boring? ___
7. Who was at the wedding? ___
8. How was the weather in India? ___

Column B

a. No, it wasn't.
b. Yes, it was.
c. For a wedding.
d. It was hot.
e. In Springfield.
f. In India.
g. Most of her friends were away.
h. All of Neeta's relatives.

B Work with a partner. Close your books. Ask and answer the questions from exercise **A**.

Student A: *Where was Jackie all summer?* Student B: *In Springfield.*

12 APPLY.

A Think of a special event in the past, such as a graduation, a wedding, or a birthday. In your notebooks, use these words as a guide and write notes about the event.

| What?   When?   Where?   Who . . . there?   . . . fun? |

B Work with a partner. Ask and answer questions about your special events. Use the past of *be*.

Student A: *What was the special event?* Student B: *It was my cousin's graduation.*
Student A: *When was it?* Student B: *In May.*

UNIT 8 LESSON 2 **255**

LESSON 3   Simple Past: Affirmative Statements

EXPLORE

1 READ the article about Andrew Evan's trip. Notice the words in **bold**.

Antarctic Adventure

Andrew Evans **had** an interesting idea. He **wanted** to travel to Antarctica. He also **wanted** a real adventure, so he **looked** at a map and **planned** a trip from his home in Washington, D.C. all the way to Antarctica.

On January 1, 2010, he **got** on a bus in Washington, D.C. and **started** his adventure. He **traveled** through nine states in the United States and 14 countries. He **took** 40 different buses and **spent** more than a thousand dollars on bus fares. Of course, the road **didn't go** all the way to Antarctica. It **ended** in Ushuaia, Argentina. From there, Andrew **traveled** by ship. Finally, on February 14, 2011, he **arrived** in Antarctica. He was very happy!

Andrew **traveled** for ten weeks. Thousands of people **followed** him online. He **shared** his travel experiences with them. He **took** photographs of the scenery and local people and **posted** them on his website. National Geographic **named** Andrew the *digital nomad*.[1] He's always traveling, and he's always connected to the Internet.

[1] **nomad:** a person who travels from place to place

▶ Andrew took this interesting photo when his bus driver stopped for a break on the Salar de Uyuni, the world's largest salt flat, Bolivia.

256   THE PAST: PART 1

2 CHECK. Read each statement about Andrew Evans' trip to Antarctica. Circle **T** for *true* or **F** for *false*.

1. Andrew Evans wanted an adventure. — T F
2. Andrew Evans started his trip in Florida. — T F
3. He traveled on 14 buses. — T F
4. He arrived in Antarctica in March. — T F
5. Andrew shared his travel experiences online. — T F

3 DISCOVER. Complete the exercises to learn about the grammar in this lesson.

A Find these sentences in the article from exercise **1**. Write the missing words.

1. He _____ to travel to Antarctica.
2. Andrew _____ for ten weeks.
3. Thousands of people _____ him online.

B Look at the verbs in the sentences from exercise **A**. What ending do all of these verbs have? What does this ending show? Discuss with your classmates and teacher.

UNIT 8 LESSON 3 257

LEARN

8.5 Simple Past: Affirmative Statements with Regular Verbs

Subject	Verb	
I	hiked	a lot on my vacation.
You	arrived	late last night.
He	started	his trip in August.
She	traveled	to Australia last summer.
We	walked	three miles yesterday morning.
You	visited	some interesting places in Mexico.
They	stayed	at a nice hotel.

1. Use the simple past to talk about completed actions.	I **finished** my homework this morning. She **worked** until seven-thirty last night.
2. For most regular verbs, add *-d* or *-ed* to the base form of the verb.*	They **lived** here twenty years ago. I **called** Lisa yesterday.
3. The simple past has the same form for all subjects.	I **walked** to the store. He **walked** to the bus stop.
4. Do not use *was* or *were* with another verb in the simple past.	✓ I visited my grandparents last week. ✗ I was visited my grandparents last week.

*See Chart 8.6 on page 259 for information on spelling rules for *-ed* forms.

4 Read each sentence and underline the verb. Is it present or past? Put a check (✓) in the correct column.

	Present	Past
1. Andrew <u>planned</u> a bus trip to Antarctica.	☐	✓
2. His trip starts in Washington, D.C.	☐	☐
3. The bus goes through the United States.	☐	☐
4. He started his adventure in August.	☐	☐
5. He traveled for ten weeks.	☐	☐
6. Thousands of people followed his adventure.	☐	☐
7. They like the stories on his Web site.	☐	☐
8. He posted his photographs online.	☐	☐
9. Andrew travels a lot.	☐	☐
10. He shares his adventures online.	☐	☐

8.6 Spelling Rules: -ed Forms

Rule	Example	
1. For most verbs, add -ed to the base form of the verb.	pack	I pack**ed** my suitcase.
2. For verbs that end in silent e, add -d.	hike	We hike**d**.
3. For one-syllable verbs that end in a consonant + vowel + consonant (CVC*), double the final consonant and add -ed.	plan	They plan**ned** their trip.
4. For two-syllable verbs that end in CVC and have the stress on the second syllable, double the final consonant and add -ed.	prefer	We prefer**red** the first hotel.
5. For two-syllable verbs that end in CVC and have the stress on the first syllable, add -ed but do not double the final consonant.	travel visit order	She travel**ed** from Mexico to Argentina last year. We visit**ed** our grandparents last weekend. I order**ed** a new backpack online.
6. For verbs that end in a consonant + vowel + -w, -x, or -y, add -ed but do not double the final consonant.	follow fix play	We follow**ed** our guide. He fix**ed** our car. They play**ed** tennis on their vacation.
7. For verbs that end in consonant + -y, change the -y to -i and add -ed.	study	I stud**ied** Japanese before my trip.

* consonant + vowel + consonant

5 Write the simple past of each verb in parentheses.

1. I ____carried____ (carry) my backpack everywhere.
2. She _____ (post) her photos online last night.
3. Jack _____ (order) a new camera before his trip.
4. We _____ (stop) at a nice restaurant for lunch.
5. They _____ (climb) two mountains last week.
6. We _____ (try) several hotels near the airport. They were all full.
7. I _____ (call) the front desk.
8. She _____ (share) her adventures with her friends and family.
9. He _____ (stay) at a small hotel.
10. They _____ (enjoy) the tour yesterday.
11. We _____ (love) the food in India. It was delicious.
12. Sue _____ (visit) a lot of interesting places on the tour.

6 PRONUNCIATION. Read the chart and listen to the examples. Then complete the exercises.

PRONUNCIATION Past -ed Endings

The -ed ending has three sounds: /t/, /d/, and /əd/.
1. Say /əd/ only after verbs that end with /t/ and /d/ sounds.
   - want – wanted
   - need – needed
2. Say /t/ after verbs that end with the sounds /f/, /k/, /p/, /s/, /ʃ/, /tʃ/, and /ks/.
   - laugh – laughed
   - stop – stopped
   - wash – washed
   - tax – taxed
   - work – worked
   - kiss – kissed
   - watch – watched
3. Say /d/ after verbs that end with the sounds /b/, /dʒ/, /g/, /l/, /m/, /n/, /ŋ/, /p/, /r/, /ð/, /v/, and /z/ sounds, and after vowel sounds.
   - rub – rubbed
   - climb – climbed
   - stir – stirred
   - play – played
   - judge – judged
   - pin – pinned
   - bathe – bathed
   - lie – lied
   - bag – bagged
   - bang – banged
   - love – loved
   - show – showed
   - pull – pulled
   - hope – hoped
   - buzz – buzzed
   - allow – allowed

See page **A4** for a guide to pronunciation symbols.

A Listen to each sentence. What sound do you hear at the end of the underlined verb? Check (✓) the correct column.

		/t/	/d/	/əd/
1.	My friend Tony and I <u>wanted</u> an adventure.	☐	☐	✓
2.	We <u>discussed</u> the trip.	☐	☐	☐
3.	We <u>decided</u> to go to Mexico.	☐	☐	☐
4.	We <u>looked</u> at a lot of travel Web sites.	☐	☐	☐
5.	We <u>discussed</u> the trip.	☐	☐	☐
6.	I <u>reserved</u> the hotel rooms online.	☐	☐	☐
7.	We <u>packed</u> our suitcases.	☐	☐	☐
8.	We <u>called</u> a taxi. It was time to go!	☐	☐	☐

B Work with a partner. Practice saying the sentences in exercise **A**. Pay attention to the pronunciation of past endings.

Puebla, Mexico, at nightfall

8.7 Simple Past Irregular Verbs: Group 1

Present	Past	Present	Past	Present	Past
buy	bought	go	went	make	made
come	came	have	had	spend	spent
do	did	hear	heard	take	took
get	got	leave	left	teach	taught

Many common verbs are irregular* in the past. They do not have -ed endings.

She goes to Italy every summer.
She **went** to Italy last summer.

I always take the bus to work.
I **took** the bus to work yesterday.

*See page A5 for a list of irregular verbs.

7 Underline the verb in each sentence. Then write the base form of the verb on the line.

1. Gina <u>went</u> to Indonesia last year. __go__
2. The trip took five hours. _____
3. They bought some postcards. _____
4. We came home late. _____
5. Unfortunately, I got sick on the trip. _____
6. We had a great time. _____
7. The plane left two hours late. _____
8. I rode a horse on my vacation. _____
9. We did the mountain hike with a guide. _____
10. I heard a loud noise in the hotel lobby. _____

REAL ENGLISH

The verb *take* is used in many different ways.

take a vacation/a trip/a break/a nap
take a test/exam
take a photograph
take the bus/a taxi/the subway/the train
take six hours/a few minutes/ a lot of time

They **took** a trip to Austria last summer.
We **took** the final exam this morning.
The trip **took** five hours.

8 Complete each sentence with the past form of the verb in parentheses.

1. The tour ____left____ (leave) at 8:30 this morning.
2. We _____ (go) to a lot of beautiful places on the tour.
3. She _____ (make) some new friends on her trip.
4. They _____ (have) lunch in a small village yesterday.
5. He _____ (get) a map at the front desk.
6. I _____ (buy) some small gifts for my family at the market.
7. They _____ (spend) ten days in Peru.
8. Our guide _____ (teach) us a few words in Spanish.

UNIT 8 LESSON 3 **261**

9 SPEAK. Work with a partner. Make sentences in the past with four of the verbs in the box. Use time expressions.

| buy | do | find | go | have | hear | take |

I bought a new phone last month.

PRACTICE

10 LISTEN.

A Listen to each sentence. Is it present or past? Put a check (✓) in the correct column.

	Present	Past
1.	☐	✓
2.	☐	☐
3.	☐	☐
4.	☐	☐
5.	☐	☐
6.	☐	☐
7.	☐	☐
8.	☐	☐

B Listen again and complete each sentence with the verb you hear.

1. We ____went____ on a trip.
2. She _____ on Monday.
3. He _____ a lot for his job.
4. You _____ at a nice hotel.
5. They always _____ their hotel reservations online.
6. I _____ my camera at the hotel.
7. I really _____ to go to Italy.
8. She really _____ her vacation last summer.

11 Complete the paragraph. Use the past tense of the verbs in parentheses.

The Inca Road

The Incas (1) __had__ (have) a huge empire¹ in South America 500 years ago. They (2) _____ (need) a way to reach all parts of their empire. The Inca road system (3) _____ (carry) people from one end of the empire to the other. It (4) _____ (have) two main roads. One road (5) _____ (go) near the ocean between Tumbes, Peru and Talca, Chile. The other road (6) _____ (cross) part of the Andes Mountains between Quito, Ecuador and Mendoza, Argentina.

Karin Muller, a filmmaker, photographer, and adventurer from Switzerland, (7) _____ (decide) to make a film about the Inca Road. She (8) _____ (follow) the ancient road and (9) _____ (travel) 4000 miles (6440 kilometers). The journey (10) _____ (take) six months. Along the way, she (11) _____ (try) many new things and (12) _____ (learn) a lot about the people. She (13) _____ (make) a film about her journey. She (14) _____ (call) the film *Along the Inca Road*.

¹ An **empire** is a group of nations controlled by one ruler.

12 EDIT. Read the paragraph about Hiram Bingham. Find and correct six more errors with regular and irregular verbs in the simple past.

Hiram Bingham

        studied
Hiram Bingham ~~studyed~~ South American history. In 1908, he get a job at Yale University in the United States and tought history. In 1908, he went to Santiago, Chile, and learned about the lost cities of the Incas. He was visit the ruins of an ancient Incan city in Choquequirao. In 1911, he go to Peru. There he heared about more ruins called "Machu Picchu." He traveled with two Peruvians along the Urubamba River near Cusco. There some people showwed them the way to some very old ruins. It was Machu Picchu!

13 LISTEN & SPEAK.

A Listen to Ana and Don talk about their trips to Machu Picchu. Then circle the correct word to complete each statement.

1. Ana and Sudie's trip **was** / **wasn't** great.

2. Cusco **is** / **isn't** very high in the mountains.

3. Don's trip **was** / **wasn't** great.

B Look at the information in the chart. Then listen again. Is the information about Ana and Sudie or Don? Check (✓) the correct column(s).

	Ana and Sudie	Don
1. always wanted to go to Machu Picchu	✓	✓
2. went with a tour group	☐	☐
3. stayed in Cusco for one night	☐	☐
4. went by train and bus	☐	☐
5. hiked on the Inca Trail	☐	☐
6. had a guide	☐	☐
7. stayed in a tent	☐	☐
8. got really sick	☐	☐

C Work with a partner. Answer the questions. Use the words in the box to help you.

three nights	four hours	a hotel	by train and bus	the Inca Trail
four days	a guide	a tent	sick	

1. Why wasn't Don's trip very good?

2. What was fun for the women?

3. What were three differences between the trips?

14 APPLY.

A Write about a place you know and your visit there. Use the simple past.

Name of the place: I went to Copán in Honduras.

Information about the place: It's very interesting. The Maya lived there...

The trip: I went there three years ago. I went by bus with my family. We visited some ancient ruins and a museum....

B Work with a partner. Share the information about your place and your visit there.

Simple Past: Negative Statements — LESSON 4

EXPLORE

1 READ the article about an interesting journey. Notice the words in **bold**.

Amazon Explorer Ed Stafford

The Amazon River is a very long river. It's almost 4000 miles (6440 kilometers) long. In 2008, Ed Stafford, an adventurer from Great Britain, started a journey down the Amazon River. He **didn't go** by boat. He walked from the beginning to the end of the river! His journey began in the Andes Mountains in Peru and ended in Brazil. It took 859 days.

Ed **didn't travel** alone. He started the trip with a friend, but after three months, his friend **didn't want** to continue. In Peru, Cho Rivera joined him. They traveled together for two years. They **didn't have** an easy journey. It was often difficult and dangerous. They got very sick, and they saw large snakes and other dangerous animals. Finally, on August 9, 2010, Ed and Cho arrived at the end of the Amazon River—the Atlantic Ocean!

▶ Ed Stafford on his 859-day hike down the Amazon River

2 CHECK. Circle the correct information to complete each statement.

1. Ed Stafford's journey began in **Peru** / **Brazil**.
2. He started his trip **alone** / **with a friend**.
3. Ed Stafford and Cho Rivera traveled together for **two months** / **two years**.
4. Their journey was **easy** / **difficult**.
5. They arrived at the **Atlantic** / **Pacific** Ocean.

3 DISCOVER. Complete the exercises to learn about the grammar in this lesson.

A Find these sentences in the article from exercise **1** on page 265. Write the missing words.

1. He _____ by boat.
2. Ed _____ alone.
3. His friend _____ to continue.

B Look at the sentences in exercise **A**. CIrcle the correct word to complete each statement. Then discuss your answer with your classmates and teacher.

1. The verbs in these sentences are **present** / **past**.
2. The verbs in these sentences are **affirmative** / **negative**.

▼ Stafford walking through a swamp, Amazon jungle, Peru

266 THE PAST: PART 1

LEARN

8.8 Simple Past: Negative Statements

Subject	Did Not/ Didn't	Base Form of Verb	
I You He She It We You They	did not didn't	arrive	last Monday.

1. Remember to use the base form of the verb after *did not/didn't*. Do not use the past form.	✓ We didn't arrive late. ✗ We didn't <u>arrived</u> late. ✓ They didn't take the bus. ✗ They didn't <u>took</u> the bus.
2. The contraction *didn't* is often used in conversation and informal writing.	A: How was the party last night? B: I **didn't go**.

4 Underline the verb in each sentence. Then change each verb from affirmative to negative.

1. Ed Stafford's journey <u>started</u> in Brazil.   Ed Stafford's journey ___*didn't start*___ in Brazil.
2. He went alone.   He _____ alone.
3. Ed and Cho traveled with a group.   Ed and Cho _____ with a group.
4. They had a guide.   They _____ a guide.
5. They took a bus to Brazil.   They _____ a bus to Brazil.
6. They bought a boat for their journey.   They _____ a boat for their journey.
7. Ed's friend wanted to continue.   Ed's friend _____ to continue.
8. They stayed in nice hotels.   They _____ stay in nice hotels.

8.9 Simple Past Irregular Verbs: Group 2

Present	Past	Present	Past	Present	Past
become	became	lose	lost	sell	sold
begin	began	know	knew	tell	told
drink	drank	meet	met	win	won
eat	ate	ride	rode	write	wrote
feel	felt	say	said		
give	gave	see	saw		

See page **A5** for a list of common irregular verbs.

5 Complete each sentence with the correct simple past form of the verb in parentheses.

1. We _____ (see) some beautiful scenery on our trip.
2. The tour _____ (begin) at 8:00 a.m.
3. I _____ (write) a blog about my trip.
4. They _____ (eat) a lot of delicious food in Thailand.
5. He _____ (drink) fresh pineapple juice in Costa Rica.
6. Our guide _____ (know) a lot about the ruins.
7. She _____ (meet) some interesting people on her trip.
8. The hotel clerk _____ (give) me a map of the city.
9. We _____ (ride) our bicycles every day on our vacation.
10. Paul and Ellen _____ (win) a trip to Hawaii.
11. We _____ (feel) very tired after the hike yesterday.
12. Victor _____ (lose) his guidebook, so he bought a new one.

8.10 Simple Past Irregular Verbs: Group 3

Present	Past	Present	Past	Present	Past
cost	cost	fit	fit	hit	hit
hurt	hurt	let	let	put	put
quit	quit	read	read	shut	shut

1. Some irregular verbs have the same form in the simple present and simple past.	I **cut** my hair every six weeks. (simple present) Meg **cuts** her hair every month. (simple present) I **cut** my hair last week. (simple past) Meg **cut** her hair last month. (simple past)
2. The past of *read* has the same form as the simple present, but the pronunciation is different.	Simple present: read /rid/ Simple past: read /rɛd/

See page **A5** for a list of irregular verbs.

6 Look at the underlined verb in each sentence. Is it present or past? Check (✓) the correct column.

	Present	Past
1. Ahn <u>reads</u> a lot of travel books.	✓	☐
2. He <u>quit</u> his job to travel.	☐	☐
3. That trip <u>costs</u> a lot of money.	☐	☐

268 THE PAST: PART 1

		Present	Past
4.	The trip <u>cost</u> $485.	☐	☐
5.	The tour bus <u>hit</u> a car.	☐	☐
6.	I <u>read</u> an article in the newspaper last week.	☐	☐
7.	He <u>hurt</u> his leg on the hike.	☐	☐
8.	She <u>put</u> the dates for the trip in her calendar.	☐	☐
9.	Lisa usually <u>puts</u> a snack in her backpack every morning.	☐	☐
10.	My sister <u>let</u> me borrow her camera.	☐	☐

7 SPEAK. Work with a partner. Complete the sentences.

1. I read _____ last week.

2. My _____ cost _____.

3. I put a / an / some / my _____ in my bag / backpack this morning.

I read an article about bears last week.

PRACTICE

8 Write the simple past of each verb.

1. write _____
2. put _____
3. become _____
4. hurt _____
5. read _____
6. drink _____
7. shut _____
8. sell _____
9. give _____
10. eat _____
11. lose _____
12. know _____
13. meet _____
14. begin _____
15. tell _____

9 WRITE & SPEAK.

A Choose five verbs from exercise **8** and write five sentences about yourself.

I drank four cups of coffee this morning.

B Work with a partner. Share your sentences from exercise **A**.

Student A: *I drank four cups of coffee this morning.*

Student B: *Really? That's a lot!*

> **REAL ENGLISH**
>
> *Really* is often used in informal conversation to show interest or surprise.
>
> A: *Where were you last week?*
> B: *I was on vacation. I went to Peru.*
> A: **Really?** *How was it?*
> B: *Fantastic!*
>
> A: *These flowers cost ten dollars each.*
> B: **Really?** *That's very expensive!*

UNIT 8 LESSON 4

10 Complete the exercises.

A Complete the paragraph with the simple past form of the verbs in parentheses.

Harriet Chalmers Adams

In the early twentieth century, most people (1) __didn't travel__ (not travel) very much. They usually (2) _____ (not visit) foreign countries. Harriet Chalmers Adams was different. She lived in the United States, and she loved adventure. In 1904, she and her husband (3) _____ (begin) a three-year journey to every country in South America. People (4) _____ (not have) cars at that time. Adams and her husband took trains and boats. They (5) _____ (travel) across the Andes Mountains on horses. She (6) _____ (no go) only to South America. She also (7) _____ (ride) a horse across Haiti.

On her trips, Adams (8) _____ (see) many interesting places and took photographs. In 1907, she (9) _____ (write) her first travel article for *National Geographic Magazine*. She also (10) _____ (sell) her photographs and (11) _____ (write) more than twenty articles. In those days, the National Geographic Society (12) _____ (not let) women join. In 1925, Adams helped start the Society of Women Geographers and (13) _____ (become) its first president.

B Read the statements about Harriet Chalmers Adams. Circle **T** for *true* or **F** for *false*.

1. People went on a lot of tours in the early twentieth century.   T   (F)
2. People didn't visit foreign countries very often.   T   F
3. Harriet Chalmers Adams didn't travel very often.   T   F
4. Adams and her husband's journey in South America took three years.   T   F
5. They drove a car across the Andes Mountains.   T   F
6. She only traveled in South America.   T   F
7. Adams didn't have a camera.   T   F
8. Chalmers started the Society of Women Geographers in 1907.   T   F

C Correct the false statements in exercise **B**. Work with a partner. Compare answers.

People didn't go on a lot of tours in the early twentieth century.

11 EDIT. Read the travel story. Find and correct six more errors with the simple past.

            made
I ~~make~~ reservations six months ago for a trip to my cousin's wedding. The night before my trip I called a taxi company for a 6:00 a.m. pick-up. The day begin with a terrible rainstorm. The taxi didn't came at 6:00 a.m. I was call the company. Nobody answered the phone, so I got in my car and drove to the airport. Unfortunately, they didn't had any parking places at the parking garage. I parked six miles from the airport. I not get my flight. They put me on a flight to another city, and I rented a car. It costed more, but I didn't miss the wedding. I even arrived an hour early!

12 LISTEN & SPEAK.

A Read the statements. Then listen and complete each statement with the affirmative or negative form of the verb in parentheses. Use the simple past.

1. Lee _____ (take) a trip to Alaska.
2. He _____ (go) on a group tour.
3. He _____ (listen) to the guide.
4. He _____ (stay) with the group.
5. He _____ (see) three bears.
6. The bear _____ (see) Lee.
7. The bear _____ (run) after Lee.
8. Lee _____ (take) a photo of the bear.

B Listen again and check your answers from exercise **A**. Then close your books and retell the story to a partner.

▲ A black bear and her two cubs

13 APPLY.

A In your notebook, use the words to make a list of typical travel problems. Use the simple past.

1. I / get / sick   *I got sick*
2. I / lose / my passport, wallet, etc.
3. Someone / take / my passport, wallet, etc.
4. I / miss / the plane, train, bus, etc.
5. I / get on / the wrong plane, train, bus, etc.
6. I / not bring / not pack / the right clothes
7. My luggage / not arrive

B Did you have any of the problems from exercise **A** on your last trip? Look at your list from exercise **A**. Check (✓) the problems you had.

C Work with a partner. Tell your partner about your experience. Where was it? When? What happened? Use the simple past.

I was on a beach in France. I went in the water, and someone took my bag. . . .

UNIT 8 LESSON 4   **271**

Review the Grammar UNIT 8

Charts 8.1, 8.5–8.10

1 Complete the article with the correct simple past form of the verbs in the boxes.

Two Famous Travelers

| ~~be~~ | be | have | leave | live | not return | travel |

Marco Polo and Ibn Battata (1) __were__ famous travelers. They both (2) _____ very interesting lives.

Marco Polo (3) _____ in the thirteenth century. He (4) _____ from Venice, Italy. In 1271, Marco Polo (5) _____ Italy with his father and uncle. They (6) _____ to Asia. They (7) _____ to Italy for more than 20 years.

| be | become | leave | not travel | read | stay | take | travel | write |

Ibn Battata (8) _____ born in Morocco in 1304. He (9) _____ Tangier in 1325 and (10) _____ 75,000 miles (120,700 kilometers). The trip (11) _____ almost 30 years. He often (12) _____ in one place for several years; he (13) _____ all the time.

Both men (14) _____ books about their travels. Many people (15) _____ their books, and Marco Polo and Ibn Battata (16) _____ famous.

Charts 8.1, 8.5–8.10

2 EDIT. Read the information about Ferdinand Magellan. Find and correct six more errors with the use of the simple past.

True or false? Ferdinand Magellan ~~is~~ [was] the first person to travel around the world.

False. Magellan planed the trip, but he didn't complete it. Magellan leaved Spain in 1519 with over 200 men on five ships. Only one of his ships went all the way around the world. It returnned to Spain in 1522. Eighteen men are on the ship. Magellan himself was not finish the journey. He was died in the Philippines in 1521.

▲ Ferdinand Magellan

272 THE PAST: PART 1

Charts 8.1–8.10

3 LISTEN & SPEAK.

A Read each statement. Then listen to the story. Circle **T** for *true* or **F** for *false*.

1. Jason Lewis and Steve Smith wanted to go around the world.   T   F
2. They didn't want to use "human power."   T   F
3. Colin Angus did not complete his trip.   T   F

B Read each statement. Then listen again. Is the statement true for Jason Lewis or Colin Angus? Put a check (✓) in the correct column.

	Jason Lewis	Colin Angus
1. He started in England.		
2. He started in Canada.		
3. He left in 2004.		
4. He went to Alaska.		
5. He went to Australia.		
6. He started the trip with a partner.		
7. He rowed a boat from Alaska to Russia.		
8. His fiancée joined him on the trip.		
9. He crossed the Equator.		
10. He finished his trip in 2007.		
11. He finished first.		
12. He road a bicycle from Costa Rica to Canada.		

C Work with a partner. Compare your answers from exercise **B**. Then ask and answer questions about the two trips.

D Read the statements below with your classmates. Do you agree or disagree? Why?

Jason Smith was the first person to go around the world under human power. Colin Angus did not go around the world.

4 SPEAK & WRITE.
Work with a partner. Write a story about two students. Complete the first two sentences with two names and the name of a place. In your notebook, write five more sentences to tell about the students' adventure.

Two students, ... and . . . ., wanted an adventure. They planned a trip to . . . .

Connect the Grammar to Writing

1 READ & NOTICE THE GRAMMAR.

A Read the blog entry. Was this trip a good experience or a bad experience? Discuss with a partner.

The End of the Trail

October 3

Today was an exciting day. We're in Canada! We reached the end of the Pacific Crest Trail this afternoon. We started at the Mexican border five months ago. We hiked every day, and now here we are!

This was an amazing experience. The scenery was beautiful. We hiked on trails high up in the mountains. It was difficult sometimes, especially when it rained. That wasn't fun at all!

Our friends from California met us at the Canadian border. We are having a great time tonight!

◀ Hikers on the Pacific Crest Trail

GRAMMAR FOCUS

In the blog entry in exercise **A**, the writer uses the simple past to talk about experiences in the past.

*Today **was** an exciting day.*
*We finally **reached** the end of the Pacific Crest Trail.*

274 THE PAST: PART 1

Write a Blog Entry about a Trip

B Read the blog in exercise **A** again. Underline the verbs in the simple past. Then work with a partner and compare answers.

C Complete this chart with information from the blog in exercise **A**.

Information about the Trip	
Place	
Events and activities	
Description of the trip	

2 BEFORE YOU WRITE. Think of one day on a trip you took. Was it a good experience or a bad experience? Where were you? What happened? Write notes in the chart. Use the chart from exercise **1C** as a model.

Information about the Trip	
Where	
Events of the day	
Description of the trip	

3 WRITE a blog entry about your trip. Use the information in your chart in exercise **2** and the paragraph in exercise **1A** to help you.

> **WRITING FOCUS   Writing Complete Sentences**
>
> A complete sentence needs a subject and verb. The subject is a noun or a pronoun.
>
> **Remember:** Complete sentences begin with capital letters and end with periods. Sometimes writers use exclamation marks (!) in informal writing to show excitement or surprise.
>
> *Today was an exciting day. We're in Canada!*

4 SELF ASSESS. Circle the subject in each sentence of your blog entry. Underline the verbs in the simple past. Use the checklist to assess your work.

- [ ] I used *was* after a singular subject. I used *were* after a plural subject. [8.1]
- [ ] I used past time expressions correctly. [8.2]
- [ ] I used the correct spelling of *-ed* forms. [8.6]
- [ ] I used the correct form of irregular verbs. [8.7–8.9]
- [ ] There is a subject and verb in each sentence. [WRITING FOCUS]

UNIT 9 Achievements

The Past: Part 2

▶ Climbers on Gasherbrum II, Karakoram Mountain Range, Pakistan

Lesson 1
page 278
Simple Past: Questions

Lesson 2
page 288
Past Time Clauses

Lesson 3
page 297
Past Progressive

Review the Grammar
page 303

Connect the Grammar to Writing
page 306

277

LESSON 1 | Simple Past: Questions

EXPLORE

1 READ the conversation about Wangari Maathai. Notice the words in **bold**.

Wangari Maathai

Brad: Hey, what are you doing?

Peter: I'm reading a book about Wangari Maathai.

Brad: Who's she?

Peter: She was a professor at the University of Nairobi in Kenya. She won the Nobel Peace Prize in 2004.

Brad: **What did she get it for?**

Peter: She got it for her work with women in Kenya and other countries in Africa.

Brad: **How did she help them?**

Peter: They didn't have enough firewood or other resources[1]. She got the idea to plant trees and started an organization called the Green Belt Movement.

Brad: So, **did she plant more trees?**

Peter: Yes, she did. Wangari Maathai and thousands of other women from rural[2] areas in Kenya planted over 50 million trees. This helped the environment, and it also helped make the women's lives better. Then other countries around the world copied the Green Belt Movement's idea and planted trees, too.

Brad: Interesting. **When did she start the Green Belt Movement?**

Peter: In the 1970s. She was an amazing woman. She worked her entire life to help people, especially women in Africa. She died in 2011.

[1] **Resources** are things that a country, an organization, or a person has and can use.
[2] A **rural** area or place is in the countryside, not in the city.

▶ Wangari Maathai in the Newlands forest in Cape Town, South Africa, in 2005

Members of the Kiharo-Kahuro Women's Group prepare young trees in rural Kenya. © Green Belt Movement

2 CHECK. Choose the correct information to complete each statement.

1. Wangari Maathai was _____.
   a. a farmer   b. a professor

2. She lived _____.
   a. in Kenya   b. in the Green Belt

3. She won _____.
   a. the Nobel Peace Prize b. a race

4. The Green Belt Movement started _____.
   a. in the 1970s   b. in 2011

3 DISCOVER. Complete the exercises to learn about the grammar in this lesson.

A Find these questions in the conversation from exercise **1**. Write the missing words.

1. What _____ she _____ it for?
2. How _____ she _____ them?
3. So, _____ she _____ more trees?
4. When _____ she _____ the Green Belt Movement?

B Look at the questions in exercise **A**. Then choose the correct words to complete each statement. Discuss your answers with your classmates and teacher.

1. *Did* is used to form _____.
   a. questions in the present   b. questions in the past   c. questions in the future

2. We use _____ of the verb after the subject in *Wh-* questions with *did*.
   a. the past form   b. the base form

UNIT 9   LESSON 1   279

LEARN

9.1 Simple Past: *Yes/No* Questions and Short Answers

Yes/No Questions

Did	Subject	Base Form of Verb
Did	I / you / he / she / it / we / you / they	help?

Short Answers

Affirmative			Negative		
Yes,	I / you / he / she / it / we / you / they	did.	No,	I / you / he / she / it / we / you / they	didn't.

1. Use *did* to form *Yes/No* questions in the simple past.

   Did you **call** Scott?

2. Use the base form of the verb after the subject in simple past *Yes/No* questions.

   ✓ **Did** you **know** her?
   ✗ Did you <u>knew</u> her?

3. **Remember:** Do not use *did* in *Yes/No* questions with *was* or *were*.

   ✓ Were they students?
   ✗ <u>Did</u> they <u>be</u> students?

REAL ENGLISH

The answers to *Yes/No* questions often do not include *Yes* or *No*.

A: *Did it rain last night?*
B: *A little.*

A: *Did you like the movie?*
B: *It was OK.*

4 Match each *Yes/No* question with the correct short answer.

1. Did you know Wangari Maathai? __d__
2. Did she win the Nobel Prize? ____
3. Did Peter know about Wangari Maathai? ____
4. Did the women in Kenya have a challenge? ____
5. Did Brad know about her? ____
6. Did the Green Belt Movement help the environment? ____

a. Yes, they did.
b. No, he didn't.
c. Yes, she did.
d. No, I didn't.
e. Yes, it did.
f. Yes, he did.

280 THE PAST: PART 2

5 Change each statement to a Yes/No question. Then complete each short answer.

1. She won a prize.
   A: <u>Did she win a prize?</u>
   B: Yes, <u>she did</u>.

2. They planted a lot of trees.
   A: _____
   B: Yes, _____.

3. She lived in Kenya.
   A: _____
   B: Yes, _____.

4. He read the book.
   A: _____
   B: No, _____.

5. We knew about her.
   A: _____
   B: No, _____.

6. She grew up in Nairobi.
   A: _____
   B: Yes, _____.

7. He finished the book.
   A: _____
   B: Yes, _____.

8. They learned about the Green Belt Movement.
   A: _____
   B: No, _____.

6 SPEAK. Work with a partner. Use the words to make Yes/No questions. Then ask and answer your questions.

we / have / homework / last night

you / do / the homework

everybody / come to class / on time / today

Student A: *Did we have homework last night?*   Student B: *Yes, we did.*

UNIT 9 LESSON 1 **281**

9.2 Simple Past: *Wh*- Questions

Wh- Word	Did	Subject	Base Form of Verb	Answers
What	did	I	buy?	A notebook and some pens.
Where	did	you	go?	Home.
When	did	she	arrive?	Last night.
Why	did	he	leave?	He felt sick. / Because he felt sick.
Who	did	they	visit?	Their uncle.
How	did	we	do?	OK.
How long	did	it	take?	Five hours.

1. **Remember:** *Wh-* questions ask for specific information.
   A: **Why did** he **arrive** late?
   B: **Because** there was a lot of traffic.

2. Put *did* before the subject in questions about the past.
   ✓ When **did** they finish?
   ✗ When they did finish?

3. Use the base form of the verb after the subject. Do not use the past form of the verb with *did*.
   ✓ How did they get there?
   ✗ How did they got there?

4. **Remember:** In conversation, the answers to *Why* questions often begin with *because*. In writing, use complete sentences to answer *Why* questions.
   A: **Why did** you **scream**?
   B: **Because** I saw a spider on my desk.

REAL ENGLISH
What for is sometimes used in place of *Why* in informal conversations.
A: *Julie went to the doctor.*
B: **What for?**
A: *She hurt her foot.*

7 Choose the correct answer for each question.

1. Where did she live?
   a. For two years.
   (b.) In Africa.

2. When did she win the prize?
   a. In 2010.
   b. She did a lot for other people.

3. Where did he go to university?
   a. In London.
   b. In 2008.

4. How did you do on the exam?
   a. Yesterday.
   b. I passed it.

5. When did you graduate from college?
   a. Last summer.
   b. In Moscow.

6. Who did she help?
   a. Her family.
   b. Yesterday.

7. What did he win?
   a. A prize.
   b. In 2006.

8. Why did he win the prize?
   a. He was an excellent student.
   b. Two years ago.

▶ Apollo 11 astronauts Neil Armstrong and Buzz Aldrin placed the American flag on the moon on July 20, 1969.

8 Look at each sentence. Write a question about the underlined word or phrase.

Neil Armstrong: The First Man on the Moon

1. Neil Armstrong's family lived <u>in Ohio, USA</u>. *Where did Neil Armstrong's family live?*
2. He went to college <u>at Purdue University</u>. _____
3. He loved <u>planes</u>. _____
4. He <u>became an astronaut</u> in 1962. _____
5. He got to the moon <u>in a rocket called *Apollo 11*</u>. _____
6. He traveled to the moon with <u>Buzz Aldrin and Michael Collins</u>. _____
7. They started their trip to the moon <u>on July 16, 1969</u>. _____
8. They landed on the moon <u>on July 20, 1969</u>. _____
9. Armstrong <u>walked on the moon</u> on July 20, 1969. _____
10. Millions of people <u>watched on TV</u>. _____
11. Armstrong won awards <u>because he was the first man on the moon</u>. _____
12. He died <u>on August 25, 2012</u>. _____

9 **WRITE & SPEAK.** Work with a partner. Use the words to make *Wh-* questions. Then ask and answer your questions.

1. How / you / get to class / today   *How did you get to class today?*
2. When / you / wake up / this morning
3. What / you / eat / for dinner / last night
4. Where / you / go / last weekend

Student A: *How did you get to class today?*   Student B: *I walked.*

UNIT 9 LESSON 1 **283**

9.3 Wh- Questions with Who or What

Who/What Questions about a Subject

Wh- Word	Verb	
Who	went	with you?
What	happened	to you?

Answers

Felix.
I hurt my hand.

Who/What Questions about an Object

Wh- Word	Did	Subject	Base Form of Verb
Who	did	you	ask?
What	did	they	do?

Answers

Professor Davis.
They went home.

1. **Remember:** Wh- questions with *Who* or *What* can be about a subject or an object.

   Question about a Subject: **Who** called?
   Question about an Object: **Who** did you call?

2. Do not use *did* when the question is about a subject.

   ✓ **What** took so long?
   ✗ What did <u>take</u> so long?

   ✓ **Who** went on the trip?
   ✗ Who did <u>go</u> on the trip?

10 Read each question. Is it about a subject or an object? Check (✓) the correct column.

	Subject	Object
1. Who won the Nobel Peace Prize last year?	✓	☐
2. Who was the first person on the moon?	☐	☐
3. What did the women do?	☐	☐
4. What happened three years ago?	☐	☐
5. Who did it?	☐	☐
6. What did she say?	☐	☐
7. Who didn't attend the meeting?	☐	☐
8. Who did you talk to?	☐	☐

11 Put the words in the correct order to make Wh- questions.

1. lived / Who / that / house / in   <u>Who lived in that house?</u>

2. she / did / ask / Who _____

3. Who / his / were / parents _____

4. she / did / What / do _____

5. Who / go / didn't _____

6. your / life / What / changed _____

7. they / did / say / What _____

8. Who / them / helped _____

284 THE PAST: PART 2

PRACTICE

12 **LISTEN** and choose the correct answer for each question.

1. a. In 1995.   (b.) In Paris.
2. a. Three years ago.   b. Yes, he did.
3. a. Very happy.   b. No, I didn't.
4. a. Someone in the library.   b. At the library.
5. a. Two weeks ago.   b. I hurt my arm.
6. a. Yes, she did.   b. She did her homework.
7. a. She got a job there.   b. In 2010.
8. a. I felt sick.   b. At 6:30.

13 Complete the interview with the correct question word. Then listen and check your answers.

Interviewer: OK, so Mr. Nash, (1) ___where___ were you born?

Nash: In Jamaica.

Interviewer: (2) _____ did you move to London?

Nash: I knew a lot of people there.

Interviewer: (3) _____ you always want to be a writer?

Nash: No, I really wanted to be a football player!

Interviewer: Really? (4) _____ happened?

Nash: I broke my ankle and had other injuries.

Interviewer: (5) _____ you a good player?

Nash: No, I really wasn't very good.

Interviewer: (6) _____ taught you to write?

Nash: My teachers.

Interviewer: (7) _____ did you write your first book?

Nash: Ten years ago. No one liked it.

Interviewer: (8) _____ did you feel about that?

Nash: I felt terrible, of course.

Interviewer: (9) _____ didn't people like it?

Nash: It really wasn't very good. It was horrible, in fact.

Interviewer: (10) _____ you want to give up?

Nash: Yes, but I continued to write, and now I'm glad.

14 SPEAK. Work with a partner. Ask and answer questions about Mr. Nash from the interview in exercise **13**.

Student A: *Where was he born?*   Student B: *In Jamaica.*

15 EDIT. Read the conversations. Find and correct five more errors with simple past questions.

1. **Jim:** Did you grow up in South Africa?
   Clive: Yes, I did.
   Jim: Did you ever s~~aw~~ ^see Nelson Mandela?
   Clive: Yes, I went to hear him speak many times.
   Jim: Did you read the new book about him?
   Clive: No, I didn't. Who did write it?
   Jim: I don't remember, but it was really good.

2. **Lily:** When they did win the prize?
   Jeff: Last week.
   Lily: How they feel?
   Jeff: They were very happy, of course.

3. **Amelia:** Were you meet the president?
   Kyle: No, I didn't. How about you?
   Amelia: I saw her, but I didn't meet her.
   Kyle: Who she met with?
   Amelia: Photographers and news reporters.

16 WRITE & SPEAK.

A Write the correct question for the underlined information in each answer.

1. Q: *Where did you grow up?*
   A: I grew up in Riyadh, Saudi Arabia.

2. Q: _____
   A: Yes, my family came from that city.

3. Q: _____
   A: I went to school in Australia.

4. Q: _____
   A: I studied biology.

5. Q: _____
   A: I did well in school.

6. Q: _____
   A: My parents helped me.

7. Q: _____
   A: I lived with my cousin in Sydney.

8. Q: _____
   A: We went to India last year.

B Ask and answer questions 1-5 from exercise **A**.

Student A: *Where did you grow up?*   Student B: *I grew up in Izmir, Turkey.*

17 LISTEN, SPEAK & WRITE.

A Read the statements about Wong How-Man. Then listen and circle **T** for *true* or **F** for *false*.

1. Wong How-Man is from the United States.   T   F

2. Wong How-Man is a writer and photographer.   T   F

B Listen again. Check (✓) the information you hear about Wong How-Man.

Name: Wong How-Man		
Lived	✓ Hong Kong	___ Beijing
Explored	___ Oceans	___ Rivers
In the 1980s	___ Led expeditions	___ Taught classes
In 1985 and 2005	___ Yangtze River	___ Mekong River
Started	___ An exploration and research society	___ A photography school

C Write as many *Yes/No* and *Wh-* questions in the past as you can about Wong How-Man.

Where did he grow up?

D Work with a partner. Ask and answer your questions from exercise **C**.

Student A: *Where did he grow up?*   Student B: *In Hong Kong.*

18 APPLY.

A Write questions in the simple past for your classmates. Use the words in the chart.

Wh- Word	Questions	Notes
Where	Where did you grow up?	Cali, Colombia (Maria)
When		
Why		
How		
What		
Who		

B Stand up and walk around the classroom. Find six classmates, and ask each person a question from exercise **A**. Write notes on your chart.

C Tell your classmates about the students you interviewed in exercise **B**.

Maria grew up in Cali, Colombia. Hamid rode his bicycle to class today. . . .

UNIT 9   LESSON 1   287

LESSON 2 | Past Time Clauses

EXPLORE

1 READ the article about Ernest Shackleton's expedition. Notice the words in **bold**.

Ernest Shackleton's Expedition

In early August 1914, members of the British Imperial Trans-Antarctic Expedition sailed for Vahsel Bay in Antarctica on a ship called the *Endurance*. Their leader was Ernest Shackleton.

Shackleton and his 27 men were 100 miles from their destination[1] **when ice surrounded[2] their ship**. For the next nine months, the ice moved their ship more than 1000 miles (1609 kilometers). Finally, **before the ice crushed[3] the ship,** the men left it and got onto the ice. The temperature was –16°F (–27°C). The men camped on the ice for several months.

In April, the ice started to melt. It was time for them to try to reach safety. They got in lifeboats[4] and started across the South Atlantic Ocean. After a week of terrible storms, they reached Elephant Island. Unfortunately, no one lived there. **After they rested for a week,** Shackleton and five of his men left Elephant Island in one of the lifeboats. They spent 17 days on the ocean **before they reached South Georgia Island.** There they walked for 36 hours over the mountains and finally reached a town.

Shackleton returned to rescue the other men on August 25, 1916. Everyone on Shackleton's expedition survived.

[1] **destination:** the place that someone is going to
[2] **surround:** to be all around something
[3] **crush:** to push or press hard
[4] **lifeboat:** a small boat used in emergencies

◀ *Endurance*, surrounded by ice

2 CHECK. Read each statement. Then circle **T** for *true* or **F** for *false*.

1. Shackleton's ship was called the *Explorer*.   T   F
2. They sailed for Vahsel Bay on December 19, 1914.   T   F
3. Ice surrounded their ship.   T   F
4. The men stayed on the ship.   T   F
5. Nobody on Shackleton's expedition died.   T   F

3 DISCOVER. Complete the exercises to learn about the grammar in this lesson.

A Look at the underlined part of each of these sentences from the article in exercise **1**. Put a check (✓) next to the ones with a subject and a verb.

1. They were 100 miles from their destination <u>when ice surrounded their ship.</u> ☐
2. <u>Before the ice crushed their ship,</u> the men left the ship and got onto the ice. ☐
3. <u>After a week of terrible storms,</u> they reached Elephant Island. ☐
4. <u>After they rested for a week,</u> Shackleton left the island in one of the lifeboats. ☐
5. They spent 17 days on the ocean <u>before they reached South Georgia Island.</u> ☐

B Discuss your answer from exercise **A** with your classmates and teacher.

UNIT 9 LESSON 2 **289**

LEARN

9.4 Past Time Clauses with *Before* and *After*

She finished school **before she moved to Seoul.**
  — Main Clause —   — Time Clause —

She moved to Seoul **after she finished school.**
  — Main Clause —   — Time Clause —

1. A clause is a group of words with a subject and a verb. A main clause can stand alone as a complete sentence.	We did our homework before dinner. — Clause —
2. A clause that begins with *before* or *after* is a time clause. A past time clause tells when an action or event happened.	They ate lunch **before they left.** We played soccer **after we ate dinner.**

3. A time clause is not a complete sentence. Do not use a time clause without a main clause.	✓ They moved to Beirut **after they got married.**
	  — Main Clause — — Time Clause —
	✗ After they got married.
	  — Time Clause —

4. A time clause can come before or after a main clause. Use a comma when a time clause is at the beginning of the sentence.	After he left work, he went to the gym. He went to the gym after he left work. Before he left work, he met with his boss. He met with his boss before he left work.

5. *Before* and *after* show the order of two actions or events.	**After** they ate dinner, they watched the game.
	  — First Event — — Second Event —
	They ate dinner **before** they watched the game.
	  — First Event — — Second Event —

> **REAL ENGLISH**
>
> *Before* and *after* are also prepositions. They can be followed by a noun.
>
> I ate breakfast **before** work.
>   Noun
>
> **After** lunch, we went to the museum.
>   Noun

4 Read each sentence. Which action or event happened first? Which action or event happened second? Write *1* for *first* and *2* for *second* below each action or event.

1. After <u>they reached land</u>, <u>two of the men went for help.</u>
              <u> 1 </u>   <u> 2 </u>

2. <u>They reached South Georgia Island</u> after <u>they spent 17 days on the ocean.</u>
              ____   ____

3. <u>They walked for 36 hours</u> before <u>they reached a town.</u>
              ____   ____

290 THE PAST: PART 2

4. Before the ice crushed the ship, the men moved onto the ice.
   _____   _____

5. He returned to rescue the others after he reached a town.
   _____   _____

6. After Shackleton rescued the other men, he became famous.
   _____   _____

7. Other men reached the South Pole before Shackleton did.
   _____   _____

8. After they rested for a week, he left the island with five of the men.
   _____   _____

5 Look at the time line for Shackleton's expedition. Then complete each sentence with *before* or *after*.

1. Shackleton and his men saw ice on the ocean ___before___ they crossed the Antarctic Circle.

2. _____ they crossed the Antarctic Circle, ice surrounded the ship.

3. _____ ice surrounded the ship, it moved 1000 miles away from the South Pole.

4. _____ they moved onto the ice, the ice carried the ship 1000 miles.

5. They moved from the ship onto the ice _____ ice began to crush the ship.

6. They moved onto the ice _____ the ship broke up.

7. The ship sank _____ the ice started to break up.

8. They got into lifeboats _____ the ice started to break up.

Shackelton's Expedition

August, 1914
← Shackleton and his men saw ice in the ocean.
← They crossed the Antarctic Circle.
← Ice surrounded the ship.
← Ice moved the ship 1000 miles.
← Ice began to crush the ship.
← They moved onto the ice.
← The ice started to break up.
← The ship sank.
← They got into lifeboats.
August, 1916

6 SPEAK. Work with a partner. Complete the sentences.

Before class, I _____ .   After I got home last night, I _____ .

Before class, I ate breakfast.

UNIT 9 LESSON 2 **291**

9.5 Past Time Clauses with *When*

I made dinner **when I got home.**
— Main Clause — — Time Clause —
They bought an apartment **when they moved to London.**
— Main Clause — — Time Clause —

1. Use *when* + the simple past to talk about an action or event that happened at a point in the past. **Remember:** A time clause is not a complete sentence. Do not use a time clause without a main clause.	✓ I had a cup of coffee **when I got to work.** ✗ When I got to work.
2. Use *when* in a time clause to talk about two actions or events in the past. The action or event in the *when* clause happened first. The action or event in the main clause happened second.	**When** the war started, they left London. — First Event — — Second Event — They left London **when** the war started. — Second Event — — First Event —
3. **Remember:** Use a comma when the time clause comes at the beginning of a sentence.	**When he got to Chicago,** he called us.

7 Change each sentence. Begin each sentence with *When*.

1. They celebrated when their team won the World Cup.

   <u>When their team won the World Cup, they celebrated.</u>

2. We had a party when my sister graduated.

   _____

3. He took a photo when he reached the top of the mountain.

   _____

4. Lisa helped me when I had a problem.

   _____

5. My parents were very happy when Neil Armstrong landed on the moon.

   _____

6. Bob texted us when he finished the race.

   _____

7. I called my mother when I heard the good news.

   _____

8. They bought their first house when they moved to Ohio.

   _____

PRACTICE

8 Read each sentence. Underline the part of the sentence that shows when the event or action happened. Which of your answers are past time clauses?

1. Emma hurt her leg <u>when she ran in a race last year.</u>   *past time clause*
2. After her injury, Emma wanted to run in another race.
3. Before the next big race, she did special exercises for her leg.
4. She was very nervous before the race.
5. After she ran the first mile, she wasn't nervous.
6. After the fifth mile, she was in first place.
7. When she won the race, everyone said, "Congratulations."
8. After she won the race, she celebrated with her friends and family.

9 Complete the sentences. Use *before, after,* or *when.* Then listen and check your answers.

JACQUES COUSTEAU

Jacques Cousteau was a famous ocean explorer. He was born in France in 1910. He learned to swim (1) __when__ he was four. (2) _____ he was thirteen, he bought his first movie camera. (3) _____ he finished school, he joined the navy.¹ (4) _____ he was 23, Cousteau was in a bad car accident. He almost died. (5) _____ his accident, he went swimming every day in the Mediterranean Sea. (6) _____ the salt water hurt his eyes, he started to wear goggles.² This changed his life. (7) _____ he used goggles, he never saw anything underwater. With goggles, he saw a lot of interesting things in the sea. (8) _____ this, he wanted to dive deeper and deeper.

¹ **navy:** a country's sailors and fighting ships
² **goggles:** plastic glasses that protect the eyes

◀ Jacques Cousteau in 1982

10 LISTEN & WRITE.

A Listen to the information about Jacques Cousteau and his family. Match each name on the left with the correct information.

1. Jacques Cousteau __b__
2. Simone _____
3. Emile _____
4. *Calypso* _____

a. an inventor
b. an underwater explorer
c. Cousteau's wife
d. Cousteau's ship

B Listen again. Number the events in the correct order.

_____ Met Emile Gagnan

_____ Helped to design an underwater camera

_____ Designed a small submarine, called "a diving saucer"

__1__ Got married

_____ Became famous after his book became a film

_____ Started to lead expeditions

_____ Designed the aqualung

_____ Bought a ship

_____ Wrote a book

▲ *Calypso* crew members used a crane to launch diving saucer *Denise* during an expedition off the coast of France.

C Complete each sentence with information from exercise **B**. Use time clauses with *before*, *after*, or *when*.

1. Cousteau met Emile Gagnan __after he got married.__

2. _____, people had no way to swim under water for long periods of time.

3. Cousteau had a way to film under water _____.

4. _____, he had a way to travel and explore the ocean.

5. _____, it became a film.

6. _____, Cousteau didn't have enough money for his expeditions.

7. _____, he became famous.

8. _____, he taught people about fish and other animals in the ocean.

294 THE PAST: PART 2

11 EDIT. Read the information about Jacques Cousteau. Add five more commas.

A Friend of the Ocean

Before Jacques Cousteau wrote *The Silent World*, he wasn't famous. After the book became a movie Cousteau led many expeditions to study the ocean. When he led expeditions a film crew went with him on his ship, the *Calypso*. He made a one-hour television show. It was very popular. When people watched this TV show they learned about the ocean. He had the TV show for nine years. Before it ended Cousteau began to see many changes and problems in the ocean. After he saw these problems he wanted to help the ocean. He started the Cousteau Society and made special television shows about problems in the ocean. Many people joined the Cousteau Society after they saw the television shows. Jacques Cousteau died in 1997 after a long career as an explorer, an inventor, and a friend of the ocean.

12 LISTEN & WRITE.

A Read each statement. Then listen to two conversations. Which statements are true? As you listen to each conversation, check (✓) the correct boxes.

	Conversation 1	Conversation 2
1. He had a good experience.	✓	☐
2. He had a bad expreience.	☐	☐
3. He felt nervous before he started.	☐	☐
4. He felt nervous after he started.	☐	☐
5. His face was red when he started.	☐	☐
6. He felt sick.	☐	☐

B Write sentences about the speakers from the conversations in exercise **A**. Use the words in parentheses and *before*, *after*, or *when*. Add other words if needed.

1. (nervous / started / his presentation)

    In conversation 1, Max _was nervous before he started his presentation._

2. (not nervous / started / the presentation)

    He _____.

3. (practiced / a lot / his presentation)

    Max _____.

UNIT 9   LESSON 2   **295**

4. (fell asleep / finished)

   His dog _____.

5. (sick / the game)

   In conversation 2, Sidney _____.

6. (left / the game / half-time)

   He _____.

7. (scored a goal / he left the game)

   His team _____.

8. (not hurt / the game)

   His stomach _____.

13 APPLY.

A Think of a time in your life when you had a challenge. Write notes in the chart.

What was the challenge?	a presentation
When was it?	in high school
How did you feel?	
What happened?	

B Write about your experience. Use *before, after,* and *when*.

When I was in high school, I gave a speech. Before the speech, I was very nervous. I did a good job. After the speech, I felt very happy. Everyone liked it.

_____

_____

_____

_____

C Work with a partner. Share your experiences from exercise **B**. Use *before, after,* and *when*.

296 THE PAST: PART 2

Past Progressive LESSON 3

EXPLORE

1 READ the article about Tenzing Norgay. Notice the words in **bold**.

Tenzing Norgay

On May 29, 1953, the leader of a climbing expedition[1] **was waiting** at a camp on Mount Everest. Two of the expedition's climbers, Edmund Hillary and Tenzing Norgay, **were trying** to reach the top of the mountain. They were not the first to try. In fact, this was Tenzing's seventh attempt.

Tenzing Norgay grew up in a very poor family in Nepal. He was a Sherpa. Sherpas are often porters.[2] They carry things for other climbers. When Tenzing was 19, **he was living** in India. He got a job on a climbing expedition. After several expeditions, he became a climber and was no longer a porter.

In 1953, Tenzing met Edmund Hillary when he joined an expedition to climb to the top of Mount Everest. It was a very difficult and dangerous expedition. Once when **they were climbing**, Hillary fell and Tenzing rescued him. Climbers from another expedition **were also trying** to reach the top of Mount Everest, but they failed.

Early in the morning on May 29, 1953, Hillary and Tenzing left their camp and continued their climb up Mount Everest. At 11:30, they reached the top.

[1] **expedition:** a journey usually made by a group for a special purpose
[2] **porter:** a person whose job is to carry things

▼ Tenzing Norgay at the top of Chukhung Peak on his way to the top of Mount Everest (1953).

2 CHECK. Read each statement. Then circle **T** for *true* or **F** for *false*.

1. Tenzing Norgay and Edmund Hillary were trying to reach the top of Mount Everest.   T   F

2. Tenzing was a Sherpa.   T   F

3. This was Tenzing's first attempt.   T   F

4. Tenzing rescued Hillary.   T   F

3 DISCOVER. Complete the exercises to learn about the grammar in this lesson.

A Find these sentences in the article from exercise **1**. Write the missing words.

1. When Tenzing was 19, he _____ in India.
   a

2. He _____ a job on a climbing expedition.
   b

3. Once when they _____, Hillary fell and Tenzing _____ him.
   c   d

4. At 11:30, they _____ the top.
   e

B Look at the verbs in exercise **A**. Then answer these questions. Discuss your answers with your classmates and teacher.

1. Which two verbs talk about an action that was happening for a period of time in the past?   a b c d e

2. Which verb talks about an action that happened when another action was in progress?   a b c d e

▼ Tenzing Norgay and Edmund Hillary drinking tea after their successful climb, Mount Everest (1953)

298

LEARN

9.6 Past Progressive

Affirmative Statements

Subject	Was/Were	Verb + -ing	
I He She	was	living	in Rio in 2009.
You We You They	were		

Negative Statements

Subject	Was Not/ Were (Not)	Verb + -ing	
I He She	was not wasn't	living	in Rio in 2009.
You We You They	were not weren't		

1. Use the past progressive to talk about an action that was in progress at a specific time in the past.

   We **were eating** dinner at 7:30 last night.
   She **was working** in Mexico City in 2011.

2. Use the past progressive to talk about an action in the past that was in progress when another action or event happened.

   We **were eating** when she **arrived**.
       Action in Progress   Second Action

4 Read the sentences. Put a check (✓) next to the sentences that have a verb in the past progressive. Then underline the verbs in the past progressive.

1. __✓__ In the early 1950s, many people <u>were trying</u> to climb to the top of Mount Everest.
2. _____ Many Sherpas were porters, but Tenzing Norgay became a climber.
3. _____ One day Hillary and Tenzing were climbing Mount Everest.
4. _____ When Hillary fell, Tenzing rescued him.
5. _____ Tenzing was living in India when he was 19.
6. _____ They were very happy when they reached the top.
7. _____ When they returned to their camp, the other climbers were waiting for them.
8. _____ They were all hoping to reach the top, but Tenzing and Hillary were the first.

5 Complete each sentence with the past progressive form of the verb in parentheses.

1. Karen and Frank __were climbing__ (climb) the mountain when the accident happened.
2. Frank _____ (work) as a guide when they first met.
3. In June 2004, we _____ (travel) in Nepal.
4. They _____ (live) in Bangkok at that time.
5. I _____ (not pay attention) when I fell down the stairs.

6. I _____ (sleep) at 11:00 p.m. last night.

7. Carol and Ed _____ (wait) for the train when we saw them.

8. I _____ (drive) home when I heard the news.

9. They _____ (talk) during the entire presentation. It was very rude!

10. We _____ (study) for the exam all last week.

9.7 Simple Past vs. Past Progressive

I **was walking** to class when I **heard** a loud noise.
   Past Progressive   *Simple Past*

Junko **was riding** her bike when it **started** to rain.
   Past Progressive   *Simple Past*

1. **Remember:** Use the simple past for completed actions.	I **called** my parents last night. He **woke up** at 6:00 a.m. this morning.
2. When one event happened while another event was in progress, use the simple past for the second action or event.	I **was watching** the game when my sister **called**. *First Action* — *Second Action*
3. Do not use the past progressive with non-action verbs.*	✓ We **saw** Gemma yesterday. ✗ We **were seeing** Gemma yesterday. ✓ Efren **knew** the answer. ✗ Efren **was knowing** the answer.

6 Circle the correct form of the verb(s) to complete each sentence.

1. My brother (**started**)/ **was starting** his own business when he was in high school.

2. He **got** / **was getting** the idea when he **helped** / **was helping** our grandmother one day.

3. She **had** / **was having** a new computer at that time.

4. She **wasn't knowing** / **didn't know** anything about computers.

5. She **didn't understand** / **wasn't understanding** a lot of things about her new computer when she **called** / **was calling** him.

6. He **gave** / **was giving** computer lessons to her once a week.

7. One of her friends **came** / **was coming** to our grandmother's house when he **taught** / **was teaching** her.

8. The friend **wanted** / **was wanting** to take lessons, too. Soon my brother **had** / **was having** a lot of students.

PRACTICE

7 Complete the paragraph. Use the simple past or past progressive of each verb in parentheses.

The Paralympic Games

The Paralympic Games are international competitions for athletes with disabilities. The idea for the games (1) _____ (begin) in 1948. At that time, many former soldiers with disabilities from the war (2) _____ (live) in England. Dr. Ludwig Guttmann (3) _____ (work) at a London hospital, and he (4) _____ (want) to help the soldiers. He (5) _____ (organize) an archery competition for people in wheelchairs. Soon there (6) _____ (be) many sport competitions for people with disabilities. Many people (7) _____ (like) Guttmann's idea, and the first Paralympics (8) _____ (take) place in 1960.

8 LISTEN & SPEAK.

A Listen to the information about the first voyage of the *Titanic*. Complete the sentences.

1. The *Titanic* was going from Southampton in ___England___ to ___New York___.
2. About _____ people were on the ship.
3. There were _____ lifeboats on the ship.
4. The *Titanic* left England on _____ 10, 1912.
5. There were _____ about icebergs.

B Circle the correct form of the verb to complete each sentence.

1. The *Titanic* **crossed** / **(was crossing)** the Atlantic Ocean on April 10, 1912.
2. The ship **had** / **was having** space for more lifeboats.
3. It was carrying 20 lifeboats, but it **needed** / **was needing** 64 for the number of passengers on the ship.
4. Other ships **knew** / **were knowing** about the icebergs and sent reports about them.
5. The captain didn't get the reports because he **had** / **was having** dinner with the passengers.
6. The ship **went** / **was going** at full speed when it hit the iceberg.
7. At first, people **didn't believe** / **weren't believing** that the *Titanic* was sinking.
8. The *Titanic* **sank** / **was sinking** on April 15, 1912.
9. Over 1500 people **died** / **were dying**.
10. It **was** / **was being** a terrible event in history.

▼ *Titanic*, Southhampton, England, April 10, 1912.

C Work in a group. Share your answers to these questions.

1. Did you know about the *Titanic* before this? How did you learn about it?

2. What other facts do you know about the *Titanic*?

3. Did you see the movie, *Titanic*? Did you like it? Why, or why not?

I knew about the Titanic *before this. I learned about it in high school . . .*

9 APPLY.

A Think of another historical event, such as the first moon landing in 1969. Write notes to answer each question about this event.

Questions	Answers
What was the event?	The first man landed on the moon.
When did it happen?	
Where did it happen?	
What happened?	
What were people doing when it happened?	
How did you learn about it?	

B Work in a group. Share your information from exercise **A** with your classmates.

C In your notebook, write about your event. Use the information from your chart in exercise **A**.

UNIT 9 Review the Grammar

Charts 9.1–9.2, 9.4–9.7

1 WRITE & SPEAK.

A Complete the sentences. Use the simple past or past progressive. Add a comma if necessary.

1. Before I ate breakfast this morning _____.
2. When I woke up _____.
3. After breakfast I _____.
4. When I was at home last night _____.
5. I was coming to class when _____.
6. I was doing my homework when _____.
7. I started school when _____.
8. Before I was born _____.

B Work with a partner. Share your sentences from exercise **A**.

Student A: *Before I ate breakfast this morning, I called my parents.*

Charts 9.1–9.2, 9.4–9.7

2 WRITE, LISTEN, & SPEAK.

A Complete the article with the correct form of each verb in parentheses. Then listen and check your answers.

Exploration of the Arctic and the Antarctic

The early 20th century was a time of great exploration. Expeditions from several countries (1) __were trying__ (try) to reach the North and South Poles. Voyages to the Arctic and Antarctic took several years and (2) _____ (be) very dangerous. Many explorers (3) _____ (die) when they (4) _____ (travel). The weather was very cold. Sometimes the temperature was only –20 degrees Fahrenheit (–29 degrees Celsius).

▲ Roald Amundsen

In 1910, several explorers (5) _____ (want) to reach the North Pole. A Norwegian, Roald Amundsen, (6) _____ (be) one of the explorers, but when he (7) _____ (prepare) for his voyage, two explorers from the United States (8) _____ (reach) the North Pole. This was bad news for Amundsen because he wanted to be first.

After the challenge of the North Pole (9) _____ (end), the race for the South Pole (10) _____ (begin). In fact, in 1910, explorers from Germany, France, Japan, Norway, and the United States all (11) _____ (plan) new expeditions to the South Pole. The explorers all (12) _____ (have) the same goal: They (13) _____ (want) to be the first expedition to reach the South Pole.

UNIT 9 REVIEW THE GRAMMAR **303**

Review the Grammar UNIT 9

B Write as many questions as you can about the information in exercise **A**. Use the simple past and the past progressive.

What were expeditions from different countries trying to do in the 1900s?

C Ask and answer your classmates' questions from **B**.

Student A: *What were expeditions from different countries trying to do in the 1900s?*

Student B: *They were trying to reach the North and South Poles.*

Charts 9.1–9.7

3 EDIT. Read the questions and answers about polar expeditions. Find and correct six more errors with simple past questions and the past progressive.

Frequently Asked Questions about Polar Expeditions

▶ Robert Peary

Q: Who **was** the first man ~~was~~ to the North Pole?

A: No one really knows. In 1909, two men from the United States, Robert Peary and Fredrick Cook, both said, "I was the first."

Q: Why so many explorers wanted to reach the poles first?

A: They were wanting to be famous.

Q: Did expeditions continued after explorers reached the North and South Poles?

A: Yes, they did.

Q: Why they continued?

A: Many explorers were scientists. They wanted to learn many things about the poles. When they were returned, they were having a lot of new information.

Charts 9.1–9.7

4 LISTEN & WRITE.

CD3-14

A Two classmates see each other after many years. Read the information in the chart. Then listen to their conversation. Is the information about Dana or Allen? Put a check (✓) in the correct column(s). Then work with a partner and compare your charts.

	Dana	Allen
Lives in Oklahoma	✓	✓
Is married		
Has two daughters		

B Listen again. Number the events in Allen's life in the correct order.

Allen
___ Graduated from high school
___ The tornado happened
___ Graduated from college
_1_ Got a job
___ Got married
___ Had a child

Dana
___ Graduated from high school
___ The tornado happened
___ Graduated from college
___ Got a job
___ Got married
___ Had a child

C Listen again. Number the events in Dana's life in the correct order. Then compare your answers from exercises **B** and **C** with a partner.

D Write about three events in Allen and Dana's lives. Use past time clauses with the past or past progressive and *before, after,* or *when.*

1. (when) Allen _was living in Oklahoma when Dana saw him._

2. (before) Allen _____.

3. (after) Allen _____.

4. (when) Dana _____.

5. (before) Dana _____.

6. (after) Dana _____.

Charts 9.1–9.7

5 WRITE & SPEAK.

A Write six important events in your life on the time line.

| I was born   now |

B Work with a partner. Discuss the events in your life. Use the information from your time line from exercise **A** and *before, after,* and *when.* Use the simple past or past progressive.

Student A: *We moved to Germany when I was six.*

Student B: *Really? Do you speak German?*

UNIT 9   REVIEW THE GRAMMAR   305

Connect the Grammar to Writing

1 READ & NOTICE THE GRAMMAR.

A Read the biography. What did Florence Nightingale do? Discuss with a partner.

Florence Nightingale

Florence Nightingale lived in the 1800s. When she was 24, Nightingale studied nursing. After she finished school, she got a job in a hospital. She became the director of the hospital after only three years. When she was 34, Nightingale took a group of nurses to help injured soldiers in Crimea. Before the nurses arrived, the hospital was very dirty. Many soldiers got diseases. After Nightingale arrived with her nurses, the number of deaths went down by 66 percent.

When she returned to England, Nightingale wrote a book about ways to improve hospital care. Her book changed the nursing profession. Her knowledge saved many people's lives.

▲ Florence Nightingale

GRAMMAR FOCUS

In the biography in exercise **A**, the writer uses past time clauses to show when events happened.

Remember: A time clause includes a word such as *before*, *after*, or *when*, a subject, and a verb.

When she was 24, Nightingale became a nurse.
After she finished school, she got a job in a hospital.

B Read the biography in exercise **A** again. Underline the past time clauses. Then work with a partner and compare answers.

C Complete the notes with information about Florence Nightingale's life with information from the biography in exercise **A**.

Florence Nightingale
1. _____lived in the 1800s._____
2. (age 24) _____.
3. _____ in a hospital.
4. _____ director of the hospital.
5. (age 34) _____ a hospital in Crimea.
Deaths _____.
6. _____ about ways to improve hospital care.

THE PAST: PART 2

Write a Biography

2 BEFORE YOU WRITE.

A Choose a person to write about. Complete the chart below with information about that person's life. What did he or she do? What were the important events in his or her life? Use the chart from exercise **1C** as a model.

1.
2.
3.
4.
5.
6.

3 WRITE a biography. Use the information in your chart in exercise **2A** and the biography in exercise **1A** to help you.

> **WRITING FOCUS** — Using *When*, *Before*, and *After*
>
> Writers use *when*, *before*, and *after* at the beginning of time clauses to show the sequence of events. They also use *before* and *after* as prepositions.
>
> **Remember:** Use a comma when the time clause is at the beginning of the sentence.
>
> <u>When she was 24,</u> Nightingale studied nursing. (time clause)
> She became the director of the hospital **after** only three years. (preposition)

4 SELF ASSESS. Read your biography. Underline the past time clauses. Then use the checklist to assess your work.

☐ I used the simple past for completed actions and the past progressive for actions that were in progress at a specific time in the past. [9.6, 9.7]

☐ I used main clauses with past time clauses. [9.4, 9.5]

☐ There is a subject and a verb in each time clause. [9.4, 9.5]

☐ I used a comma after a time clause at the beginning of a sentence. [9.4, 9.5]

☐ I used *when*, *before*, and *after* to show the sequence of events. [WRITING FOCUS]

UNIT 10 Human and Animal Encounters

Adjectives and Adverbs

◀ A diver has a close encounter with a southern right whale, Auckland Islands, New Zealand.

Lesson 1
page 310

Adjectives; Using Nouns as Adjectives

Lesson 2
page 320

Adverbs of Manner and Adjectives

Lesson 3
page 329

Adjectives and Adverbs with *Too, Very,* and *Enough*

Review the Grammar
page 336

Connect the Grammar to Writing
page 338

LESSON 1　Adjectives

EXPLORE

1 READ the article about the fennec fox. Notice the words in **bold**.

Fennec Foxes

The fennec fox lives in the Sahara and in other parts of North Africa. Everything about this **small** fox helps it in the desert. For example, it is **cream-colored**. The fox's **sandy** color helps it hide in the desert. The fennec fox also has very **large** ears. Its ears keep its body **cool**. This is **important** because the desert gets very **hot** during the day.

The fennec fox has **thick** fur. This keeps it warm at night and cool during the day. The **thick** fur on its feet also helps protect it when it walks or runs across the **hot desert** sand.

Several other things help the fennec fox live in the desert. For one thing, it's a **nocturnal** animal, so it's **active** at night. During the day, it lives under the ground in its den.[1] Another thing that helps this fox is its **excellent** hearing. This helps it find and catch **small** animals to eat, such as mice, reptiles, and insects. When the fox hears a **small** animal under the sand, it starts to dig. The fennec fox also doesn't need a lot of water. This is **helpful** because the desert doesn't get much rain. The fennec fox is truly a **desert** animal.

Related Articles

What's the Sahara **like** at night?
How big is the Sahara?
What kinds of animals live in the Sahara?
What's life **like** for nocturnal animals?

[1] **den:** the home of some kinds of animals

◂ The fennec fox lives in the desert.

▲ A family of fennec foxes

2 CHECK. Match the first part of each sentence in Column A with the second part in Column B. Write the letter on the line.

Column A

1. The sandy color of its fur __c__.
2. Its big ears _____.
3. Its thick fur _____.
4. Its excellent hearing _____.
5. The small amount of water it needs _____.

Column B

a. helps it in the dry desert
b. keep its body cool
c. helps it hide
d. keeps it warm at night and cool during the day
e. helps it find food

3 DISCOVER. Complete the exercises to learn about the grammar in this lesson.

A Find these sentences in the article from exercise **1** on page 310. Write the missing words.

1. Everything about this _____ fox helps it in the desert.
2. The fennec fox also has very _____ ears.
3. The fennec fox has _____ fur.
4. Another thing that helps this fox is its _____ hearing.
5. This is _____ because the desert doesn't get much rain.

B Look at the words you wrote in exercise **A**. What do these words describe? Choose your answer. Then discuss your answer with your classmates and teacher.

These words describe _____ in the sentences.

   a. the subjects   b. the verbs   c. the nouns

LEARN

10.1 Modifying Nouns with Adjectives

Noun	Be	Adjective
The article	is	interesting.
The foxes	are	small.

	Adjective	Noun
It's an	interesting	article.
They are	small	foxes.

1. **Remember:** Adjectives describe or modify nouns or pronouns.	The desert is **hot**. She is **friendly**.
2. **Remember:** Adjectives often come after the verb *be* and modify the subject. They can also come before nouns.	They are **nice**. They are **nice** people. That **tall** man over there is Lee's brother.
3. **Remember:** Use *a* or *an* before an adjective + singular noun. Use *a* before a consonant sound. Use *an* before a vowel sound.	She's **a** good student. He's **an** excellent teacher.
4. **Remember:** The form of an adjective does not change. An adjective is the same for singular and plural nouns and pronouns.	✓ That flower is **beautiful**. ✓ Those flowers are **beautiful**. ✗ Those flowers are beautifuls.
5. Some adjectives after the verb *be* are followed by specific prepositions.	I'm **afraid** of snakes. I'm **worried** about the test. Sugar isn't **good** for you.
6. Use *very* to make an adjective stronger.	Antarctica is **very** cold. My backpack is **very** heavy.

REAL ENGLISH

Like *very*, *really* makes an adjective stronger. *Really* is less formal than *very*.

*It was **really** cold last night.*
*That movie is **really** funny.*

4 Underline the adjectives in the paragraph. Draw an arrow from each adjective to the word it modifies.

Arabian Camels

Arabian camels live in the sandy desert. They are perfect animals for life in this difficult climate. Long eyelashes protect them from blowing sand. They have large feet, so they don't sink into deep sand. They can go for a long time without food or water. They truly are desert animals.

▲ Rothschild giraffes eat from a table at Giraffe Manor in Nairobi, Kenya.

5 Complete each sentence with an adjective from the box. Add *a* or *an* if necessary. Many answers are possible.

| bad | dangerous | good | intelligent | nice | scary | strong |
| beautiful | friendly | huge | interesting | noisy | small | tall |

1. Giraffes are very _____tall_____.
2. Cats are _____ pets.
3. A fennec fox is _____ animal.
4. Grizzly bears are _____ animals.
5. A dog is _____ pet.
6. Snakes aren't _____.
7. Ants are _____ insects.
8. An elephant is _____ animal.
9. Sharks are _____.
10. A lion is _____ animal.

6 WRITE & SPEAK. Write four sentences with adjectives about animals. Use the adjectives from exercise **5** and add an article if necessary. Then share your sentences with a partner.

My dog is a good pet.   I don't like cats. They aren't friendly.

UNIT 10 LESSON 1 313

10.2 Adjectives with *How* and *What* Questions

Questions	Answers
How + Be . . . ?	
How are you?	I'm fine.
How's the pizza?	It's good.
How + Adjective + Be . . . ?	
How tall is your brother?	Six feet.
How bad was the storm?	Very bad.
What + Be . . . Like?	
What's Boston **like**?	It's great. I love Boston.
What are your roommates **like**?	They're nice. I like them a lot.

1. Questions with *How + be*, *How + adjective*, and *What . . . like* ask for descriptions. The answers are often adjectives.

   A: **How's** that book?
   B: It's interesting.

   A: **How cold is** Antarctica?
   B: It's freezing!

   A: **What's** Rosa's brother **like**?
   B: He's very funny.

2. **Be careful!** Questions with *What + be . . . like* and *What do/does . . . like* are not the same.

   A: **What's** she **like**?
   B: She's nice. I like her.

   A: **What does** she **like**?
   B: Tennis and funny movies.

REAL ENGLISH

What kind of . . . asks for specific information.

A: **What kind of** music do you like?
B: *Rock music.*

A: **What kind of** ice cream is that?
B: *Chocolate.*

---

7 Read each conversation. Then choose the correct word(s) to complete A's question.

1. A: _____ the Sahara Desert like?   (a.) What's   b. What does
   B: It's hot and dry.

2. A: _____ is the Sahara Desert?   a. How big   b. How hot
   B: It's huge!

3. A: _____ the weather like at night there?   a. What's   b. How's
   B: It's cool.

4. A: _____ that article about meerkats?   a. How was   b. What was
   B: It was very interesting.

▲ A family of meerkats

5. A: _____ meerkats?
   B: They're small.
   a. How big are b. What is

6. A: What _____ like?
   B: They're very friendly.
   a. is a meerkat b. are meerkats

7. A: _____ was the test?
   B: Very hard.
   a. How long b. How difficult

8. A: _____ John like?
   B: He's funny and smart.
   a. What does b. What's

9. A: How _____ are you?
   B: I'm 21.
   a. tall b. old

10. A: How _____ the weather today?
    B: It's really cold.
    a. cold b. 's

11. A: What _____ your city like?
    B: It's really nice.
    a. does b. 's

12. A: How _____ your family?
    B: There are only four of us.
    a. big is b. is

8 SPEAK. Work with a partner. Ask and answer questions 10–12 in exercise **7**. Use your own answers, not the answers in the book.

Student A: *How's the weather today?*   Student B: *It's sunny and windy.*

UNIT 10　LESSON 1　315

10.3 Using Nouns as Adjectives

	Noun as Adjective	Noun
He is an	animal	doctor.
She is a	tour	guide.

1. Nouns are often used to describe or modify other nouns.	I made a big salad in a **salad** bowl. (= This is a bowl for salad.)
2. Nouns used as adjectives are similar to adjectives. They are used in the singular, not in the plural.	✓ She's a **horse** trainer. (= She trains horses.) ✗ She's a <u>horses</u> trainer.
3. Some nouns used as adjectives end in *-ing*.	We went on a **camping** trip. It's a huge **shopping** center.
4. With *a* and *an*, nouns used as adjectives follow the same rules as nouns.	She's **a bus** driver. He's **an art** teacher.

9 Underline the noun used as an adjective in each sentence.

1. The <u>desert</u> sand is hot.
2. I need a new pencil case.
3. We live in a tall apartment building.
4. It's a very good English program.
5. That biology class is difficult.
6. The hotel has a swimming pool.
7. Where did I put my math book?
8. This is a great shoe store.

10 Complete each sentence. Use nouns as adjectives. Add *a* or *an*.

1. He's a trainer for animals. He's _____an animal trainer_____.
2. It's a park for wildlife. It's _____.
3. It's an elephant. It's a baby. It's _____.
4. I'm a driver. I drive a taxi. I'm _____.
5. He's a teacher. He teaches science. He's _____.
6. It's a report. It's about the weather. It's _____.
7. We're students. We go to college. We're _____.
8. It's an assignment. It's for homework. It's _____.
9. They're workers. They work for the government. They're _____.
10. It's a room. It's for exercise. It's _____.

316 ADJECTIVES AND ADVERBS

PRACTICE

11 Read the paragraph. Underline the adjectives and circle the nouns used as adjectives. Then draw an arrow to the nouns they modify.

Saltwater Crocodiles

(Saltwater) crocodiles are <u>large</u> animals. They are dangerous, too. On the Adelaide River near Darwin, Australia, they are also tourist attractions. Tour boats take people along the river. The tour guides put small pieces of meat on metal poles. Then they hold the poles out over the side of the boat. The crocodiles jump up and take the meat. Fifty years ago, crocodile hunters killed almost all of the crocodiles. The Australian government passed a strict[1] law to protect these crocodiles, and they are now common in Australia.

[1] A **strict** law is very clear and needs to be followed.

▲ A saltwater crocodile jumps for meat, Adelaide River, Northern Territory, Australia.

12 WRITE & SPEAK.

A Complete the e-mail with adjectives and nouns used as adjectives from the box. Add *a* or *an* if necessary. Then work with a partner and compare your answers.

| boat | close | exciting | huge | nervous | scary | small | tour |

Hi Jess,

Greetings from Australia! We're are having a wonderful time here. We went on (1) __an exciting__ tour today! It was (2) _____ trip on the Adelaide River near Darwin. We saw (3) _____ crocodiles! The crocodiles swam near the boat, and the boat was (4) _____, so I was a little (5) _____ at first. The (6) _____ guide held some meat up over the crocodiles, and the crocodiles jumped up right next to the boat. One was really (7) _____ to us. It was really (8) _____! That's all for now! Take care.

Paula

UNIT 10 LESSON 1 317

B Work with a partner. Ask and answer the questions about the information in exercise **A** on page 317.

How was the tour?
What kind of trip did she take?
What were the crocodiles like?

How big was the boat?
Was she nervous?
How close were the crocodiles?

Student A: *How was the tour?*
Student B: *It was exciting.*

13 LISTEN & WRITE.

A Listen to the information about Brian Skerry. Then write the answers to the questions.

1. What is Brian Skerry's job? _____

2. How does he feel about his job? _____

B Look at the words. Then listen again and match each adjective or noun used as adjective in column A with the correct noun in column B. Write the letter on the line.

Column A

1. shark __c__
2. work ____
3. clear ____
4. huge ____
5. rare ____
6. amazing ____
7. underwater ____
8. exciting ____

Column B

a. assignment
b. job
c. fin
d. photographer
e. photos
f. kind of shark
g. water
h. shark

◀ An oceanic whitetip shark has white on the top of its fin.

▲ An oceanic whitetip shark with a diver in the background

C Look at the underlined part of each sentence on the right. Write a question about the underlined word or phrase.

1. _What kind of photographer is Skerry?_ Skerry is an <u>underwater</u> photographer.
2. _____ His job is <u>exciting and dangerous</u>.
3. _____ The shark was <u>very</u> dangerous.
4. _____ The shark was <u>huge</u>.
5. _____ His photographs were <u>amazing</u>.
6. _____ The shark was <u>very</u> close.
7. _____ Whitetip sharks are <u>very</u> rare.
8. _____ The water was <u>very clear and blue</u>.

D Work with a partner. Ask and answer your questions in exercise **C**.

14 APPLY.

A Work with a partner. Choose one of the jobs listed. Then write an interview for a person with that job. Use questions with *How + be, How + adjective, What . . . like,* and *What kind of . . . ?*

tour guide on the Adelaide River   underwater photographer   wild animal photographer

Student A: *What do you do?*   Student B: *I'm a tour guide on the Adelaide River.*

B Role-play your interview from exercise **A** for your classmates.

UNIT 10   LESSON 1   **319**

LESSON 2 Adverbs of Manner and Adjectives

EXPLORE

1 **READ** the news article about a gorilla encounter. Notice the words in **bold**.

Gorilla Encounter[1]

In Uganda, 300 gorillas move around **freely** in Bwindi Impenetrable[2] National Park. The park **carefully** controls the number of visitors. Tourists usually follow guides through the forests to see the gorillas, but one morning, a family of gorillas walked into the tourists' camp. A wildlife photographer, John King, wanted to photograph them. He sat down next to a path and waited **patiently**. The gorillas walked **slowly** past King. Then one gorilla **suddenly** stopped and sniffed[3] him. It touched his hair **lightly**. He sat **quietly** and looked down. The gorillas all sat behind King and looked at him.

King didn't **seem afraid**. In fact, he **looked happy**. Later, he said, "These gorillas were interacting with me just like I was one of their own, and it happened completely **naturally**. Who knows why it happened?" Maybe it was his black shirt and silver hair. The big male silverback gorillas have black and silver fur, so perhaps they thought he was a gorilla!

[1] **encounter:** an unplanned meeting
[2] **impenetrable:** hard or impossible to enter or pass through
[3] **sniff:** to smell something

2 CHECK. Read the statements. Circle **T** for *true* or **F** for *false*.

1. Gorillas are in cages in the Bwindi Impenetrable National Park. T (F)
2. A family of gorillas came out of the forest into a camp. T F
3. The gorillas were afraid of the photographer. T F
4. He enjoyed this experience. T F
5. He thinks the gorillas were interested in his camera. T F

3 DISCOVER. Complete the exercises to learn about the grammar in this lesson.

A Find these sentences in the news article from exercise **1**. Write the missing words.

1. The park _____ controls the number of visitors.
2. He sat down next to the path and waited _____.
3. The gorillas walked _____ past King.
4. Then one gorilla _____ stopped and sniffed him.
5. It touched his hair _____.

B Look at the words you wrote in exercise **A**. What do these words describe? Circle your answer. Then discuss your answer with your classmates and teacher.

These words describe _____ in the sentences.   a. nouns   b. verbs   c. adjectives

LEARN

10.4 Adjectives vs. Adverbs of Manner

1. **Remember:** Adjectives describe or modify nouns. Adverbs of manner describe or modify action verbs.	I'm **careful**. (Adjective) I drive **carefully**. (Adverb) I always **drive carefully**. (*Carefully* describes *drive*.)
2. Do not use an adverb to modify a noun.	✓ She is happy. ✗ She is happily.
3. Do not use an adverb before an object.	✓ I **carefully** drove my new car. ✗ I drove carefully my new car.
4. To form adverbs of manner, add *-ly* to most adjectives.*	beautiful (Adjective) beautifully (Adverb)
5. *Well* is the adverb form of the adjective *good*.	She's a **good** driver. (Adjective) She drives **well**. (Adverb)

*See page **A3** for more information on spelling rules for adverbs.

4 Underline the adverb in each sentence. Draw an arrow to the verb it describes.

1. The park <u>carefully</u> controls the number of visitors.
2. The gorillas move freely in the park.
3. John King sat beside the path and waited patiently.
4. The gorillas walked slowly past King.
5. One of the gorillas touched his hair lightly.
6. King sat quietly.
7. I read the news article quickly.
8. We did the exercise carefully.

5 Look at the <u>underlined</u> adjectives. Then complete each sentence with the correct adverb.

1. That bird is very <u>loud</u>. It sings very ___loudly___.
2. The gorillas were <u>quick</u>. They ran _____.
3. The scientists are very <u>careful</u>. They work _____.
4. The photographer has a <u>good</u> camera. It works _____.
5. Everyone was <u>silent</u>. We sat _____.

322 ADJECTIVES AND ADVERBS

6. She was very calm. She walked very _____ and watched the bear.

7. Those tourists were very rude. They acted very _____.

8. Our guide was very clear. He explained everything very _____.

6 SPEAK. Work with a partner. Use two of the adverbs from exercise **5**. Say sentences about yourself.

Student A: *I wake up slowly.*

Student B: *I walk to the bus quickly.*

10.5 Linking Verbs + Adjectives

Subject	Linking Verb	Adjective
I	am	warm.
Jonathan	looks	tired.

1. Linking verbs connect, or link, subjects and adjectives. The adjective modifies the subject.

   Be, become, feel, get, look, seem, smell, sound, stay, and *taste* are linking verbs.

   We **are** hungry.
   The sky **became** cloudy.
   He **feels** happy.

2. Some verbs can be action verbs or linking verbs; for example: *get, feel, look, smell, sound,* and *taste.*

   The flower **smells** good. (*smell* = linking verb)
   Noun   Adjective
   I **smelled** the flower. (*smell* = action verb)

REAL ENGLISH

The adjectives *afraid, asleep, alone,* and *awake* are only used after the verb *be.* They are never used before nouns.

✓ The baby's **asleep**.
✗ The asleep baby.

I was **awake** at 4:00 a.m.
We weren't **afraid**.
Joe is **alone** in his office right now.

7 Underline the linking verbs in these sentences. Then circle the adjectives and adverbs. Draw an arrow back to the words they modify.

1. The gorillas were (interested) in the photographer.

2. He didn't seem afraid. In fact, he acted bravely.

3. She looked happy as she looked at the photographs.

4. I love these flowers. They smell wonderful.

5. I had a headache last night. I felt fine this morning.

6. Most people feel nervous when they make presentations.

7. Please taste this soup. Does it taste OK?

8. I need to buy some warm clothes. The weather is getting cold.

9. You sound upset. Did something happen?

10. I'm very tired today. I didn't sleep well last night.

8 SPEAK. Work with a partner. Complete the sentences with linking verbs. Use your own ideas.

1. I'm _____cold_____.

2. I feel _____.

3. _____ (*name of classmate*) seems _____.

4. _____ (*name*) looks _____.

5. _____ (*food*) tastes _____.

10.6 Adverbs and Adjectives with the Same Form

1. Some adjectives and adverbs have the same form: *early, fast, hard, late*	He's a **fast** runner. (*fast* = adjective) He runs **fast**. (*fast* = adverb)
2. **Remember:** Some adjectives end in *-ly*: lonely, ugly, friendly.	She's a **friendly** person.

REAL ENGLISH

In everyday conversation and informal writing, we use *slow* as an adjective and adverb. In formal writing, we use *slowly*.

Informal: He does everything slow.
Formal: He does everything slowly.

9 Look at the underlined word in each sentence. Is it an adjective or an adverb? Check (✓) the correct column.

	Adjective	Adverb
1. The homework was <u>hard</u>.	✓	☐
2. Marcy seems very <u>friendly</u>.	☐	☐
3. Drive <u>slowly</u>. The roads are icy tonight.	☐	☐
4. They were driving <u>fast</u> when they saw the police car.	☐	☐
5. Julie won the race <u>easily</u>.	☐	☐
6. We worked <u>hard</u> and finished on time.	☐	☐

	Adjective	Adverb
7. When you're feeling <u>lonely</u>, please call me.	☐	☐
8. The horse didn't look <u>fast</u>, but it won the race.	☐	☐
9. Walk <u>fast</u>, OK? We're late!	☐	☐
10. Sorry I'm late. The bus was really <u>slow</u>.	☐	☐
11. I have an <u>early</u> class.	☐	☐
12. The train was <u>late</u> this morning.	☐	☐

PRACTICE

10 Circle the correct words to complete the story. Then work with a partner and compare answers.

A Helpful Chimpanzee

Geza Teleki is a primatologist. He studies chimpanzees. One day he saw some chimps go into the woods (1) **quick** / **(quickly)**. He was (2) **curious** / **curiously**, so he followed them. He followed the chimpanzees for several hours in the woods. Then the chimpanzees stopped and began to eat fruit from the trees. Teleki (3) was **hungry** / **hungrily**. His stomach was making (4) **loud** / **loudly** noises. The fruit looked (5) **good** / **well**. He wanted to eat some, too. He tried to reach the fruit in the trees, but it wasn't (6) **easy** / **easily**. The fruit was very (7) **high** / **highly** in the trees. Teleki tried to use a stick to knock the fruit from the tree, but it didn't work very (8) **good** / **well**. He didn't get any fruit. One of the young chimps was watching him (9) **careful** / **carefully**. The chimp picked a piece of fruit from the tree and gave it to him. Teleki was very surprised. The young chimp understood Teleki's problem and helped him solve it. They are very (10) **intelligent** / **intelligently** animals.

◀ A young chimpanzee in the Tai Forest, Tai National Park, Ivory Coast, Africa

11 Work with a partner. Complete each sentence with a verb and an adverb from the box.

Verbs				Adverbs			
arrive	read	study	yell	carefully	fast	loudly	softly
drive	speak	swim	walk	early	hard	quickly	slowly

1. When I'm late for work or class, I _____walk fast._____
2. When I'm talking to someone in a noisy place, I _____.
3. When I see a shark at the beach, I _____.
4. When I have a big test, I _____.
5. When I'm reading a test question, I _____.
6. When I'm talking to someone in the library, I _____.
7. When I'm going to the airport for an international flight, I _____.
8. When I'm in my car and it's raining or snowing, I _____.

12 **EDIT.** Read the safety tips. Find and correct six more errors with adverbs or adjectives and linking verbs.

Safety Tips for Encounters with a Wild Animal

Welcome to our Wildlife Park. Stay ~~safely~~ safe. There are a lot of wild animals in this area. Here are some important safety tips:

- Carry a can with rocks in it. Shake loudly the can. Wild animals usually stay away when they hear people.
- During a wild animal encounter, do not look directly at the animal. Look down.
- Do not run. Walk quiet away.
- Do not climb a tree. Many animals climb trees good.
- When you see baby animals, do not stand between them and their mothers.
- Speak softly.
- On a tour, follow closely your guide.
- Try to stay calmly.
- If an animal runs direct at you, try to look large and tall. Hold your arms and a jacket above your head.

326 ADJECTIVES AND ADVERBS

▲ Jambo the gorilla at the Jersey Zoo (now the Durrell Wildlife Park), Jersey, Channel Islands

13 LISTEN & SPEAK.

A Listen to a true story about an unusual animal encounter. Then choose the correct answer.

1. Where did this story happen?   a. In a wildlife park.   b. In the wild.
2. Did the gorilla hurt the boy?   a. Yes.   b. No.

B Listen again. Read the statements. Circle **T** for *true* and **F** for *false*.

1. The boy didn't want to see the gorillas.	T	(F)
2. He wanted to get very close to the gorillas.	T	F
3. He hit his head hard when he fell.	T	F
4. A 400-pound gorilla named Jambo quickly ran over to the child.	T	F
5. Jambo touched the boy gently on the back.	T	F
6. Jambo sat next to the boy and yelled loudly.	T	F
7. Jambo ran away quickly.	T	F
8. The zookeepers moved slowly.	T	F

C Work with a partner. Compare your answers from exercise **A**. Then correct the false statements to make them true.

1. The boy ~~didn't want~~ *wanted* to see the gorillas.

D Work in a group. Discuss these questions.

1. How did the boy feel before he fell?
2. How did he feel when he woke up?
3. How did Jambo act with the boy?
4. Did Jambo's actions surprise you?

UNIT 10   LESSON 2   **327**

▲ A common house mouse searches for a snack.

14 APPLY.

A Think about an encounter with an animal. Write notes in the chart about the experience. Use the questions in the chart to help you.

What kind of animal was it? Describe it. Use adjectives.	a little mouse
How did you feel? Use adjectives.	
Describe the experience. Was it funny, exciting, scary? Use adjectives.	
What happened? Use adverbs.	

B In your notebook, write about this animal encounter. Use adjectives and adverbs to make your story interesting.

I moved into a new apartment. When I turned on the oven for the first time, a little mouse ran out from behind the stove. I was really scared. I screamed loudly and . . .

C Work in a group. Share your stories with your classmates.

328 ADJECTIVES AND ADVERBS

Adjectives and Adverbs with *Too, Very,* and *Enough*

LESSON 3

EXPLORE

1 READ the article about the Iberian lynx. Notice the words in **bold**.

Save the Iberian Lynx

Is the world **big enough** for both humans and wild animals? Cities are expanding[1] **very quickly** into the countryside. When human activity is **too close** to wild animal habitats,[2] it causes problems for the animals.

This is the case with the Iberian lynx in Spain, for example. People started to move into the lynx's native habitat in the mountains. They cut down trees and grew olives on the hillsides. This forced the lynx into smaller areas in the mountains. Now the Iberian lynx is almost extinct; only a few hundred are still alive. They live **too far** from each other to grow in number.

Is it **too late** to save the Iberian lynx? People in Spain have a plan. They are removing olive trees in the mountains and planting native trees. They want to grow a forest **big enough** for the lynx to live in. They hope the forests will grow **quickly enough** to save the Iberian lynx.

[1] **expand:** get bigger
[2] **habitat:** the area in which an animal or plant usually lives

▲ An Iberian lynx in motion. Wildlife experts in Spain track the Iberian lynx with the help of a special collar.

UNIT 10 LESSON 3 **329**

2 CHECK. Choose the correct answer for each question.

1. What happened to the lynx's habitat?   a. animals moved in   (b.) people moved in
2. How many Iberian lynx are there?   a. a few hundred   b. a few thousand
3. Where do Iberian lynx live?   a. in the desert   b. in the mountains
4. What is the plan to help the lynx?   a. plant trees   b. make new farms

3 DISCOVER. Complete the exercises to learn about the grammar in this lesson.

A Find these sentences in the article from exercise **1** on page 329. Write the missing words.

1. Cities are expanding _____ into the countryside.
2. When people move _____ to wild animal habitats, it causes problems for the animals.
3. Is it _____ to save the Iberian lynx?
4. They want to grow a forest _____ for the lynx to live in.

B Look at your answers from exercise **A**. Choose the correct answer to the question below. Then discuss your answer with your classmates and teacher.

Which word has a negative meaning?   a. too   b. very   c. enough

◂ Close-up of an Iberian lynx

330

LEARN

10.7 Too/Very + Adjective or Adverb

Too + Adjective or Adverb
I don't want to go outside. It's **too cold**. (*too* + adjective)
I didn't understand them. They spoke **too quickly**. (*too* + adverb)

Very + Adjective or Adverb
I don't want to go outside. It's **very cold** (*very* + adjective)
They finished the assignment early. The worked **very quickly**. (*very* + adverb)

1. *Too* has a negative meaning. It means "more than necessary." Use *too* + adjective or adverb when there is a problem or a negative result.	The hotel is **too noisy**. (Negative result: We can't sleep at night.) He was driving **too fast**. (Negative result: He got a ticket.)
2. **Remember:** Use *very* to make an adjective or adverb stronger. *Very* does not mean the same thing as *too*. It does not have a negative meaning.	✓ The people were **very friendly**. ✗ The people were <u>too</u> friendly. ✓ We studied **very hard**. ✗ We studied <u>too</u> hard.

4 Circle the correct word to complete each sentence.

1. People are moving **(too)** / **very** close to the lynx's habitat. It's causing problems for the animals.

2. The Iberian lynx is a **too** / **very** beautiful animal.

3. The lynx's habitat is **too** / **very** small. The animals don't have enough space.

4. The article about the Iberian lynx was **too** / **very** interesting.

5. The information was **too** / **very** helpful.

6. Everyone in our class is **too** / **very** nice. It's a great class.

7. I didn't finish the assignment last night. It was **too** / **very** long.

8. Amy is **too** / **very** smart. She always gets good grades.

5 SPEAK. Work with a partner. Complete each sentence with *too* or *very* and an adjective.

The weather today is . . .   *The weather today is very nice.*

This city is . . .

My friends are . . .

UNIT 10 LESSON 3 **331**

10.8 Adjective or Adverb + *Enough*

	Adjective/Adverb	Enough	
It's	cold	enough	for gloves and a hat today.
He did	well		to pass the course.

1. After an adjective or an adverb, *enough* means "to a necessary or satisfactory extent."	We voted this year. We are **old enough**. I missed the bus. I didn't run **fast enough**.
2. Put *enough* after adjectives and adverbs.	✓ This room is <u>big</u> enough for our meeting. ✗ This room is <u>enough big</u> for our meeting.
3. *Enough* is often followed by an infinitive.	He's tall **enough** <u>to touch</u> the ceiling. I'm not strong **enough** <u>to lift</u> that heavy box.

6 Complete each sentence with the word(s) in parentheses and *enough*.

1. Our classroom is _____not big enough_____ (not big) for all the students.

2. He didn't speak _____ (loudly) during his presentation. It was difficult to hear him.

3. She didn't explain the information _____ (clearly). We didn't understand.

4. They didn't do _____ (well) to pass the test.

5. He didn't do his homework _____ (carefully). He makes a lot of mistakes.

6. It's _____ (not warm). Please turn up the heat.

7. I can't hear the music. It's _____ (not loud). Please turn it up.

8. It feels _____ (cold) to snow!

9. Is your sister _____ (old) to live alone?

10. She's _____ (not old) to drive.

7 Work with a partner. Complete each sentence with *enough* or *not enough* and an adjective.

I am . . .
This classroom is . . .
This building is . . .

I'm not tall enough to play basketball.

332 ADJECTIVES AND ADVERBS

PRACTICE

8 Match each sentence in Column A with a sentence in Column B. Write the letter on the line.

Column A

1. He's not studying hard enough. _g_
2. She's running very fast. ____
3. It's raining too hard. ____
4. He's reading very carefully. ____
5. It's not warm enough. ____
6. He's working too hard. ____
7. It's too hot in here. ____
8. You're driving too slowly. ____

Column B

a. Please turn up the heat.
b. He needs to relax and take a vacation.
c. Come on. Hurry up!
d. Let's stay home.
e. Let's open the window.
f. She's winning the race.
g. His grades are terrible.
h. He wants to understand the information.

9 Complete the conversation with *too, very,* or *enough* and the adjectives in parentheses. Then listen and check your answers.

Ethan: Look. This is (1) ___very interesting___ (interesting). There's a new exhibit at the zoo.

Emma: I don't like to go to zoos. I feel (2) _____ (sad) when I see the animals in those little cages.

Ethan: Me, too. The areas for the animals aren't (3) _____ (big), especially for the large animals such as lions and tigers.

Emma: Yeah, I agree with you, but zoos want to show the animals. When the exhibits are (4) _____ (large), sometimes people don't see any animals. The animals usually don't stay (5) _____ (close) to the windows of the exhibit, so it's difficult to see them.

Ethan: You're right. That's (6) _____ (true). The animals are often (7) _____ (far) from the windows for anyone to see them.

Emma: My friends and I want to go on a safari someday. In Africa, animal parks are (8) _____ (big) for the animals. The animal parks help protect the animals.

Ethan: I know, but safaris are (9) _____ (expensive).

Emma: That's true. They're (10) _____ (expensive) for me right now. Maybe someday!

10 EDIT. Read the news article. Find and correct five more errors with *too, very,* or *enough.*

ZOO NEWS

The City Zoo

The City Zoo is planning to expand. Right now the zoo isn't ~~enough~~ large ^enough for all of the animals. Many animal exhibits are too small. There isn't enough land to expand on this site. The zoo tried very hard to buy more land in the city, but the land was enough expensive. Last week, the zoo bought the old Cherry Hill Farm. "We are too happy about this," says the zoo director. "The Cherry Hill Farm is too large. The property is big enough for us to build a new zoo." Plans for the new exhibits are too exciting. They include natural habitats. These are enough big for the animals.

▲ A child watches a polar bear at a zoo exhibit.

11 LISTEN & SPEAK.

A Listen to the conversations. Match each topic with the correct conversation.

Conversation 1 _____   a. A bear

Conversation 2 _____   b. A new exhibit for night animals

Conversation 3 _____   c. The weather

B Listen again. The speakers in the conversations do not always agree with each other. After you listen, work with a partner and make sentences for each conversation. Use *very, too, enough,* and the words in the boxes.

Conversation 1

| cold | hard | warm | windy |

Mindy: We're having a picnic at the zoo. Do you want to come with us?

Eduardo: Isn't it _____ and cold? The wind is blowing _____ to eat outside.

Mindy: No, it isn't. It's _____ to eat outside.

334 ADJECTIVES AND ADVERBS

Conversation 2

| crowded | dark | hot | interesting | slowly |

Sam: It's a beautiful exhibit. It's _____.

Liz: I didn't like it. It was _____.

Sam: Of course it was. It has to be _____ for the animals. They're nocturnal. When it's light, they go to sleep.

Liz: I know, but it was also _____, and it was _____. There were too many people in there, and everyone was walking _____. I didn't like it at all.

Conversation 3

| big | huge | small |

Marta: Isn't that bear cute?

David: Well, grizzly bears are _____ to be cute.

Marta: This exhibit isn't really _____ for a huge bear, is it?

David: You're right. It's _____.

C With your partner, practice saying the conversations in exercise **B**.

▲ The slender loris is a nocturnal animal. It lives in forests in Sri Lanka and southern India.

12 APPLY.

A Work in a small group. Share your answers to these questions.

1. What animals are interesting to you? Why?

2. What do you think about zoos? Are the animal exhibits big enough? Do the animals live freely enough? Do zoos help or hurt animals? How?

3. Why do you like or dislike zoos?

B Write four or five sentences to explain your answer to question 3 in exercise **A**.

_____
_____
_____
_____
_____

Review the Grammar UNIT 10

Charts 10.1, 10.4–10.8

1 Circle the correct words to complete the paragraph.

A Dangerous Situation

Mattias Klum is a famous photographer. He takes (1) **(beautiful)** / **beautifully** photographs of animals. Once when he was in Borneo, he saw a king cobra. The cobra was lying (2) **quiet** / **quietly** near a small river. King cobras are very (3) **dangerous** / **dangerously** snakes. Klum wanted to take a photograph of the cobra, but he wasn't (4) **quick** / **quickly** enough to get a (5) **good** / **well** photograph.

Klum (6) **quick** / **quickly** ran along the river and tried to find a (7) **good** / **well** place to take a photograph. He jumped into the river, and then he saw the cobra. It was in the water moving (8) **direct** / **directly** in front of him. It was very (9) **close** / **closely** to Klum. The cobra raised its head out of the water and tried to bite him. Klum used his camera to protect his legs. It was a very (10) **dangerous** / **dangerously** situation for Klum. His (11) **quick** / **quickly** action worked (12) **good** / **well**. The snake didn't bite him, and he took some (13) **amazing** / **amazingly** photographs of the cobra.

▲ A king cobra

Charts 10.1, 10.3–10.7

2 EDIT. Read the e-mail. Find and correct six more errors with adjectives and adverbs.

From: Davis, Pam
To: Martin, Judy
Subject: Dugong

Hi Judy,

I had an amaze day today. [*amaze* corrected to *amazing*] I saw a dugong. It was huge! The water was clearly and quiet. It wasn't very deeply. I saw perfectly the dugong. It was moving slowly along the bottom and it was eating the seagrass. Every few minutes it swam up and quick put its nose out of the water. It seemed very gently. No one was afraid of it. There aren't many dugongs anymore. They're endangered. I was luckily to see one!

Pam

▲ A dugong

336 ADJECTIVES AND ADVERBS

Charts 10.1, 10.3–10.7

3 LISTEN, WRITE & SPEAK.

A Dugongs are endangered animals. Why? Listen and check (✓) the reasons you hear.

CD3-24

1. _✓_ the supply of seagrass
2. ____ the water temperature
3. ____ hunters
4. ____ large tour boats
5. ____ nets on large fishing boats
6. ____ the number of baby dugongs
7. ____ disease

B Complete each sentence with information from the listening. Add a verb and use the word in parentheses with *too, very,* or *enough*. Then listen again and check your answers.

CD3-24

1. The supply of sea grass __is not large enough__ (large).
2. Seagrass _____ (slowly).
3. Hunters _____ them _____ (easily) because dugongs _____ (slowly).
4. Fishing boats _____ dugongs _____ (frequently) because dugongs _____ (fast).
5. The number of dugongs _____ (quickly).

Charts 10.1, 10.4, 10.7 & 10.8

4 READ & SPEAK.
Work with a partner. Partner A, read the information about giant pandas on this page. Partner B, read the information about Mexican gray wolves on page **A6**. Then close your books. Tell your partner about the animal. Use adjectives, adverbs, *too, very,* and *enough*.

Partner A

Giant Pandas

Giant pandas are black and white bears. They are very shy. In Chinese, their name means "Large Bear-Cat." In the past, they lived in China, Myanmar, and North Vietnam. Now they only live in a small area of China. Giant pandas are very rare. They are endangered because people moved into their habitats, so their habitats are not big enough for them.

UNIT 10 REVIEW THE GRAMMAR 337

Connect the Grammar to Writing

1 READ & NOTICE THE GRAMMAR.

A Read the paragraph. How does the writer feel about snakes? What encounters did she have with snakes? Discuss with a partner.

My Feelings about Snakes

I am afraid of snakes. In my hometown, there are a lot of huge snakes. They are very dangerous. One time, I almost stepped on a snake when I was walking in my yard. I was walking slowly, so I didn't step on it, but it was very scary. Another time, I went on a camping trip, and a big snake crawled into our tent. Fortunately, I saw it before it got dark. Of course, I screamed loudly, and my father ran quickly to help. That was my last camping trip.

GRAMMAR FOCUS

In the paragraph in exercise **A**, the writer uses adjectives and nouns used as adjectives to modify nouns and pronouns. The writer also uses adverbs to modify verbs.

I am **afraid** of snakes.
     Adjective

I was walking **slowly**, so I didn't step **directly** on it.
         Adverb   Adverb

B Read the paragraph in exercise **A** again. Underline the adjectives and nouns used as adjectives. Circle the adverbs of manner. Then work with a partner and compare answers.

C Write notes in the chart to answer the questions about the information in the paragraph in exercise **A**.

What is the topic of the paragraph?	The writer's feelings about snakes.
How does the writer feel about them?	
Why? What encounters or experiences did the writer have with snakes?	

338 ADJECTIVES AND ADVERBS

Write about an Animal

2 BEFORE YOU WRITE. Complete the chart with information about an animal you feel strongly about. Use the questions to write notes about your ideas. Use the chart from exercise **1C** as a model.

What is the topic of your paragraph?	My feelings about _____
How do you feel about it / them?	
Why do you feel this way? Write about an encounter or experience.	

3 WRITE a paragraph. Use the information in your chart in exercise **2A** and the paragraph in exercise **1A** to help you.

> **WRITING FOCUS   Using Adverbs and Adjectives to Add Interest**
>
> Writers use adjectives and adverbs to add interest to their writing.
>
> GOOD: *In my hometown, there are a lot of snakes.*
> BETTER: *In my hometown, there are a lot of **huge** snakes. They are very **dangerous**.*
>
> GOOD: *I screamed, and my father ran to help.*
> BETTER: *I screamed **loudly**, and my father ran **quickly** to help.*

4 SELF ASSESS. Read your paragraph. Underline the adjectives. Circle the adverbs of manner. Then use the checklist to assess your work.

- [ ] I used adjectives and nouns used as adjectives to describe nouns and pronouns. [10.1, 10.3, 10.5]
- [ ] I used adverbs to describe action verbs. [10.4, 10.6]
- [ ] I used adjectives (not adverbs) after linking verbs. [10.5]
- [ ] I used adjectives and adverbs to add interest to my writing. [WRITING FOCUS]

UNIT 11 Challenges and Abilities

Modals: Part 1

▲ BASE jumper Miles Daisher during a jump from the New River Gorge Bridge on Bridge Day, October 22, 2009, Fayetteville, West Virginia, USA

Lesson 1
page 342

Can/Could

Lesson 2
page 352

Be Able To; Know How To

Lesson 3
page 359

And, But, and *So;* Contrasts after *But*

Review the Grammar
page 367

Connect the Grammar to Writing
page 370

LESSON 1   Can/Could

EXPLORE

1   READ the article about Yves Rossy. Notice the words in **bold**.

Look! I can fly!

The passengers on a plane in Switzerland were surprised when they looked out the windows. A man was flying next to the plane!

The passengers were not imagining[1] things. Yves Rossy, or "Jetman," **can fly**. Rossy wears a large V-shaped wing with very small jet engines on it. A helicopter takes Rossy up. Then he falls back first out of the helicopter. When he starts the jet engines in his wing, he **can go** between 200 and 300 miles per hour (between 320 and 480 kilometers per hour)!

Rossy's wing is about six feet (two meters) wide. It weighs 120 pounds (55 kilograms). With the wing, he **can fly** for eight minutes. He **can't fly** any longer than that because there isn't enough fuel[2] for the engines. When he wants to land, he opens his parachute.[3] On one flight, he had some trouble: He **couldn't open** his parachute. Finally, at 1500 feet (457 meters) above the ground, he **was able to open** it and landed safely.

[1] **imagine:** to picture something in your mind
[2] **fuel:** a substance such as oil or gasoline that is burned to provide energy
[3] **parachute:** something that helps people float slowly to the ground from high in the air

---

DISCUSS THIS ARTICLE

D.J. Butler
   Interesting! **Where can I learn** to fly?
   July 17, 10:21 AM

Arlene Sargeant
   Can anyone buy a wing like this?
   July 17, 10:40 AM

Sarah8201
   Why couldn't he open his parachute? That's really scary!
   July 17, 10:42 AM

◀ "Jetman" Yves Rossy over Lake Lucerne, Switzerland

342   MODALS: PART 1

2 CHECK. Read the statements. Circle **T** for *true* or **F** for *false*.

1. Yves Rossy uses a big wing with small jet engines to fly.　　T　F
2. Rossy flies very fast with his jet wing.　　T　F
3. Rossy flies for 200 minutes.　　T　F
4. The wing uses all the fuel in 80 minutes.　　T　F
5. Rossy lands with a parachute.　　T　F

3 DISCOVER. Complete the exercises to learn about the grammar in this lesson.

A Find these sentences in the article from exercise **1**. Write the missing words.

1. Yves Rossy, or "Jetman," _____.
2. He _____ any longer than that because there isn't enough fuel for the engines.
3. On one flight, he had some trouble: He _____ his parachute.

B Look at the sentences from exercise **A**. Then choose the correct word to complete each statement. Discuss your answers with your classmates and teacher.

1. We use *can* and *can't* to show ____.　　a. ability　　b. necessity
2. *Could* and *couldn't* show possibility in the ____.　　a. present　　b. past
3. The verb after *can* or *could* ____ a final *-s*.　　a. has　　b. doesn't have

UNIT 11　LESSON 1　343

LEARN

11.1 Can/Could for Ability and Possibility: Statements

Affirmative

Subject	Can/Could	Base Form of Verb
I, You, He, She, It, We, You, They	can	fly.
	could	

Negative

Subject	Can't/Couldn't	Base Form of Verb
I, You, He, She, It, We, You, They	can't / cannot	fly
	couldn't / could not	

1. Use *can* to talk about present and future ability or possibility. Use *could* to talk about ability or possibility in the past.	**I can speak** Spanish. (present) We **can** talk later. (future) My grandfather **could run** ten miles when he was young. (past)
2. *Can* and *could* are modals. A modal verb changes the meaning of the main verb. *Can* and *could* add the meaning of ability or possibility to the main verb.	He **can** speak German. I **can't** speak German. I **couldn't** speak German before this class.
3. Use the base form of the verb after *can* and *could*. *Can* and *could* keep the same form for all subjects.	✓ I **can ride** a bicycle. ✓ She **could ride** a bicycle. ✗ She can rides a bicycle. ✗ She could to ride a bicycle.
4. *Can't* and *couldn't* are used in speaking and informal writing. *Cannot* and *could not* are used in formal writing.	I **can't** ice skate. She **couldn't** drive. Children under 15 **cannot** drive. We **could not** understand him.

4 Complete each sentence with *can*, *can't*, *could*, or *couldn't* and the verb in parentheses.

1. Rossy _____can fly_____ (fly) with special jet wings.

2. The jet wing uses a lot of fuel, so Rossy _____ (stay) in the air for more than eight minutes.

3. You _____ (learn) more about Rossy online.

4. One time, Rossy _____ (open) his parachute. That was scary!

5. A long time ago people _____ (travel) by plane.

6. The plane _____ (leave) because the weather was bad.

7. Some planes _____ (go) very long distances now.

8. The pilot _____ (see) very far because it was very cloudy.

344 MODALS: PART 1

5 PRONUNCIATION. Read the chart and listen to the examples. Then complete the exercises.

PRONUNCIATION — Can/Can't

Pay attention to the vowel sounds in *can* and *can't*.

In affirmative statements with *can* + verb, *can* is usually pronounced /kən/, and the main stress of the sentence is on the ability that follows.

I can speak Spanish. = I /kən/ speak **Spanish**.   He can swim = He /kən/ **swim**.

In negative statements, *can't* is usually pronounced /kænt/, and it is stressed to emphasize the lack of an ability.

I can't speak Arabic. = I /**kænt**/ speak Arabic.   He can't ski. = He /**kænt**/ ski.

See page **A4** for a guide to pronunciation symbols.

A Listen to each sentence. Do you hear *can* or *can't*? Check (✓) the correct column.

	Can	Can't		Can	Can't
1.	☐	✓	6.	☐	☐
2.	☐	☐	7.	☐	☐
3.	☐	☐	8.	☐	☐
4.	☐	☐	9.	☐	☐
5.	☐	☐	10.	☐	☐

B Work with a partner. Complete the sentences.

1. I can _____.

2. I can't _____.

Student A: *I can speak three languages.*

Student B: *I can't ice skate.*

▶ An ice skater on frozen Canyon Ferry Lake, Montana, USA

UNIT 11   LESSON 1   **345**

11.2 *Can/Could* for Ability and Possibility: Questions

Yes/No Questions

Can/Could	Subject	Base Form of Verb
Can Could	you he she they	swim?

Short Answers

Affirmative	Negative
Yes, I/he/she/they can. could.	No, I/he/she/they can't. couldn't.

Wh- Questions

Wh- Word	Can/Could	Subject	Base Form of Verb
Who			ask?
What		I	make?
When	can	you	talk?
Where	could	he	meet?
How		she	find it?
How far		we	run?
How fast		you	fly?
How many languages		they	speak?

Answers

The librarian.
Goulash and pasta.
Tomorrow afternoon at three.
At the coffee shop.
Ask at the front desk.
Three miles.
Two hundred miles per hour.
Four.

1. *Can* and *could* come before the subject in *Yes/No* questions and most information questions.	**Can** you speak Korean? Where **can** we get some coffee? How **could** he do that?
2. Use *How far* to ask questions about distance.	A: **How far** can you swim? B: About a mile.
3. Use *How fast* to ask questions about speed.	A: **How fast** can it go? B: Eighty miles per hour.
4. **Remember:** *Wh-* questions with *Who* or *What* can be about a subject or an object.	Questions about a Subject: **Who** can speak Russian? (**Igor** can.) **What** can happen? (**Anything** can happen.) Questions about an Object: Who can we **ask**? (We can ask **Mary**.) What can she **play**? (She can play **tennis**.)

6 Change each statement into a *Yes/No* question. Then complete the short answer for each question.

1. I can ice skate.   A: <u>Can you ice skate?</u>
   B: Yes, <u>I can</u>.

2. I can ski.   A: _____
   B: No, _____.

3. We could understand the article.   A: _____
   B: No, _____.

346 MODALS: PART 1

4. She can play the piano.   A: _____
                                    B: Yes, _____ .

5. He could sing very well.   A: _____
                                    B: No, _____ .

6. I can drive a car.   A: _____
                                    B: Yes, _____ .

7. My brother can cook.   A: _____
                                    B: Yes, _____ .

8. They could swim.   A: _____
                                    B: No, _____ .

7 Read each statement. Write a *Wh-* question about the underlined information.

1. A marathon runner can run 26.2 miles. _____How far can a marathon runner run?_____
2. That plane can fly 400 miles per hour. _____
3. Astronauts can travel into space. _____
4. The teacher can help me. _____
5. I can speak three languages. _____
6. We can play tennis. _____
7. You can see the Northern Lights in Iceland. _____
8. They can meet at 2:00. _____
9. They can get to Paris by boat or plane. _____
10. He could swim a mile when he was younger. _____

8 SPEAK. Ask your classmates questions about the activities in the box. Use *Can you . . . ?* Write the names of students who say *Yes* next to each activity. Do not use a student's name more than once.

Student A: *Can you ride a horse?*   Student B: *Yes, I can.*

ice skate _____	ski _____
speak Arabic _____	play the piano _____
ride a horse _____	drive a car _____
cook _____	swim _____

UNIT 11 LESSON 1 **347**

PRACTICE

9 Complete the paragraph with *can, can't, could, couldn't* and the verb in parentheses.

Frequently Asked Questions: The Amphicar

What is an Amphicar?

An Amphicar is a very unusual car. (1) It <u>can travel</u> (travel) on the road or in the water.

What is the history of the Amphicar?

A man named Hans Trippel made the first Amphicar in Berlin, Germany in 1962. It (2) _____ (go) 70 miles per hour (112 kilometers per hour) on the road, but in the water it (3) _____ only _____ (go) seven mph (11 kph). That didn't worry four Englishmen who in 1965 took two Amphicars across the English Channel! Everyone was surprised that the cars (4) _____ (do) this. In the 1960s, people (5) _____ (buy) an Amphicar for about $3000. Now, you (6) _____ (not buy) a used Amphicar for less than $30,000. Trippel's company sold almost 4000 cars, but it closed in 1968. The car (7) _____ (not pass) the new air pollution[1] tests.

Can you find Amphicars anywhere now?

Yes, you can. In many places, Amphicar owners have "swim-ins." They usually meet at a lake where they (8) _____ (drive) into the water together.

[1] **pollution:** the process of making water, air, or land dirty and dangerous

▼ A 1964 Amphicar on the River Thames near Staines, England in 1998

10 EDIT. Read the conversation about flying cars. Find and correct five more errors with *can, can't, could,* or *couldn't*.

Dad:	Here's an interesting ad. It says, "Yes, cars can ~~flies~~ fly!"
Daughter:	That's crazy. Cars can't to fly!
Dad:	Well, I saw a flying car when I was a child.
Daughter:	Really? Could it flies?
Dad:	Yes, but it couldn't goes very fast.
Daughter:	Where you can drive it? You can't drive a car with wings on the highway.
Dad:	Sure you can. The wings fold up, and you can to drive it on the highway.

348 MODALS: PART 1

11 Look at each answer. Write a question about the underlined phrase.

Frequently Asked Questions: Flying Cars

1. Q: <u>Can cars really fly?</u>

   A: <u>Yes</u>, cars really can fly!

2. Q: _____

   A: <u>Yes</u>, companies could build flying cars more than fifty years ago.

3. Q: _____

   A: The flying cars can travel <u>on roads and in the air</u>.

4. Q: _____

   A: <u>No</u>, they can't take off from the highway. You need a flat place with no other cars, such as an airport.

5. Q: _____

   A: The cars can go <u>100 miles per hour</u>.

6. Q: _____

   A: The cars can carry <u>two people</u>. They're very small.

7. Q: _____

   A: You can fit <u>two suitcases</u>. Not all flying cars have this much room, but a couple of them do.

8. Q: _____

   A: You can learn more about them <u>online</u>.

▶ A flying car over farmland near Giessen, Germany in 1997

12 LISTEN, WRITE & SPEAK.

A Look at the photos and the information about three flying cars. Then listen to information about these flying cars. Write the name of each flying car.

| SkyRunner | Transition® | PAL-V |

1. Name: _____
   Air speed: _____ mph (185 kph)
   Distance: 490 miles (787 km)
   Passengers: 2
   Other: the wings fold

2. Name: _____
   Air speed: _____ mph (177 kph)
   Distance: _____ miles (563 km)
   Passengers: _____
   Other: flies like a tiny helicopter;
   drives like a _____

3. Name: _____
   Air speed: 55 mph (88 kph)
   Distance: 200 miles (321 km)
   Passengers: _____
   Other: a parasail

350 MODALS: PART 1

B Listen again. Complete the chart in exercise **A** with information about each flying car.

C Write sentences about each flying car. Use information from the chart in exercise **A**. Use *can* or *can't*.

1. The Transition can fly 115 miles per hour.
2. _____
3. _____
4. _____
5. _____
6. _____

D Work with a partner. Ask and answer questions about the flying cars.

Student A: *Can the SkyRunner fly 115 miles per hour?*

Student B: *No, it can't.*

13 APPLY.

A Work in a group with four or five students. You are at a flying car show. Choose one of the roles below.

Student A wants to buy a flying car.

Student B wants to buy a flying car.

Student C is a salesperson for the Transition®.

Student D is a salesperson for the SkyRunner.

Student E is a salesperson for the PAL-V.

B Role-play a conversation at the flying car show. Students A and B ask Students C, D, and E questions about their flying cars. Students C, D, and E answer the questions about their cars. Which car do you want to buy?

Student A: *How far can the SkyRunner fly?*

Student D: *It can fly 200 miles.*

Student C: *The Transition® can fly 490 miles.*

Student B: *How fast can the PAL-V fly?*

Student E: *It can fly 110 miles per hour.*

C Which car do Students A and B want to buy? Why? Write three sentences about each student.

Abdul likes the Transition® because he can drive it on the road and keep it at his house. It can fly... Beatrice likes the SkyRunner because...

UNIT 11   LESSON 1   351

LESSON 2   Be Able To; Know How To

EXPLORE

1 READ the article about Winter the dolphin. Notice the words in **bold**.

Winter the Dolphin

One day, a fisherman in Florida saw a dolphin in the water. When he got close to it, he **was able to see** the dolphin's problem. Lines from a crab trap[1] were wrapped around the dolphin's tail and mouth. The dolphin **wasn't able to get** free from the lines. The fisherman called for help, and a rescue team took the dolphin to an aquarium. However, the people at the aquarium **weren't able to save** its tail.

This was a big problem because dolphins use their tails to move through the water. With no tail, the dolphin **wasn't able to swim** very well. The little dolphin named Winter was in danger. The people at the aquarium **didn't know how to keep** Winter strong. Then, Kevin Carroll and Dan Strzempka heard about Winter's problem. They **knew how to help**. Their company made artificial[2] legs and arms for people. They **were able to** make a new tail for Winter.

It wasn't easy, but they did it! With the artificial tail, Winter **was able to move** through the water like a dolphin again.

[1] **trap:** a device to catch something, for example, an animal
[2] **artificial:** made by a person, not by nature

▶ Winter with her new tail at the Clearwater Marine Aquarium, Clearwater, Florida, USA

2 CHECK. What is the correct order of these events in the article from exercise **1**? Write numbers 1–5 next to each sentence.

____ A rescue team took the dolphin to an aquarium.

____ The dolphin got an artificial tail.

____ A fisherman saw the dolphin.

____ The dolphin lost its tail.

____ Kevin Carroll and Dan Strzempka helped the dolphin.

3 DISCOVER. Complete the exercises to learn about the grammar in this lesson.

A Find these sentences in the article from exercise **1**. Write the missing words.

1. The dolphin _____ get free from the lines.

2. However, the people at the aquarium _____ save its tail.

3. With the new tail, Winter _____ move through the water like a dolphin again.

B Look at the sentences from exercise **A**. What do these words tell us? Choose your answer. Then discuss your answer with your classmates and teacher.

1. We use *wasn't able to* when ____.

   a. something wasn't necessary   b. something wasn't possible

2. The verb after *be able to* ____ the base form.

   a. is   b. isn't

UNIT 11 LESSON 2 353

LEARN

11.3 Be Able To

Affirmative Statements

Subject	Be Able To	Base Form of Verb	
I	am able to / was able to		
He / She	is able to / was able to	fix	their car.
You / We / They	are able to / were able to		

Negative Statements

Subject	Be Not Able To	Base Form of Verb	
I	'm not able to / wasn't able to		
He / She	isn't able to / wasn't able to	fix	their car.
You / We / They	aren't able to / weren't able to		

Yes/No Questions

Is he **able to fix** their car?
Was he **able to fix** their car?
Are they **able to help**?
Were they **able to help**?

Short Answers

Affirmative		Negative	
Yes, he	is. / was.	No, he	isn't. / wasn't.
Yes, they	are. / was.	No, they	aren't. / weren't.

---

1. To talk about ability or possibility, use *be able to*. It has the same meaning as *can*.
   I'm able to swim. = I can swim.
   Are you able to swim? = Can you swim?

2. To talk about abilities and inabilities in the past, use *was able to* or *were able to*.
   He **was able to meet** with us yesterday.
   We **weren't able to finish** the assignment.

3. To form the negative of *be able to*, put *not* after *be*.
   ✓ **I'm not able to talk** right now.
   ✗ I <u>don't</u> able to talk right now.

   ✓ **I was able to answer** all the questions.
   ✗ I <u>didn't</u> able to answer all the questions.

---

4 Change each sentence from the present to the past.

1. The dolphin isn't able to swim.   The dolphin ___wasn't able to swim___.
2. The fisherman is able to help.   The fisherman _____.
3. The rescuers aren't able to save its tail.   The rescuers _____ its tail.
4. The two men are able to make a new tail.   The two men _____ a new tail.
5. The dolphin is able to move normally.   The dolphin _____ normally.
6. We are able to see dolphins in Florida.   We _____ dolphins in Florida.
7. The dolphin is able to swim very well.   The dolphin _____ very well.
8. We aren't able to see the aquarium.   We _____ the aquarium.

5 Write *Yes/No* questions about abilities in the past. Use the words in parentheses and *be able to*. Then complete the short answer.

1. (you / swim)
A: When you were a child, <u>were you able to swim?</u>
B: Yes, <u>I was</u>.

2. (you / understand / that question)
A: _____
B: No, _____.

3. (you / finish / your homework)
A: _____
B: Yes, _____.

4. (the students / finish / the test)
A: _____
B: No, _____.

5. (Fred / go / to the movies)
A: _____
B: No, _____.

6. (your parent / go / with you)
A: _____
B: Yes, _____.

7. (you / fall asleep / last night)
A: _____
B: No, _____.

8. (you / hear / the bell)
A: _____
B: No, _____.

9. (they / do / the exercise)
A: _____
B: Yes, _____.

10. (she / find / her book)
A: _____
B: Yes, _____.

11. (Oleg / talk to / his teacher)
A: _____
B: No, _____.

12. (you / see / anything)
A: _____
B: No, _____.

6 **WRITE & SPEAK.** List three things you were not able to do in the past, but are able to do now. Then share your sentences with a partner. Use the verbs in the box or your own ideas.

buy	go	read	understand
drive	play	speak	use

I wasn't able to speak English before I came here.

I wasn't able to drive when I was fifteen.

UNIT 11 LESSON 2

11.4 Know How To

Affirmative Statements
He **knows how to read** a map.
They **know how to ski**.

Negative Statements
He **doesn't know how to fly** a plane.
They **don't know how to skate**.

Yes/No Questions
Do you **know how to ski**?
Does he **know how to skate**?

Short Answers	
Affirmative	Negative
Yes, I **do**.	No, I **don't**.
Yes, he **does**.	No, he **doesn't**.

1. *Know how to* means you have a skill or ability to do something from practice or experience. It is similar to *can*.	I **know how to** swim. = I can swim. **Do** you **know how to** swim? = Can you swim?
2. Use *do/does* to make this expression negative or interrogative.	A: **Do** you **know** how to fix a car? B: No, I **don't**.
3. The past of *know* is irregular: *knew*. Use *knew how to* to talk about a skill or ability in the past.	I **knew** how to read before I started school.
4. Use *can*, not *know how to*, when an ability does not come from practice or experience.	✓ I **can** open the door for you. ✗ I <u>know how to</u> open the door for you. ✓ Fish **can** swim. ✗ Fish <u>know how to</u> swim.

REAL ENGLISH

Learn how to is used to talk about an ability or skill we don't have, but want to learn.

I want to **learn how to** ski. Do you know where I can take lessons?

7 Change each affirmative statement to a negative statement.

1. They know how to play tennis. <u>They don't know how to play tennis.</u>
2. I know how to fly a plane. _____
3. He knows how to speak Chinese. _____
4. We know how to solve the problem. _____
5. She knows how to cook. _____
6. I knew how to swim. _____
7. They knew how to help. _____
8. We knew how to find the answer. _____
9. Ted knows how to fix your computer. _____
10. Lori knew how to get there. _____

8 Use the words in parentheses to write Yes/No questions. Use *know how to* in the present.

1. (you / fly a plane) Do you know how to fly a plane?
2. (your son / ride a bicycle) _____
3. (they / dance the tango) _____
4. (you / play the guitar) _____
5. (he / scuba dive) _____
6. (they / take good photographs) _____
7. (I / play golf) _____
8. (she / fix a car) _____
9. (he / make cookies) _____
10. (you / use this vending machine) _____

9 SPEAK. Work with a partner. Ask and answer questions about ability. Use *know how to* and the words in the box.

| cook | fly a plane | play tennis | ride a horse |
| drive a car | make coffee | play the piano | surf |

Student A: *Do you know how to surf?*

Student B: *No, I don't.*

PRACTICE

10 Match each question in Column A with the correct answer in Column B. Write the letter on the line.

Column A

1. Were you able to read before you started school? _b_
2. Do you know how to ride a motorcycle? ____
3. Does a dolphin know how to swim? ____
4. Does your grandmother know how to use a computer? ____
5. Were people able to fly in the nineteenth century? ____
6. Was I able to finish the last lesson? ____
7. Are dogs able to talk? ____
8. Do babies know how to walk? ____

Column B

a. No, I don't.
b. No, I wasn't.
c. Yes, you were.
d. No, they don't.
e. Yes, she does.
f. No, they weren't.
g. No, they aren't.
h. Yes, it does.

11 **EDIT.** Read the questions and answers about doctors in the past. Find and correct five more errors with *be able to* and *know how to*.

Ask the Doctor

Q: When people were sick in the old days, were doctors able ^to help them?

A: In the past, many people died because doctors didn't able to save them. Doctors didn't know to help very sick people.

Q: Were women able to being doctors?

A: In some countries, they did. But in most countries, women weren't able to be doctors. They wasn't able to go to medical school.

12 LISTEN & SPEAK.

A Listen to the information about Sophie Germain. Then choose the correct answers.

1. When did Sophie Germain live?
   a. in the 1900s
   b. in the 1800s
   c. in the 1700s

2. Why was her life difficult?
   a. Education for women was not common.
   b. She wasn't a good student.

B Listen again. What things was she able to do? Put a check (✓) next to the activities.

1. ☐ study math when her parents were awake
2. ☐ study late at night
3. ☐ attend college
4. ☐ write to a professor
5. ☐ sign her letter "Sophie Germain"
6. ☐ learn math from a college professor
7. ☐ solve difficult math and physics problems
8. ☐ help people build tall buildings

C Work with a partner. Ask and answer *Yes/No* questions about Sophie Germain. Use *be able to* and *know how to*.

Student A: *Was she able to go to college?*   Student B: *No, she wasn't.*

13 APPLY. Work in a group. How is life different for women now? Ask and answer questions about the activities in the box. Use *Were women able to . . .* and *Are women able to . . . ?*

| become doctors | become the leader of the country | drive cars | vote |
| buy houses | have jobs outside the home | wear pants | |

Student A: *Are women able to vote in the United States?*

Student B: *Yes, they are now. They weren't able to vote before 1920.*

And, But, and *So* **LESSON 3**

EXPLORE

1 READ the article about athletes with disabilities. Notice the words in **bold**.

Challenges for Athletes

In 1904, George Eyser competed in gymnastics in the Olympics. He won three gold medals, two silver medals, and a bronze medal. He was a great athlete, **but** he was also an unusual athlete. As a child, he lost his leg in a train accident, **so** he had an artificial leg. It was made of wood.

Eyser isn't the only athlete with a physical disability to compete in the Olympics. Im Dong Hyun is almost blind, **but** he won gold medals in archery with his team from South Korea. Natalia Partyka from Poland was born with only one arm, **but** she competed in the Olympics in table tennis.

Many more athletes with disabilities compete in the Paralympic Games. These take place every four years in the winter and summer. The first Games were in 1960, **and** 400 athletes from 23 countries competed. Now, more than 4000 athletes from more than 160 countries compete. Like George Eyser, these athletes focus on the competition, not on their disabilities.

▲ Hannah Cockroft of Great Britain on her way to her second gold medal at the 2012 Summer Paralympic Games in London, England

2 CHECK. Read the statements. Circle **T** for *true* or **F** for *false*.

1. George Eyser won seven medals in the Olympics.   T   F
2. Eyser had only one arm.   T   F
3. Im Dong Hyun's team won gold medals.   T   F
4. The Paralympic Games are only in the summer.   T   F
5. In the first Paralympic Games, 400 athletes competed.   T   F

3 DISCOVER. Complete the exercises to learn about the grammar in this lesson.

A Find these sentences from the article from exercise **1** on page 359. Write the missing words.

1. He was a great athlete, _____ he was also an unusual athlete.
2. As a child, he lost his leg in a train accident, _____ he had an artificial leg.
3. The first Games were in 1960, _____ 400 athletes from 23 countries competed.

B Look at the sentences and words you wrote in exercise **A**. Then choose the correct word to complete each statement. Discuss your answers with your classmates and teacher.

1. Use ____ to add information.   a. and   b. but   c. so
2. Use ____ to show a contrast or add surprising information.   a. and   b. but   c. so
3. Use ____ to show a result.   a. and   b. but   c. so

▼ David Weir of Great Britain wins the gold medal in the men's 1500-meter T54 final at the 2012 Summer Paralympic Games in London, England

LEARN

11.5 And, But, So

I can speak Spanish, **and** I also speak a little Italian.
— Independent Clause —   — Independent Clause —

She can't read Farsi, **but** she can speak it.
— Independent Clause —   — Independent Clause —

I lived in Costa Rica, **so** I can understand Spanish.
— Independent Clause —   — Independent Clause —

1. *And, but,* and *so* are often used to connect two sentences or independent clauses. **Remember:** A clause is a word group with a subject and a verb. An independent clause can stand alone as a complete sentence.	He was a very fast runner. He won a lot of races. He was a very fast runner, **so** he won a lot of races. Larry ran very fast, **but** he didn't win the race. — Independent Clause — — Independent Clause —
2. Put a comma before *and, but,* or *so* when you connect two independent clauses.	Pablo plays soccer, **and** he likes tennis, too. I can play the piano, **but** I'm not very good. Mina felt sick yesterday, **so** she didn't run in the race.
3. Use *and* to add information.	I ran in the race, **and** I finished it in 35 minutes.
4. Use *but* to show a contrast or add surprising information.	They tried hard, **but** their team didn't win.
5. Use *so* to show a result.	She broke her leg, **so** she couldn't run in the race.

REAL ENGLISH

In conversation, we often use parts of sentences.

But I like it.
So we did it.

This is not correct in writing. Use complete sentences in writing.

My science class is difficult, but I like it.
Our teacher gave us homework, so we did it.

4 Connect the two sentences. Use the word in parentheses.

1. He didn't win. He did very well. (but) _He didn't win, but he did very well._

2. He had an artificial leg. He could walk. (so) _____

3. He was in an accident. He lost his leg. (and) _____

4. She had an artificial leg. She could run very fast. (but) _____

5. She entered the race. She won. (and) _____

6. The Games were very popular. Tickets sold fast. (so) _____

7. Ava is strong. She's not fast. (but) _____

8. They were very fast. They won a lot of races. (so) _____

5 Circle the correct word to complete each sentence.

1. We lost the game, **and** / **(but)** we had fun.
2. He ran in the marathon, **and** / **but** he did very well.
3. We read an article about sports, **and** / **so** it was very interesting.
4. She didn't understand the assignment, **and** / **so** she asked her teacher for help.
5. They want to learn French, **but** / **so** they're taking classes twice a week.
6. I don't have any sisters, **but** / **and** I have two brothers.
7. Anil missed the bus, **but** / **so** he was late for work.
8. My history class is difficult, **and** / **but** I like it a lot.

6 SPEAK. Work with a partner. Complete the sentences.

I can speak English, but I …
English grammar is difficult, but …
The weather today is good/terrible, so …
Today we're sitting in class, and …

I can speak English, but I can't speak Chinese.

11.6 Contrasts after *But*

Affirmative Clause	But	Negative Clause
We're ready,	but	they aren't.
I was there,		she wasn't.
He plays tennis,		I don't.
We can speak Korean,		they can't.
They could go,		we couldn't.

Negative Clause	But	Affirmative Clause
We aren't ready,	but	they are.
I wasn't there,		she was.
He doesn't play tennis,		I do.
We can't speak Korean		they can.
They couldn't go		we could.

1. The clause after *but* is often shortened.	I'm ready for the race, but he isn't. (= I'm ready for the race, but he isn't ready for the race.) She plays soccer, but her brother doesn't. (= She plays soccer, bur her brother doesn't play soccer.) We can't speak French, but they can. (= We can't speak French, but they can speak French.)
2. Do not shorten the clause after *but* if the verb is different from the verb in the first clause.	✓ I'm studying, but my brother is working. ✗ I'm studying, but my brother is.

362 MODALS: PART 1

7 Circle the correct word to complete each sentence.

1. I can ski, but my parents **can** / **(can't)**.
2. My brother likes baseball, but I **do** / **don't**.
3. We watched the game, but she **did** / **didn't**.
4. He doesn't compete in races, but his brother **does** / **doesn't**.
5. He's an athlete, but they **are** / **aren't**.
6. I wasn't in the race, but my friends **were** / **weren't**.
7. Marie wasn't able to finish the race, but I **was** / **wasn't**.
8. I don't know how to swim, but he **does** / **doesn't**.
9. She finished the race, but I **did** / **didn't**.
10. We're tired today, but she **is** / **isn't**.

8 Complete each sentence with the correct affirmative or negative form of *be*, *do*, or *can*.

1. That exercise isn't difficult, but this one _____is_____.
2. My sister is a very good athlete, but I _____.
3. We can't go, but they _____.
4. He knows her, but I _____.
5. Claudia can't speak Arabic, but Noor _____.
6. I ate breakfast, but you _____.
7. She likes to go shopping, but I _____.
8. They didn't get lost, but we _____.

9 SPEAK. Work with a partner. Make sentences about some differences between you and your partner. Use *but* and the correct form of *be*, *do*, and *can*.

| am/is | do/does | like/like to |
| can | don't/doesn't | _____ (your idea) |

I like to wake up early, but Cara doesn't.

Monica can speak Portuguese, but I can't.

I'm married, but Antonio isn't.

I don't play soccer, but Ahmed does.

UNIT 11 LESSON 3

PRACTICE

10 Match the beginning of each sentence in column A with the correct ending in column B.

Column A

1. I can't speak Spanish, but __d__.
2. Yesterday Ed and Al went to work, but _____.
3. I can speak Chinese, so _____.
4. Last year, she didn't run the marathon, but _____.
5. My brother is a fast runner, but _____.
6. Anita can swim very well, and _____.
7. He hurt his foot, so _____.
8. She was tired after the race, so _____.
9. I went to the game last night, and _____.
10. The game was very exciting, and _____.

Column B

a. this year she did
b. he's not well
c. today they didn't
d. I can speak Italian
e. she went to bed early
f. we had great seats
g. I saw Peter and Jun there
h. he couldn't finish the race
i. I want to go to Hong Kong to study
j. she can scuba dive, too

11 Complete the conversations with *and, but,* and *so.* Then listen and check your answers.

Conversation 1

Andres: I really want to play in the game tomorrow, (1) ___but___ I can't.

Jill: Why not?

Andres: Well, I was practicing yesterday, (2) _____ I hurt my foot.

Jill: That's too bad. Ted is sick, (3) _____ he can't play either.

Conversation 2

Yuri: Terry won the bike race yesterday, (4) _____ we're having a party for her. Are you free on Friday night?

Liam: That's great, (5) _____ I have plans for dinner with my parents. What time is the party?

Yuri: The party's at 8:00, (6) _____ it's at Carol's house.

Liam: Oh, well, we usually eat dinner at 6:00, (7) _____ Carol lives near me, (8) _____ I can go to the party after dinner.

Conversation 3

Jason: It's noon, (9) _____ I'm thinking about lunch. Do you want to join me?

Ed: Sorry. I just finished breakfast, (10) _____ I'm not hungry.

Jason: Hi, Mark. Ed isn't hungry, (11) _____ I am. How about lunch?

Mark: Oh, I'm sorry. That sounds good, (12) _____ I have a lot of work today.

12 EDIT.
Read the paragraph about Aimee Mullins. Find and correct five more errors with the use of *but, and,* and *so.*

Aimee Mullins

When Aimee Mullins was born, she didn't have bones in part of her legs, ~~but~~ *so* she couldn't walk. The doctors talked to her parents, so they decided to amputate[1] part of her legs. Some people have trouble with artificial legs, and Mullins doesn't. She learned to walk with them, but they were a normal part of her life. In high school, Aimee played softball, and in college she competed in many track and field events. In the Paralympics, she ran 100 meters in 17.01 seconds, so she jumped 3.14 meters in the long jump. Aimee Mullins has a physical disability, and that doesn't slow her down.

[1] **amputate:** to cut off surgically

13 LISTEN & WRITE.

A Listen to information about three famous people. What were their challenges and achievements? Put a check (✓) in the correct column.

		Walt Disney	Bruce Hall	Beethoven
Challenges	• couldn't hear	☐	☐	☐
	• couldn't see	☐	☐	☐
	• had very little money	✓	☐	☐
Achievements	• artist and businessperson	☐	☐	☐
	• underwater photographer	☐	☐	☐
	• music composer	☐	☐	☐

B Work with a partner. Write three sentences about each famous person from exercise **A**. Use the words from list A and list B with *and, but,* and *so.*

1. Walt Disney

List A
family / poor
not be / a good student
start / a company

List B
get / a job
leave / high school
do very well

(so) _Walt Disney's family was poor, so he got a job._

(and) _____

(and) _____

UNIT 11 LESSON 3 **365**

2. Bruce Hall

   List A

   be blind
   hear about stars
   learn to scuba dive

   List B

   be / a photographer
   not see / them
   take / underwater photographs

▲ An example of Bruce Hall's underwater photography.

(but) _____

(but) _____

(so) _____

3. Beethoven

List A	**List B**
be / a great musician	write / music
become / a composer	lose / his hearing
become / deaf	continue to write / music

(and) _____

(but) _____

(but) _____

14 APPLY.

A Work in a small group. Discuss these questions.

1. Think of three or four people who had challenges in their lives. They can be famous people or people you know. Who are these people? What challenges did they face?

Michael J. Fox is an actor. He got a disease, but he didn't stop acting.

2. What did he or she do about this challenge or situation?

Michael J. Fox started an organization to make money for research about his disease . . .

B Write five or six sentences about one of the people from exercise **A** and his or her challenges. Use *and, but,* and *so* in your sentences.

C Share your sentences with your classmates.

366   MODALS: PART 1

UNIT 11 Review the Grammar

Charts 11.1–11.4

1 Complete the conversations. Use words from the box. There are two possible answers for some of the sentences. You can use the words more than once.

can	Can you	know how to
can't	Do you know how to	don't know how to

1. A: Excuse me. (1) _Can you / Do you know how to_ read Chinese?
   I (2) _____ read this street sign.
   B: I'm sorry. I (3) _____ read Chinese either.

2. A: This door is stuck! I (4) _____ open it.
   B: Let me try. No, I (5) _____ open it either. Is it locked?

3. A: (6) _____ fix computers? My computer isn't working.
   I (7) _____ turn it on.
   B: Yes, I (8) _____ fix some computer problems. Let me look at it.

4. A: (9) _____ solve this math problem?
   I (10) _____ do it.
   B: No, I'm sorry. I (11) _____ do it either.

Charts 11.1–11.3

2 READ & SPEAK.

A Read the story about National Geographic photographer, Alison Wright. Underline the forms of *be able to* and *could/couldn't*.

Alison Wright

Alison Wright is a photographer and writer. She travels to remote villages, places far away from cities and airports. She takes photographs of the people there and writes about their lives. Several years ago, she was traveling on a bus on a remote mountain road in Laos when a truck hit the bus. She was able to get out of the bus, but she had a broken back and many other injuries. She couldn't move, and she wasn't able to breathe very well. No one could help her because she was very far away from any doctors or hospitals. She waited for ten hours. Finally, someone came by in a small truck and saw her. He put her in the back of his truck and drove for eight hours to a small hospital in Thailand. A doctor there was able to save her life, but she had serious injuries. She returned to her home in the United States and had more than 20 operations. When she left the hospital, she couldn't walk very well, and she wasn't able to travel. However, she didn't give up. She became stronger and exercised every day because she had a dream: she wanted to climb Mount Kilimanjaro. Four years later, she did it. She was able to climb Mount Kilimanjaro!

Review the Grammar UNIT 11

B Work with a partner. Compare your answers from exercise **A** on page 367.

C Role-play an interview between Alison Wright and a reporter. Partner A is the reporter. Partner B is Alison Wright. Use information in the story and your imagination.

Reporter: *Where was the accident?*

Alison: *In Laos.*

Reporter: *Were you able to breathe?*

Alison: *Yes, I was, but I couldn't breathe very well.*

Charts 11.5–11.6

3 EDIT. Read the paragraph about Bethany Hamilton. Find and correct seven more mistakes with *and*, *but*, and *so*.

Bethany Hamilton

Bethany Hamilton grew up in Hawaii, ~~but~~ *and* she was an excellent surfer. She won many competitions, but she was the number 1 surfer for the 13-year-old age group. One day, she was on her surfboard with one arm in the water, but a shark bit her. People nearby took her to the hospital, so doctors couldn't save her arm. She lost her arm, so she got back on her surfboard one month after the shark attack. Most people can't surf with one arm, and Bethany can. She entered a competition four months after the attack, so she won fifth place. A year later, she entered a national competition, and she won! Bethany faced a huge challenge when she lost her arm, and she didn't give up.

▶ Bethany Hamilton at Super Girl Pro (2013), Oceanside, California, USA

Charts 11.1–11.4

4 LISTEN & SPEAK.

A Listen to the conversation. Then complete the sentences.

1. Tami and Richard tried to get away from the hurricane, but _they couldn't_.
2. Most waves don't turn a boat upside down, but _____.
3. When Tami woke up the next day, she thought Richard was on the boat, but _____.
4. Tami tried to find Richard, but _____.
5. Tami survived the hurricane, but _____.
6. Many people don't know how to use the sun for location, but _____.
7. Tami wanted to use the engine, but _____.
8. Most people don't sail again after a terrible experience, but _____.

B Listen again. Then work with a partner. Use *and, but,* or *so* to combine the sentences.

1. Tami wanted to see the ~~world. She~~ *world, so she* helped people sail their boats across the ocean.
2. A hurricane was coming. Tami and Richard didn't know.
3. The hurricane was moving toward them. They changed direction.
4. A huge wave turned the boat over. It caused a lot of damage in the boat.
5. Tami looked for Richard. She didn't find him.
6. Tami's trip to Hawaii took 41 days. She survived.
7. It was a terrible experience. Tami still likes to sail.
8. Tami is a brave woman. She's a good sailor.

C Work with a partner. Discuss these questions.

1. Can you imagine a trip across an ocean in a sailboat? Why, or why not?
2. What surprised you about this story?

Connect the Grammar to Writing

1 READ & NOTICE THE GRAMMAR.

A Read the story. What was the challenge? Discuss with a partner.

My Cousin's Challenge

My cousin got very sick when she was 14 years old. She was in the hospital for two weeks, and she couldn't go to school for a month. She wasn't able to sit up, so she couldn't do any homework. When she finally went back to school, she didn't know how to do any of the math problems, and she was behind in all her courses.

Before my cousin got sick, she wasn't really a very good student, but she decided to change. She studied every weekend, and she also studied with a tutor after school. Finally, she was able to catch up with the other students. She studied hard every day, and after high school she went to a very good university. I am very proud of her.

GRAMMAR FOCUS

In the story in exercise **A**, the writer uses *couldn't* and *be able to* to describe abilities or inabilities in the past.

She **couldn't** go to school for a month.
She **wasn't able to** sit up.

B Read the story in exercise **A** again. Underline the modals and expressions that show ability or inability. Then work with a partner and compare answers.

C Complete the chart with information from the story in exercise **A**. What challenges did the writer's cousin face? What actions helped her with this challenge?

My Cousin's Challenge	
Challenges	Actions
got sick
was in the hospital	

370 MODALS: PART 1

Write about a Challenge

2 **BEFORE YOU WRITE.** Think of a person who faced a challenge (you or another person). What challenge did this person face? What actions helped this person with the challenge? Write notes in the chart. Use the chart in exercise **1C** as a model.

_____ Challenge	
Challenges	Actions

3 **WRITE** a paragraph about this person's challenge. Use the information from your chart in exercise **2** and the story in exercise **1A** to help you.

> **WRITING FOCUS** Combining Sentences with *And*, *But*, and *So*
>
> Writers use *and*, *but*, and *so* to join two independent clauses. This helps show the relationship between ideas and adds variety to their writing.
>
> *She was in the hospital for two weeks,* **and** *she couldn't go to school for a month.*
>
> *She wasn't able to sit up,* **so** *she couldn't do any homework.*
>
> *Finally, she was able to go back to school,* **but** *she had a hard time.*

4 **SELF ASSESS.** Read your story. Underline *and*, *but,* and *so*. Then use the checklist to assess your work.

- ☐ I used the base form of the verb after *can/can't* and *could/couldn't*. [11.1–11.2]
- ☐ I used the correct forms of *be able to*. [11.3]
- ☐ I used *know how to* when I wrote about a skill from practice or experience. [11.4]
- ☐ I used a comma before *and*, *but,* and *so*. [11.5]
- ☐ I used *and*, *but,* and *so* to join two independent clauses and add variety to my sentences. [WRITING FOCUS]

UNIT 11 CONNECT THE GRAMMAR TO WRITING 371

UNIT 12 Amazing Places
Comparative and Superlative Adjectives

▲ Horseshoe Bend on the Colorado River, near Page, Arizona, USA

Lesson 1
page 374

Comparative Adjectives

Lesson 2
page 383

Superlative Adjectives

Lesson 3
page 391

Possessive Pronouns; *Whose*

Review the Grammar
page 399

Connect the Grammar to Writing
page 402

LESSON 1   Comparative Adjectives

EXPLORE

1 READ the article about Mount Everest and K2. Notice the words in **bold**.

Two Amazing Mountains

Two mountains in the Himalayas are very well known around the world: Mount Everest and K2. Mount Everest is **more famous than** K2 because it's the highest mountain in the world. However, K2 is **more difficult** to climb and **more dangerous**. In fact, very few climbers reach the top of K2. About 20 percent of all climbers die in their attempt.

What makes K2 **more challenging**[1] **than** Mount Everest? First, the weather on K2 is often **worse than** on Mount Everest. High winds, storms, and heavy snow make the climb very difficult. K2 is also **steeper than** Mount Everest. The climb to the top typically takes ten days **longer** as well. It usually takes 75 days to climb K2. The average expedition to climb Mount Everest is about 65 days.

[1] **challenging:** very difficult

▶ An expedition climbs K2.

2 CHECK. Read the list of adjectives in the chart. Which mountain does each adjective describe? Check (✓) the correct column. Then compare your answers with a partner.

Adjective	Mount Everest	K2
higher	✓	
more famous		
more difficult		
more challenging		
steeper		
more dangerous		

3 DISCOVER. Complete the exercises to learn about the grammar in this lesson.

A Find these sentences in the article from exercise **1**. Write the missing words.

1. Mount Everest is _____ K2 because it's the highest mountain in the world.

2. However, K2 is _____ to climb and _____ .

3. What makes K2 _____ Mount Everest?

4. First, the weather on K2 is often _____ on Mount Everest.

B Look at these sentences from exercise **A**. What do these words show? Circle **T** for *true* or **F** for *false* for each statement below. Then discuss your answers with your classmates and teacher.

1. These words show differences between two things.   T   F

2. These words show how two things are similar.   T   F

LEARN

12.1 Comparative Forms of Short Adjectives

	Be	Comparative Adjective	Than	
Ted	is	older	than	his brother.
Lucia		younger		Katya.
Planes	are	faster		buses.

1. Use a comparative adjective + *than* to talk about the difference between two people, places, or things.	Eduardo is **taller than** Joe. Brazil is **larger than** Colombia. My computer is **smaller than** my notebook.
2. *Than* is not necessary when the second item in the comparison is understood by both the speaker and the listener.	A: Do you prefer this hotel or the Grand Hotel? B: The Grand Hotel. It's **nicer**.
3. For short adjectives (one syllable), add *-er* to the end of the adjective.	old → old**er** new → new**er** high → high**er**
4. When a short adjective ends in CVC*, double the final consonant and add *-er*.	big → big**ger** fat → fat**ter**
5. When a short adjective ends in *-e*, add *-r*.	nice → nice**r**
6. Some adjectives have irregular comparative forms.	good → **better** bad → **worse** far → **farther**

REAL ENGLISH

One is often used with comparatives to avoid repeating the noun, or when the noun is understood by both the speaker and the listener.

This house is older than that **one**. (one = house)

A: Is this table OK?
B: That **one**'s bigger. Let's sit there.

*consonant + vowel + consonant

4 Complete each sentence with the comparative form of the adjective in parentheses. Add *than* when necessary.

1. Mount Everest is _____higher than_____ (high) K2.

2. K2 is _____ (low) Mount Everest.

3. K2 is _____ (steep) Mount Everest.

4. The weather on K2 is _____ (bad) on Mount Everest.

5. The weather on Mount Everest is _____ (good) the weather on K2.

6. The climb to the top of Mount Everest is _____ (short) the climb to the top of K2.

7. The climb to the top of K2 is _____ (hard) the climb to the top of Mount Everest.

8. Expeditions to the top of Mount Everest are long, but expeditions to the top of K2 are _____ (long).

376 COMPARATIVE AND SUPERLATIVE ADJECTIVES

5 SPEAK. Compare people in your class. Use the comparative form of the adjectives in the box.

| tall | short | old | young |

Junko is taller than Sonia.

12.2 Comparative Forms of Long Adjectives

	Be	Comparative Adjective	Than	
This hotel	is	more famous	than	that one.
The new store	is	more expensive	than	the old store.
The brown shoes	are	more comfortable	than	the blue ones.

1. For long adjectives (two or more syllables), put *more* before the adjective to make the comparative form.
   - modern → **more** modern
   - careful → **more** careful
   - expensive → **more** expensive

2. When a long adjective ends in consonant + *-y*, change the *-y* to *-i* and add *-er*.
   - easy → easi**er**
   - pretty → pretti**er**
   - friendly → friendli**er**

3. Some short adjectives are used with *more than*.
   - Soccer is **more** fun **than** golf.

REAL ENGLISH

Add *-er* to some two-syllable adjectives to make the comparative form.

- quiet → quiet**er**
- simple → simpl**er**
- narrow → narrow**er**

6 Complete each sentence with the comparative form of the adjective in parentheses.

1. (interesting) The movie about Mt. Everest was <u>more interesting than</u> the book.
2. (expensive) Paris is _____ Lisbon.
3. (quiet) Quebec City is _____ Mexico City.
4. (beautiful) The beach is _____ the city.
5. (sunny) Miami is _____ Seattle.
6. (crowded) Mumbai is _____ Toronto.
7. (relaxing) A vacation in Hawaii is _____ a vacation in New York City.
8. (busy) People in big cities are _____ people in small towns.
9. (noisy) Bangkok is _____ Boston.
10. (scary) The climb to the top of K2 is _____ the climb to the top of Mount Everest.

7 WRITE & SPEAK. Use the adjectives from the box to compare two places or things. Then share your sentences with a partner.

| crowded | expensive | famous | interesting | pretty |

Istanbul is more interesting than Orlando.
My sunglasses were more expensive than my shoes.

12.3 Questions with Comparatives

Yes/No Questions

Be	Subject	Comparative Adjective	
Is	Brazil	larger than	Canada?
Are	planes	faster than	trains?

Short Answers

No, it isn't.
Yes, they are.

Questions with *Which* and *Who*

Wh- Word	Noun	Be	
Which	café	is	better?
	shoes	are	more expensive, the red ones or the blue ones?
Which		is	bigger, Tokyo or Osaka?
Who		is	older, you or your sister?

Answers

The Bistro.
The blue ones.
Tokyo.
My sister.

1. **Remember:** The verb comes before the subject in *Yes/No* questions with *be*.

   Is Mount Everest higher than K2?
   Are you taller than your brother?

2. *Wh-* questions with *Which* or *Who* are often about a subject.

   Which mountain is higher?
   Who is taller, you or your brother?

8 Put the words in the correct order to make *Yes/No* questions and questions with *Which*.

1. higher / is / Which / mountain

   Which mountain is higher?

2. hotel / is / Which / cheaper

   _____

3. Which / difficult / more / course / is

   _____

4. new / your / bigger / Is / apartment

   _____

5. your / new / Is / farther away / apartment

   _____

6. worse / is / rain or snow / Which

   _____

7. closer / Which / is / bus stop / to your house

   _____

8. neighborhood / Which / safer / is

   _____

9 Read each statement. Write a question about the underlined word(s) or phrase(s).

1. Monaco is smaller than Grenada.
   _____Which is smaller_____ , _____Monaco_____ or _____Grenada_____ ?

2. No, Australia isn't bigger than Russia.
   _____?

3. The bus is more convenient than the subway.
   _____, _____ or _____?

4. My parents' house is nicer than my apartment.
   _____, _____ or _____?

5. My brother is older than my sister.
   _____, _____ or _____?

6. No, my city isn't larger than New York.
   _____?

7. English is more difficult than my language.
   _____, _____ or _____?

8. Shopping online is more fun than shopping in a store.
   _____, _____ or _____?

10 SPEAK. Work with a partner. Ask and answer questions 6–8 from exercise **9**. Use your own answers, not the answers in the book.

Student A: *Is your city larger than New York City?*

Student B: *Yes, it is. Mexico City is huge!*

UNIT 12 LESSON 1 **379**

PRACTICE

11 WRITE, READ & SPEAK.

A Complete the conversation with the comparative form of the adjectives in parentheses.

Kay: Guess what? We're going to Rome in January!

Alex: Rome, Italy? In the middle of winter? Isn't it (1) __better__ (good) to go there in the summer?

Kay: Maybe, but airfares are much (2) _____ (low) in the winter.

Alex: Well, sure. They're (3) _____ (cheap) because no one wants to go there then.

Kay: That's true. In the summer, it's a lot (4) _____ (crowded). I like to go to places in the winter when it's (5) _____ (quiet). I like the off season.

Alex: Yes, but the off season is usually (6) _____ (cold) and (7) _____ (rainy), too.

Kay: That's OK. Even in the rain, no city is (8) _____ (interesting) than Rome!

B Work with a partner. Read the conversation from exercise **A**. Then discuss these questions.

1. Why is Kay going to Rome now?
2. What do you think? Is it better to go to a place in the off season? Why, or why not?
3. Do you go to places in the off season? Where?

12 EDIT. Read the questions and answers on the travel site about Edinburgh, Scotland. Find and correct five more errors with comparative adjectives.

Edinburgh, Scotland

Q: I'd like to visit Edinburgh, Scotland. Airfares are ~~more good~~ *better* in the winter. Is the winter a good time to visit?

A: Edinburgh is a great place to visit any time of the year! Of course, the temperatures in the winter are cold than in the summer, but it's usually not very cold. Also, in the winter, the days are more short than in the summer.

Q: Which is a better place to stay, a hotel or a bed and breakfast?

A: It's usually easier to meet people in a bed and breakfast, and they are often cheap than hotels. Sometimes, they are more far from the center of the city than hotels, so be sure to look on a map.

13 READ, WRITE & SPEAK.

A Read the information in the chart. Then use the adjectives from the box below to write sentences comparing the two mountains.

	Mount Everest	Mount Kilimanjaro
1. Height	29,035 feet	19,340 feet
2. Difficulty	4 out of 5*	1 out of 5*
3. Length of expedition	65 days	8 days
4. Weather	bad	not usually bad
5. Number of climbers per year	400+	20,000+

(* Scale: 1 = easy; 5 = very difficult)

| bad | crowded | dangerous | difficult | high | long | popular |

Mount Everest is higher than Mount Kilimanjaro.

B Work with a partner. Compare your sentences from exercise A.

C Ask and answer questions about the differences between Mount Everest and Mount Kilimanjaro. Use the information from exercises A and B.

Student A: *Which mountain is higher?*   Student B: *Mount Everest.*

14 SPEAK & LISTEN.

A Work with a partner. Look at the photos. How are the two places different?

Phuket, Thailand

Prague, Czech Republic

UNIT 12 LESSON 1 **381**

B Listen and complete the chart with information about Phuket and Prague.

	Phuket	Prague
Description	Tropical beaches, mountains, jungle	Beautiful city with many historical buildings
Average rainfall each year	____ inches (160 cm)	____ inches (50 cm)
Good weather	February to April	July and August
Average high temperature	____ °F (33°C)	____ °F (21°C)
Tourists	____ million each year	____ million each year
Tourist activities or attractions	Beaches, scuba diving, swimming, safaris	Historic places such as the Old Town Square, Prague Castle, and the Charles Bridge, museums, cafés, and parks

C Work with a partner. Ask and answer questions about Phuket and Prague. Use the comparative form of the adjectives from the box.

close	exciting	hot/warm	old
cold/cool	fun	interesting	relaxing
entertaining	historic	modern	sunny/rainy

Student A: *Which place is colder?* Student B: *Prague.*

Student A: *Is Phuket colder than Prague?* Student B: *No, it isn't. Prague is colder than Phuket.*

D Work in a group. You just won a free trip to one of the places from exercise **A**. You can go camping in Phuket, or you can go to a very luxurious hotel in Prague. Which trip do you want to take? Why? Discuss your ideas.

Student A: *I want to go to Prague and stay in a hotel.*

Student B: *Me, too. A hotel is nicer than a tent.*

Student C: *I don't. I want to go to a beach in Phuket. It's more relaxing.*

15 APPLY.

A Compare two places you know. Write five sentences in your notebook.

Mexico City is bigger than Miami, Florida.

Mexico City is more crowded than Miami.

B Work with a partner. Share your sentences from exercise **A**. Then ask and answer questions about your places. Use *Yes/No* questions and questions with *which*.

Student A: *Which city is more expensive?*

Student B: *Miami.*

Superlative Adjectives — LESSON 2

EXPLORE

1 READ the article about the National Museum of Anthropology. Notice the words in **bold**.

The National Museum of Anthropology

The National Museum of Anthropology[1] (Museo Nacional de Antropología) in Mexico City is **the largest** museum in Mexico, and it is one of **the most interesting** museums in the world. As you walk through the exhibits, you learn about the history of ancient[2] cultures in Mesoamerica: the area from central Mexico through Belize, Guatemala, El Salvador, Honduras, Nicaragua, and northern Costa Rica. Each room in the museum has artifacts[3] from a different region and culture.

The museum has **the biggest** collection in the world of artifacts from life before the Spanish arrived in the Americas. Two of **the most famous** artifacts in this museum are the huge Aztec sunstone and a beautiful jade[4] mask.

The museum doesn't just have exhibits about ancient cultures. There are also exhibits about life in different parts of Mexico today. A visit to this museum is **the best** way to learn about Mexican culture, both old and new.

[1] **anthropology:** the study of people and their cultures
[2] **ancient:** very old
[3] **artifacts:** objects used by people a very long time ago
[4] **jade:** a green or white stone used for jewelry or ornaments

◀ Jade death mask of Mayan King Pakal, National Museum of Anthropology,

2 CHECK. Read the questions. Circle *Yes* or *No*.

1. Is the National Museum of Anthropology the largest museum in Mexico?   Yes   No
2. Is it one of the most interesting museums in the world?   Yes   No
3. Does it have many artifacts from life before the Spanish arrived in the Americas?   Yes   No
4. Does the museum only have artifacts from Mexico?   Yes   No

3 DISCOVER. Complete the exercises to learn about the grammar in this lesson.

A Find these sentences in the article from exercise **1** on page 383. Write the missing words.

1. The National Museum of Anthropology in Mexico City is _____ _____ museum in Mexico, . . .

2. . . . and it is one of _____ _____ _____ museums in the world.

3. The museum has _____ _____ collection of artifacts from life before the Spanish arrived in the Americas.

B Look at the sentences from exercise **A**. What do these words show? Circle **T** for *true* or **F** for *false* for each statement. Then discuss your answers with your classmates and teacher.

1. We use these words to talk about differences between two things.   T   F
2. We use these words to talk about how one thing is different from many others.   T   F

◀ Stone of the Sun (Aztec Calendar), National Museum of Anthropology. Mexico City, Mexico

LEARN

12.4 Superlative Forms of Short Adjectives

	The	Superlative Adjective	
That's		newest	building in the city.
This is	the	largest	classroom in the building.
Benny's is		closest	restaurant to our office.

1. The superlative form shows that one person, place, or thing is different from others in some way.	Roberto is **the tallest** student in our class. That's **the oldest** building in the city.
2. For short adjectives (one syllable), add *-est* to the adjective to make the superlative form.	young → the young**est** old → the old**est**
3. When a short adjective ends in CVC*, double the consonant and add *-est*.	big → the big**gest** thin → the thin**nest**
4. When a short adjective ends in *-e*, add *-st*.	nice → the nice**st**
5. *The* comes before a superlative adjective.	✓ Dilma is **the youngest** student in our class. ✗ Dilma is youngest student in our class.
6. Some adjectives have irregular superlative forms.	good → **the best** bad → **the worst** far → **the farthest**

*consonant + vowel + consonant

4 Complete each sentence with the correct superlative form of the adjective in parentheses.

1. It is ___the largest___ (large) museum in Mexico.

2. The museum is _____ (good) way to learn about history and culture.

3. It has _____ (big) collection of artifacts from Mesoamerica.

4. The Uffizi Gallery in Florence, Italy, is one of _____ (old) museums in the world.

5. _____ (cheap) way to get to the museum is by subway.

6. This is _____ (small) room in the museum, but the exhibit is very interesting.

7. That museum has one of _____ (nice) restaurants in the city.

8. _____ (fast) way to get to the museum is by taxi.

> **REAL ENGLISH**
>
> The superlative form is very common after *one of*. Use a plural noun after *one of* + superlative.
>
> He's **one of the youngest** people in the school.
> That's **one of the most famous** restaurants in Rome.

12.5 Superlative Forms of Long Adjectives

	The Most	Adjective	
This is	the most	beautiful	park in Paris.
That is		expensive	hotel in the world.

1. For long adjectives (two or more syllables), put *the most* before the adjective to make the superlative form.

    modern → the most modern
    useful → the most useful
    beautiful → the most beautiful

2. When a long adjective ends in consonant + -y, change the -y to -i and add -est.

    easy → eas**iest**
    pretty → prett**iest**
    friendly → friendl**iest**

REAL ENGLISH

The infinitive (*to* + verb) often follows the superlative.

Flying is the fastest way **to travel**.
Chinese is the most difficult language **to learn**.
The Super Mall is the best place **to shop**.

5 Complete each sentence with the superlative form of the adjective in parentheses.

1. (modern) The United Arab Emirates has ____the most modern____ cities in the world.
2. (expensive) The Ginza in Tokyo is one of _____ places to shop.
3. (beautiful) Central Park is _____ park in New York City.
4. (interesting) The history exhibit was _____ part of the museum.
5. (famous) The Louvre is _____ museum in the world.
6. (crowded) That's _____ street in the city.
7. (helpful) This guide book is _____.
8. (exciting) Seoul is the _____ city in South Korea.

▼ People walk by a modern building in Seoul, South Korea.

6 SPEAK. Work with a partner. Talk about places in your country such as cities, buildings, and museums. Use the superlative form of the words in the box and your own ideas.

| beautiful | crowded | exciting | famous | interesting | ugly |

Times Square is one of the most famous places in New York City.

12.6 Questions with Superlatives

Yes/No Questions

Be	Subject	Superlative	
Is	that store	the best	place to shop?
Are	they	the most difficult	units in the book?

Short Answers

No, it isn't.
Yes, they are.

Questions with Who/What

Who/What	Be	Superlative	
Who	are	the most interesting	students in our class?
What	is	the best	place to shop?

Answers

Ed and Sue are.
The Bistro.

1. **Remember:** The verb comes before the subject in *Yes/No* questions with *be*.

   Is this museum the best one?
   Are you the oldest person in your family?

2. **Remember:** The word order in a question does not change when a question with *Who* or *What* asks about a subject.

   Who is the youngest person in the class?
   What's the hottest place on Earth?

7 Use the words in parentheses to write questions with the superlative.

1. (Who / old person) _Who is the oldest person_ in your family?
2. (What / good place) _____ to study?
3. (this supermarket / cheap) _____?
4. (What / interesting museum) _____ to visit?
5. (Who / your good friend) _____?
6. (Which city / big) _____ in your country?
7. (you / young) _____ in your family?
8. (What / nice restaurant) _____ in this city?

8 SPEAK. Work with a partner. Ask and answer questions from exercise **7**.

Student A: *Who's the oldest person in your family?*

Student B: *My grandmother. She's 90.*

PRACTICE

9 Complete the paragraph with the superlative form of the adjectives in parentheses.

The Most Famous Canals of the World

China's Grand Canal is among (1) __the oldest__ (old) and one of (2) _____ (long) canals in the world, but there are interesting canals in many parts of the world. The Canal du Midi in southern France is also one of (3) _____ (early) canals. (4) _____ (important) canals today for shipping are the Suez Canal and the Panama Canal. (5) _____ (busy) canal in the world is the Kiel Canal in Germany. About 35,000 ships pass between the North Sea and the Baltic Sea through this canal every year. One of (6) _____ (new) canals in the world is the Narmada Canal in India. Some canals aren't used for shipping any more, but they are popular destinations for tourists. (7) _____ (good) way to see the canals is on a boat, of course! (8) _____ (popular) canals for cruises are in France and Great Britain.

10 EDIT. Read the information. Find and correct five more errors with the superlative form of adjectives.

The Best Place to . . .

Every year National Geographic asks some of ^the most adventurous explorers for their ideas about the best places to have exciting experiences. Here are some of their favorites.

- The better place to surf in the world is the Mentawai Islands in Indonesia.
- Most challenging place to kayak is the Yarlung Tsangpo River in the Himalayan Mountains.
- The more difficult downhill ski race is Hahnenkamm in Austria.
- One of the hardest trip is across the entire Sahara Desert in North Africa.
- The most amazing place to scuba dive is in the Galápagos Islands in Ecuador.
- The taller mountain in South America is Aconcagua in Argentina.

▶ A surfer in the Mentawai Islands, Indonesia

▲ The driest place in the world

11 SPEAK.

A Work with a partner. Partner A, look at this page. Partner B, look at page **A6**.

B Ask Partner B questions to complete the chart. Then answer B's questions.

Partner A: *What is the biggest art museum in the world?*

Partner B: *What do you think?*

Partner A: *I think it's the Louvre.*

Partner B: *No, the Metropolitan Museum is the biggest. It's in New York.*

Geography Trivia

Big art museum? Metropolitan Museum	High waterfall? _____	Small country? _____
The largest country in the world is Russia.	Dry place? _____	The biggest desert in the world is the Sahara.
The largest islands in the world are Australia and Greenland.	The smallest ocean in the world is the Arctic.	Long river? _____

12 LISTEN & SPEAK.

A Listen to the conversations. What activity do the speakers want to do? Match each conversation with the correct topic. Write the letter on the line.

    Conversation 1 _____   a. look at wildlife

    Conversation 2 _____   b. go shopping

    Conversation 3 _____   c. visit museums

B Listen again. Match each place with its attraction. Write the letter on the line.

1. Zurich _____   a. wildlife

2. The Galápagos Islands _____   b. a shopping street

3. Berlin _____   c. museums

C Complete the statements with information from the listening. Use the superlative form of the adjectives in the box.

| big | expensive | famous | good | rich | unusual |

1. Berlin has some of the best museums in Europe.
2. The Louvre in Paris _____.
3. The Hermitage Museum _____.
4. The Galápagos Islands _____.
5. Zurich _____.
6. _____ shop at these very expensive places.

D Compare your sentences from exercise **C** with a partner.

E Work with a partner. What is the best place in your area to do the activities listed?

| eat lunch | go for a walk | look at wildlife | shop for clothes |
| enjoy a beautiful view | live | ride a bicycle | shop for groceries |

The best place to shop for clothes is . . .

13 APPLY.

A Work with a partner. Write a "Top-ten" list for a visitor to your city. Think about restaurants, parks, stores, museums, and so on. Use the superlative form of the adjectives in the box or your own ideas. Use each adjective only once.

amazing	famous	interesting	old
beautiful	good	large	popular
cheap	high	modern	small
expensive	historical	new	dangerous

Top-Ten List

San Francisco, California
1. The most beautiful park is Golden Gate Park.

B Share your list with your classmates.

390 COMPARATIVE AND SUPERLATIVE ADJECTIVES

Possessive Pronouns; *Whose* — **LESSON 3**

EXPLORE

1 **READ** the article about Frank Gehry. Notice the words in **bold**.

Frank Gehry: An Unusual Architect

Modern architecture is changing the look of our cities. Frank Gehry, a Canadian architect, is making us think about architecture in new ways.

It's easy to spot[1] a Gehry building. When you see one, you immediately think, "**Whose** crazy idea was that?"

Gehry's buildings are unique.[2] Most buildings have straight lines, but not Gehry's. **His** have curved lines. Also, most buildings have soft colors such as gray, brown, or white, but not Gehry's. **His** are bright and surprising. For example, the Experience Music Project (EMP) museum in Seattle, Washington, is red, gold, and purple!

Gehry's most popular building is the Guggenheim Museum in Bilbao, Spain.

Some people love Gehry's style, but others don't like it at all. **Whose** opinion do *you* agree with?

[1] **spot:** to find with your eyes; to see or notice
[2] **unique:** one of a kind

▲ The Guggenheim Museum in Bilbao, Spain, designed by Frank Gehry

UNIT 12 LESSON 3 **391**

▶ Cleveland Clinic Lou Ruvo Center for Brain Health by Frank Gehry, Las Vegas, Nevada, USA

2 CHECK. What makes Gehry's buildings different from other buildings? Complete the chart below with the descriptions from the box.

| bright colors | ~~curved lines~~ | soft colors | straight lines | surprising colors |

Gehry's Buildings	Other Buildings
curved lines	

3 DISCOVER. Complete the exercises to learn about the grammar in this lesson.

A Find these sentences in the article on page 391. What does *His* mean in each sentence? Choose the correct answer for each sentence.

1. <u>His</u> have curved lines.

   a. Gehry   b. Gehry's buildings   c. most buildings

2. <u>His</u> are bright and surprising.

   a. Gehry   b. most buildings   c. the colors of Gehry's buildings

B Discuss your answers from exercise **A** with your classmates and teacher.

392 COMPARATIVE AND SUPERLATIVE ADJECTIVES

LEARN

12.7 Possessive Pronouns

	Possessive Adjective	Noun
That is	my	car.
	your	
	his	
	her	
	our	
	your	
	their	

	Possessive Pronoun
That car is	mine.
	yours.
	his.
	hers.
	ours.
	yours.
	theirs.

1. Use a possessive pronoun in place of a possessive adjective + noun.	A: Is this your phone? B: It's **her phone**. = It's **hers**.
2. When a possessive pronoun replaces a singular noun, use the singular form of the verb.	This is my **book**. **Hers** <u>is</u> on the desk. These are my **keys**. **His** <u>are</u> on the desk.
3. Do not put a noun after a possessive pronoun.	✓ The book is **mine**. ✗ That is <u>mine</u> book.

REAL ENGLISH

Possessive pronouns are often used to make comparisons.

*Edgar's house is bigger than **mine**.*
*My car is older than **yours**.*

4 Read the sentences. Circle the possessive pronouns. Then draw an arrow back to the noun that each possessive pronoun replaces.

1. Their buildings are traditional, but (his) are not.
2. His colors are bright and surprising, but theirs are different.
3. Our architecture is very different from theirs.
4. San Francisco is my favorite city. What's yours?
5. His apartment is bigger than hers.
6. That notebook isn't his. He took my notebook by mistake.
7. Is that my phone or yours?
8. Please call me on John's phone. I left mine at home. Here's his number.

5 Change the underlined words in each sentence to a possessive pronoun.

1. This isn't my house. It's <u>my parents' house</u>. _____theirs_____

2. I like this apartment. It's more convenient than <u>my apartment</u>. _____

3. My city is modern. <u>Your city</u> is very old. _____

4. I told her about my country, and she told me about <u>her country</u>. _____

5. I like this neighborhood better than <u>their neighborhood</u>. _____

6. My husband's favorite restaurant is Vito's. <u>My favorite restaurant</u> is Café India. _____

7. Takeshi's class is in Room 203. <u>Our class</u> is in Room 205. _____

8. Here's my address. What's <u>your address</u>? _____

12.8 Wh- Questions with Whose

Questions with Whose			Answers
Whose	Noun		
Whose	car	did you take?	We took Sara's car.
	idea	was it?	It was mine.
	book	is this?	It's Brent's.

1. We often use *Whose* + noun for questions about possession.	A: **Whose computer** is this? B: It's Gemma's.
2. It is not necessary to state the noun when it is understood by both the speaker and the listener.	A: Look at that beautiful car in the parking lot. B: **Whose** is it? A: **Whose** are these? B: They're mine.
3. **Be careful!** *Whose* and *Who's* (*Who is*), sound the same.	A: **Whose** apartment is best for the party? B: Tom's is. A: **Who's** your favorite classmate? B: Tom is.
4. Be careful about the word order in questions with *Whose* + noun.	Question about a Subject: A: <u>Whose car</u> **goes** faster? B: Carl's does. Question about an Object: A: Whose car **did** <u>you</u> **take**? B: We took Sally's.

394 COMPARATIVE AND SUPERLATIVE ADJECTIVES

6 Complete each question with *Whose* or *Who's*.

1. __Whose__ apartment is bigger, yours or mine?
2. _____ city is warmer in January, yours or Kareem's?
3. _____ your teacher?
4. _____ class are you in?
5. _____ backpack is this?
6. _____ the student from Australia?
7. _____ next?
8. _____ sitting behind Tara?
9. _____ book is this?
10. _____ jacket is on the chair?

7 Read each statement. Make a question about the underlined words.

1. It was <u>Helen's</u> idea. __Whose idea was it?__
2. Those are <u>Ali's</u> glasses. _____
3. It's <u>Linda's</u> notebook. _____
4. <u>My</u> apartment is closer than Jane's. _____
5. It's <u>Greg's</u> turn. _____
6. That's <u>Susan's</u> pen. _____
7. That's <u>my</u> phone. _____
8. <u>Julie's</u> car is behind ours. _____
9. We used <u>John's</u> computer. _____
10. I borrowed <u>David's</u> book. _____

8 SPEAK. Work with a partner. Point to things in the room. Ask and answer questions with *Whose*.

Student A: *Whose is this?*

Student B: *It's Hiro's.* OR *It's mine.*

PRACTICE

9 Circle the correct words to complete the conversation.

Felix: (1) **Our** / **Ours** class is ending soon. Let's have a party.

Alicia: Good idea, but (2) **who's** / **whose** apartment is big enough for (3) **our** / **ours** whole class? (4) **My** / **Mine** isn't. It's too small. How about (5) **your** / **yours** ? Is it big enough? You live with (6) **your** / **yours** cousin, right?

Felix: Yes, but (7) **our** / **ours** place isn't big enough either. There isn't even enough space for (8) **our** / **ours** furniture!

Alicia: How about Camila's apartment? She lives with her sister. I think (9) **their** / **theirs** place is pretty big.

Felix: Yeah, it's big enough, but (10) **their** / **theirs** apartment isn't very close.

Alicia: True. How about Lenny's? His apartment is closer.

Felix: Oh, good idea!

Alicia: Do you want to ask him?

Felix: Well, he's really more (11) **your** / **yours** friend, not (12) **my** / **mine**. I don't know him very well.

Alicia: Yeah, but (13) **who's** / **whose** idea was this party anyway, huh?

Felix: OK, OK. I'll ask him.

10 **EDIT.** Read the conversation. Find and correct five more errors with possessive pronouns and questions with *Whose*.

Meg: I just finished the design for our architecture class a few minutes ago. Did you finish ~~your~~ *yours* yet?

Toshi: Yes, I finished mine last night. Juan and Tony finished their last week. They're always ahead of everyone else.

Meg: Did they show you theirs?

Toshi: No, they didn't want to show it to me because my wasn't finished yet.

Meg: I'm sure their is good. Their designs are always really good. Who's design is that over there?

Toshi: Oh, that's Ana's.

Meg: Whose Ana?

Toshi: She's Diana's roommate. Her designs are always very unusual.

11 LISTEN & SPEAK.

A Look at the photos. Then listen to the description of each building. Match the buildings to their architects. Write the letter on the line.

_____ 1. Zaha Hadid

_____ 2. Jacques Herzog and Pierre de Meuron

_____ 3. Frank Gehry

B Complete the paragraph about the buildings in exercise **A**. Use *his, her, hers, their,* and *theirs*.

Three Different Designs

These three buildings, by different architects, are great examples of modern architecture. (1) _____ designs are all unusual. Gehry's building is different from the others because he uses bright colors and different shapes. Hadid's building has a traditional shape, and some people say (2) _____ design is easier to look at than Gehry's. (3) _____ has smooth lines and curves, while (4) _____ doesn't. Herzog and de Meuron's building is famous for its unique shape. Unlike Gehry's and Hadid's buildings, (5) _____ has no straight lines, and the outside of (6) _____ building has white letters all over it.

C Take a survey. Ask five classmates the questions in the chart and take notes on their answers. Use *his, hers,* or *theirs* in your questions and answers.

Classmate's Name	Whose building do you like?	Whose building don't you like?

Student A: *Whose building do you like?*

Student B: *Zaha Hadid's building is my favorite. I like hers because . . .*

D Look at your notes from exercise **C**. Which building was the most popular? Report to the class.

12 APPLY.

A Art museums are often in very unusual buildings. In your notebook, draw a design for a modern art museum. Think about these questions when you draw your design.

Is the design modern or traditional?   Are the windows large or small?

Does it have curved or straight lines?   Are the colors bright or soft?

B Work in a group. Discuss and compare your designs from exercise **A**. Decide on the best one. Use *mine, yours, his, hers,* or *theirs* in your discussion.

Student A: *Let's look at yours first.*

Student B: *Yours is good. It's better than mine, but I really like Helen's.*

Student C: *Yes, I like hers, too.*

C In your notebook, write five sentences about the designs from exercise **B**. Compare your design with your classmates' designs.

My design is more traditional than Helen's.

Hers is more modern. It's very unusual.

Mine has . . .

UNIT 12 Review the Grammar

Charts
12.1–12.4
12.5–12.6

1 READ, WRITE & SPEAK.

A Read the information in the chart. Then complete each sentence with the comparative or superlative form of the adjective in parentheses.

The Largest Pyramids in Egypt			
	The Red Pyramid	The Great Pyramid	The Pyramid of Khafre
Name of Pharaoh	Sneferu	Khufu	Khafre
Original height	341 feet	480.6 feet	471 feet
Size	59.7 million cubic feet	591.1 million cubic feet	78 million cubic feet
Year built	around 2581 B.C.	around 2560 B.C.	around 2532 B.C.

The Pyramids

One of (1) __the most famous__ (famous) places in the world is in Egypt. It's the site of the Pyramids of Giza. Many people go there to see the Great Pyramid. The Great Pyramid is, of course, (2) _____ (large) pyramid in Egypt. It is also (3) _____ (tall). Khufu's son, Khafre, also built a pyramid in Giza. It is (4) _____ (small) than the Great Pyramid, but it looks (5) _____ (tall) because it's on a hill.

The (6) _____ (popular) pyramids in Egypt are the Pyramids of Giza, but many people also visit the Red Pyramid, the pyramid for Khufu's father, in Dahshur. Some people say the Red Pyramid is (7) _____ (good) than the Great Pyramid because it's a quiet place to visit. It's (8) _____ (far) from Cairo, so there aren't a lot of tourists there.

The Red Pyramid is (9) _____ (old) true pyramid in the world. It is also (10) _____ (small) of all of the Egyptian pyramids. It is definitely an interesting pyramid to visit.

B Work with a partner. Ask and answer five questions about the pyramids. Use *Yes/No* questions and *Wh-* questions with *Which* and *Whose*. Use the information in the chart in exercise **A**.

Student A: *Whose pyramid was the largest?*

Student B: *Khufu's. Whose pyramid was the smallest?*

Review the Grammar — UNIT 12

2 EDIT. Read the information about the Anasazi cliff dwellings. Find and correct five more errors with the comparative and superlative forms of adjectives.

The Anasazi Cliff Dwellings

Mesa Verde National Park in Colorado has *the* most interesting ruins in the United States. They are ancient cliff dwellings—homes in cliffs. They belonged to the Anasazi people. The Anasazi were Native Americans. They were some of the earlyest people in North America. They lived in the Mesa Verde area from 600 to 1300. The Mesa Verde National Park has 600 cliff dwellings. There were two types of rooms in the dwellings. *Kivas*, or round rooms, were for families, so they were largest than the other kind of room.

Next to Mesa Verde National Park is the Ute Mountain Tribal Park. Mesa Verde is crowded than the Ute Park, so Ute Park is sometimes a best park to visit. It also has beautiful cliff dwellings. It's one of the most interesting place to visit in North America.

▲ Ruins of the Anasazi Cliff Palace, Mesa Verde National Park, Colorado

Charts 12.1, 12.2, 12.5, 12.6

3 LISTEN, WRITE & SPEAK.

A Listen to the conversation. Then choose the correct answer for each question.

CD3-46

1. What are they discussing?   a. hotels near Mesa Verde   b. tours of Mesa Verde

2. Do they make a final decision?   a. Yes.   b. No.

B Listen again. Complete the chart with information about the ways to visit Mesa Verde. Write **NI** if no information is given.

CD3-46

Type	Length	Cost	Other Information
Bus tour	4 hours		
Van tour			
Jeep tour			
Car rental			

COMPARATIVE AND SUPERLATIVE ADJECTIVES

C Write sentences about the ways to visit Mesa Verde. Use comparatives and superlatives of the adjectives in parentheses.

1. (long)

    The bus tour is longer than the jeep ride.

    The van tour is the longest.

2. (cheap)

3. (comfortable)

4. (fun)

5. (educational)

6. (expensive)

D Work with a partner. Ask and answer questions about the ways to visit Mesa Verde.

Student A: *Which tour is the longest?*   Student B: *The van tour.*

4 APPLY. Work with a partner. Discuss these questions.

1. From exercise **3**, what do you think is the best way to see Mesa Verde? Why?

    The best way to see Mesa Verde is by jeep because. . . . The bus tour is more . . . , but it's . . .

2. What's the most famous historical site in your area? What are some ways people can visit it (bus tour, walking tour, and so on)? What is the best way to visit it? Why?

    _____ is the most famous site in _____. You can visit it on a bus tour or on a walking tour. The best way to visit it is a bus tour because . . .

UNIT 12 REVIEW THE GRAMMAR **401**

Connect the Grammar to Writing

1 READ & NOTICE THE GRAMMAR.

A Read the comparison. What two places does the writer compare? Discuss with a partner.

Two Beaches

I like to go to two different beaches in Hawaii, Waimea and Waikiki. Waimea is my favorite. It is <u>farther</u> from my home <u>than</u> Waikiki is, but it is one of the most beautiful beaches on the whole island.

Sometimes the waves in Waimea are very big. Then I go to Waikiki because it's a safer place to swim. The waves at Waikiki are always smaller than the waves at Waimea. Waikiki Beach is more crowded than Waimea, but it is closer to my home, so it's more convenient. I'm very lucky to live in Hawaii.

▲ Waimea Beach, Oahu, Hawaii, USA

B Read the comparison in exercise **A** again. Underline the comparative and superlative adjectives. Then work with a partner and compare answers.

C Complete the chart with information from the comparison in exercise **A**. What are the differences between Waikiki and Waimea?

Two Beaches	
Waimea	Waikiki
farther from home	

GRAMMAR FOCUS

In the comparison in exercise **A**, the writer uses comparative and superlative adjectives to describe how the beaches are different from each other and from other beaches.

Remember: Use comparative adjectives to compare two things. Use superlative adjectives to compare three or more things.

It is **farther** from my home **than** Waikiki is, but it is **one of the most beautiful beaches** on the whole island.

402 COMPARATIVE AND SUPERLATIVE ADJECTIVES

Write a Comparison between Two Places

2 BEFORE YOU WRITE. Choose two places to compare. How are these places different from each other? Complete the chart with the differences between the two places. Use the chart from exercise **1C** as a model.

Two Places	
_____ (place 1)	_____ (place 2)

3 WRITE a comparison between two places. Use the information from your chart in exercise **2** and the paragraph in exercise **1A** to help you.

> **WRITING FOCUS**   Pronouns
>
> Writers use pronouns to refer to something a second time and not repeat the same noun. This helps make their sentences and paragraphs more interesting and helps make them sound more natural.
>
> With no pronouns:
>
>   *I go to two different beaches in Hawaii, Waikiki, and Waimea. Waimea is my favorite. Waimea is farther from my home than Waikiki, but Waimea is one of the most beautiful beaches on the whole island.*
>
> With pronouns:
>
>   *I go to two different breaches in Hawaii, Waikiki and Waimea. Waimea is my favorite. **It** is farther from my home than Waikiki, but **it** is one of the most beautiful beaches on the whole island.*

4 SELF ASSESS. Read your comparison. Underline the comparative and superlative adjectives. Then use the checklist to assess your work.

- [ ] I used the comparative adjectives correctly. [12.1–12.2, 12.3]
- [ ] I used the superlative adjectives correctly. [12.4–12.5, 12.6]
- [ ] I used a plural noun after *one of the* (adjective) + *-est*. [12.4]
- [ ] When I referred to a noun for the second time, I used a pronoun. [WRITING FOCUS]

UNIT 13 Customs and Traditions

Modals: Part 2

▼ Lanterns float into the night sky during the Yee Peng Festival in Chiang Mai, Thailand.

Lesson 1
page 406

Should/Shouldn't

Lesson 2
page 413

May and *Can*; *Have To/Don't Have To*

Lesson 3
page 422

Can/Could/Would: Polite Requests and Offers

Review the Grammar
page 428

Connect the Grammar to Writing
page 430

405

LESSON 1 Should/Shouldn't

EXPLORE

1 READ the e-mails about advice for a trip to Japan. Notice the words in **bold**.

Subject: A Business Trip to Tokyo

Hi Taka,

I'm going to Tokyo next week to meet with some clients.[1] Do you have any advice for me? This is my first trip to Japan. **Should I take** anything special with me? What's your schedule like this week? I'd like to take you to lunch. Are you free on Thursday?

Peter

[1] **client:** a customer

Hi Peter,

Thursday isn't good for me. How about Friday? Here's some advice in the meantime[2].

You **should take** some small gifts for your clients. I usually buy something from a gift shop. They don't have to be expensive.

Don't forget your business cards! In Japan, people exchange[3] business cards when they first meet, so be prepared. Keep them in your jacket. You **shouldn't keep** them in your wallet or in the pocket of your pants. When you present your card, you **should hold** it with both hands. When you get business cards from people at a meeting, you **should place** each card carefully on the table in front of you when you sit down. More advice at lunch.

Best,
Taka

[2] **in the meantime:** in the period between two events
[3] **exchange:** give and take

▼ Sunset, Tokyo, Japan

406   MODALS: PART 2

▲ Business people bow to each other at the Tokyo Stock Exchange.

2 CHECK. Look at each action in the chart. Does Taka think it is a good idea or a bad idea? Put a check (✓) in the correct column.

		Good idea	Bad idea
1.	Take small gifts for clients.	✓	
2.	Forget your business cards.		
3.	Keep business cards in the pocket of your pants.		
4.	Hold your business card with both hands.		
5.	Put business cards in front of you on the table at a meeting.		

3 DISCOVER. Complete the exercises to learn about the grammar in this lesson.

A Find these sentences in the e-mails from exercise **1**. Write the missing words.

1. You ____should take____ some small gifts for your clients.

2. You _____ them in your wallet or in the pocket of your pants.

3. When you present your card, you _____ it with both hands.

4. When you get business cards from people at a meeting, you _____ each card carefully on the table in front of you when you sit down.

B Look at your answers from exercise **A**. What do these words tell us? Choose the correct words to complete each statement. Then discuss your answer with your classmates and teacher.

1. We use *should* and *shouldn't* to ____.

   a. discuss a problem

   b. give advice

2. The verb after *should* ____.

   a. changes form

   b. is the base form of the verb

UNIT 13   LESSON 1   **407**

LEARN

13.1 *Should* for Advisability: Statements

Affirmative Statements		
Subject	*Should*	Base Form of Verb
I You He She It We You They	should	wait.

Negative Statements		
Subject	*Shouldn't*	Base Form of Verb
I You He She It We You They	shouldn't should not	wait.

1. Use *should* and *shouldn't* to give advice.	You **should study** for the test. You **shouldn't go** to a party the night before a test.
2. *Should* is a modal. Use the base form of the verb after *should* and *shouldn't*.	✓ He **should stay** home. ✗ He should <u>to</u> stay home.

4 Use *should* or *shouldn't* and the verb in parentheses to complete each sentence.

1. (buy) I _____should buy_____ a small gift.
2. (have) He _____ his business cards ready.
3. (not keep) You _____ your cards in your pants pocket.
4. (bring) Everyone _____ a lot of business cards.
5. (not be) We _____ late for the meeting.
6. (read) We _____ more about the history of the city.
7. (ask) He _____ his Japanese friends for advice.
8. (learn) She _____ some Japanese words.

5 WRITE & SPEAK. Write three sentences about yourself. Use *should* or *shouldn't* and the verbs from the box or your own ideas. Then share your sentences with a partner.

do	eat	go to bed	sleep	study
drink	exercise	practice	speak	walk

Student A: *I shouldn't speak Spanish in class.*

Student B: *I should exercise every day.*

408 MODALS: PART 2

13.2 *Should* for Advisability: Questions

Yes/No Questions

Should	Subject	Base Form of Verb
Should	she / we	leave?

Short Answers

	Subject	Should/ Shouldn't
Yes,	she / we	should.
No,		shouldn't.

Wh- Questions

Wh- Word	Should	Subject	Base Form of Verb	
What	should	I	bring?	
Where		she	stay?	
When		he	leave?	
Why		you	arrive	early?
Who		we	ask?	
How		they	get	there?

Answers

Some small gifts.
At the Grand Hotel.
At 3:00.
Because it's polite.
Paola.
By subway.

Should comes before the subject in *Yes/No* questions and in most information questions.

Should she try again?
What **should** we tell her?

6 Use the words in parentheses to make *Yes/No* questions and *Wh-* questions with *should*.

1. A: ___Should I bring___ (I / bring) a gift? B: Yes, you should.
2. A: _____ (we / shake / hands)? B: Yes, we should.
3. A: _____ (When / I / be) there? B: At around 10:30.
4. A: _____ (What / he / wear)? B: A suit.
5. A: _____ (they / call) the office? B: Yes, they should.
6. A: _____ (Who / she / ask)? B: Her manager.
7. A: _____ (How / we / get) there? B: By subway.
8. A: _____ (Where / we / meet)? B: In the coffee shop.
9. A: _____ (she / be) on time? B: Yes, she should.
10. A: _____ (Why / we / arrive) early? B: It's the custom.

PRACTICE

7 Complete the statements and questions in the conversation. Use *should* or *shouldn't* and the words in parentheses. Then listen and check your answers.

Sidney: Do you know much about German culture? I'm going to Berlin on a business trip next month.

Darcy: I know one thing. (1) __You shouldn't be__ (you / not / be) late! Germans are very punctual.

Sidney: That's right. (2) _____ (I / be) on time for my meetings. (3) _____ (I / take) gifts with me?

Darcy: That's a good question. I don't know. (4) _____ (You / ask) Greta. She's from Germany.

Sidney: You're right! In fact, if I'm not mistaken, I think she's from Berlin! What else (5) _____ (I / ask) her?

Darcy: Well, (6) _____ (you / wear) formal clothes, or is it OK to dress informally?

Sidney: Good idea. Also, (7) _____ (I / call) people by their first names? I know in some countries it's better to use Mr. and Ms.

Darcey: Right. That's important. (8) _____ (You / look for) information about German business customs online. You can probably find a lot of helpful information there.

Sidney: That's true. Thanks. Maybe (9) _____ (I / buy) a guidebook, too. Well, (10) _____ (we / hurry). It's time for our meeting with the director.

▼ Potsdamer Platz, the financial district of Berlin, Germany

410 MODALS: PART 2

8 READ, WRITE & SPEAK.

A Read each situation. Then put the words in the correct order to make questions.

Situation 1

Chris Mackenzie owns a company in Canada. She sells her products in many other countries. She got an e-mail from a new international client. The e-mail began, "Dear Mr. Mackenzie."

1. (explain / Should / his mistake / she) _Should she explain his mistake?_

Situation 2

Chris usually shakes hands at business meetings. She knows this is not common in her client's country.

2. (she / greet / How / them / should) _____

Situation 3

Chris and her assistant Tim Hubbard arrive at the meeting. The client offers them coffee.

3. (Should / say / "No, thank you"/ they) _____

4. (should / When / they / talk about / business) _____

Situation 4

Something surprises Chris. When she asks her client questions, he answers Tim. When her client asks questions, he asks Tim, not Chris.

5. (she / Should / say something) _____

B Work with a partner. Discuss the questions from exercise **A**.

Student A: *Should she explain his mistake?*   Student B: *Yes, she should.*

9 LISTEN & WRITE.

A Read the chart. Then listen to advice about doing business in South Africa, Thailand, and the United States. Where is each piece of advice important? Check (✓) the correct column(s).

	Activities	South Africa	Thailand	USA
1.	Arrive exactly on time or early for a meeting.			✓
2.	Take time to talk about topics such as health or family before you "talk business."			
3.	Don't put someone's business card in your pocket.			
4.	Don't use your left hand to give something.			
5.	Don't touch someone's head or pass anything above someone's head.			
6.	Don't show the bottom of your foot.			

B Make sentences about the information from the chart in exercise **A**. Use *should* or *shouldn't*.

1. In the United States, _you should be exactly on time or early for a meeting_.
2. In South Africa, _____.
3. In South Africa, _____.
4. In Thailand, _____.
5. In Thailand, _____.
6. In Thailand, _____.

10 APPLY.

A What are some important business customs in your country? Think of customs for greetings, introductions, conversations, meetings, or gifts. Write sentences with *should* or *shouldn't*.

1. _In my country, you shouldn't ask people about their salary._
2. _____
3. _____
4. _____
5. _____

B Work in a group. Share your sentences from exercise **A**. Are any of your customs similar?

▲ Morning rush hour at Grand Central Station, New York City, USA

412

May and Can; Have To/Don't Have To   LESSON 2

EXPLORE

1 READ the blog about some unusual laws. Notice the words in **bold**.

You can't do that here!
Strange Laws from around the World   Tuesday, August 8

When a government makes a law, we usually understand the reason. For example, in Greece, women **can't wear** high heels[1] at historic sites because high heels may damage the ancient steps. That makes sense, but **why can't** women **wear** high heels in the beach town of Carmel, California, in the United States? On the Isle of Capri in Italy, you **can wear** sandals with high heels, low heels, and anything in between, but you **can't wear** noisy sandals! What's the reason for that?

Here are some other unusual laws from around the world.

- In Florida, USA, single women **cannot parachute** on Sundays.
- In Victoria, Australia, you **can't change** a light bulb. Only an electrician **can do** that.
- In Vermont, USA, women **can have** false[2] teeth, but they **have to** get permission in writing from their husbands.
- In Moscow, Russia, you **can't drive** a dirty car.
- In Singapore, you **can't sell** gum.
- In France, you **can't name** a pig Napoleon.

▼ Female skydiver

3 COMMENTS

POSTED BY MAC

Funny! **Do** people **have to follow** these laws now?
April 27, 4:56 P.M.

POSTED BY BRAD

This isn't true. People **can change** their own light bulbs in Australia. They **don't have to call** an electrician anymore. That's crazy!
April 28, 12:05 A.M.

POSTED BY RALPH

I heard something strange about England. You **have to be** careful when you put a stamp with a king or queen on a letter. The stamp **can't be** upside down. Is this really a law?
April 28, 12:30 A.M.

[1] **high heels:** a kind of shoes for women that make them taller
[2] **false:** not real

UNIT 13   LESSON 2   **413**

2 CHECK. Complete each law in the left-hand column with the correct phrase on the right. Write the letter on the line.

1. Single women can't parachute on Sundays _____.
2. Only an electrician can change a light bulb _____.
3. You can't drive a dirty car _____.
4. You can't name a pig Napoleon _____.
5. Women can't have false teeth without permission from their husbands _____.

a. in Australia
b. in Florida
c. in France
d. in Russia
e. in Vermont

3 DISCOVER. Complete the exercises to learn about the grammar in this lesson.

A Find these sentences in the blog in exercise **1** on page 413. Write the correct words.

1. On the Isle of Capri in Italy, you __can wear__ sandals with high heels, low heels, and anything in between, but you _____ *noisy* sandals.
2. In Florida, USA, single women _____ on Sundays.
3. In Moscow, Russia, you _____ a dirty car.

B Look at your answers from exercise **A**. Then choose the correct answer to complete the statement. Discuss your answer with your classmates and teacher.

We use *can, can't,* and *cannot* to talk about _____.

a. difficult situations
b. advice
c. rules and laws

▼ A shoemaker's workshop, Capri, Italy

13.3 *Can/May* for Permission

Affirmative Statements

Subject	Can	Base Form of Verb	
I She They	can	park	there.

Negative Statements

Subject	Can't	Base Form of Verb	
I She They	can't cannot	park	there.

Yes/No Questions

Can/May	Subject	Base Form of Verb	
Can	I	leave	early today?
May	we		

Short Answers

Sure.
Yes, of course.
Sorry, not today.

Wh- Questions

Wh- Word	Can/ Can't	Subject	Base Form of Verb	
When	can	we	begin	the test?
Where	can	I	use	my phone?
Why	can't	he	drive?	

Answers

In a few minutes.
Outside or in the hallway.
Because he's too young.

1. Use *can* and *can't* to talk about permission. Use *can* to request or give permission. Use *can't* to refuse a request for permission.	They **can** enter now. We're ready. You **can't** come in now. I'm sorry.
2. **Remember:** *Can, can't,* and *may* are modals. Use the base form of the verb with *can, can't,* and *may*.	You **can** leave early today. We **can't** use our phones in class. **May** I sit here?
3. **Remember:** *Can, can't,* and *may* come before the subject in questions.	**May** I have some tea? Where **can** I park?
4. Use *may* to ask for permission. *May* is more formal than *can*. *May* is most often used with *I* and *we*.	**May** I have a cookie? **May we** take photos in the museum?
5. Use short answers to agree to requests for permission.	A: **Can** I take this chair? B: Sure. / Of course.
6. Use *Sorry* or *I'm sorry, . . .* (and give a reason) to refuse requests for permission.	A: **Can** I borrow your laptop tonight? B: I'm sorry, it's not working.

REAL ENGLISH

Could is also used to ask for permission. It is more polite than *can*, but not quite as formal as *may*. We do not use *could* in the answer.

A: **Could** I leave early today?
B: Sure. / OK. / Yes, you can leave right after the test.

4 Complete the statements. Use *can* or *can't* and the words in parentheses.

1. <u>You can't drive</u> (You / not drive) a dirty car in Russia.
2. In Australia, _____ (people / change) their own light bulbs. They don't need to call an electrician.
3. In the United States, _____ (people / vote) when they are 18 years old.
4. _____ (You / not travel) to many countries without a passport.
5. In France, _____ (people / bring) their dogs to restaurants.
6. _____ (You / not park) here. The sign says, "No Parking."
7. _____ (You / not take) photos in the museum.
8. _____ (We / drink coffee) in class. Our teacher says it's OK.

5 Complete each question or request. Use *can* or *may* and the words in parentheses.

1. A: <u>May I sit</u> (I / sit) here?
   B: Yes, of course you can.
2. A: _____ (my / brother come), too?
   B: Sure, he's welcome to join us.
3. A: _____ (I / have) a piece of cake?
   B: No, sorry. It's for the party.
4. A: _____ (I / bring) a friend to the party?
   B: Of course.
5. A: _____ (When / we / eat) the cookies?
   B: After dinner.
6. A: _____ (I / take) one of these magazines?
   B: Sure. They're free.
7. A: _____ (Where / we / park)?
   B: Across the street.
8. A: _____ (Why / we / not go) to that restaurant?
   B: Because we're wearing shorts. It's a very formal restaurant.

13.4 Have To for Necessity: Statements

Affirmative

Subject	Has To/Have To	Base Form of Verb
He She It	has to	stay.
I You We You They	have to	

Negative

Subject	Doesn't Have To/Don't Have To	Base Form of Verb
He She It	doesn't have to	stay.
I You We You They	don't have to	

1. To say that something is necessary, use *has to* or *have to*. *Have to* and *need to* mean the same thing.	I **have to** go. She **has to** work today.
2. *Have to* is a modal. Use the base form of the verb after *has/have to* and *doesn't/don't have to*.	We **have to leave** at six-thirty. She **doesn't have to go**.
3. To say that something is not necessary, use *doesn't have to* or *don't have to*.	I **don't have to** go. He **doesn't have to** pay.
4. *Had to* and *didn't have to* are the past forms of *have to*.	She **had to** leave early. We **didn't have to** work yesterday.
5. **Be careful!** *Have to* and *have* do not mean the same thing.	I **have to** get a job. (= It is necessary to get a job.) I **have** a job. (= I work.)

REAL ENGLISH

Must is stronger than *have to*. It is often used to talk about rules or laws.

> You **must be** at the airport two hours early.
> Students **must bring** their IDs to the exam.

6 Complete each sentence with the affirmative or negative of *have to*.

1. We're late! We ___have to hurry___ (hurry).
2. I can't talk right now. I _____ (catch) the bus.
3. I _____ (work) late tonight. My boss needs this report tomorrow.
4. This is important. He _____ (come) with us.
5. The concert is free. We _____ (not pay).
6. That restaurant is never crowded. We _____ (not make) a reservation.
7. The test is tomorrow. We _____ (study).
8. I don't want to stay up late tonight. I _____ (get up) early tomorrow.

7 WRITE & SPEAK. List some things that you *have to do* or *don't have to do* today. Then share your sentences with a partner.

Student A: *I have to go to the doctor.* Student B: *I don't have to cook dinner tonight.*

UNIT 13 LESSON 2 **417**

13.5 *Have To* for Necessity: Questions

Yes/No Questions

Do/Does	Subject	Have To	Base Form of Verb
Do	you	have to	go?
Does	she		

Short Answers

	Subject	Do/Don't Does/Doesn't
Yes,	I	do.
No,	she	doesn't.

Wh- Questions

Wh- Word	Do/Does	Subject	Have To	Base Form of Verb
When	do	you	have to	leave?
What		we		write?
Where		they		go?
Who	does	he		call?
Why		she		study?

Answers

Soon.
A short paragraph.
To the post office.
His manager.
She has a test tomorrow.

Use the auxiliary* verb *do* or *does* before the subject in questions with *have to*.

Do you have to work this weekend?
When **does** he have to leave?

✓ What **do you** have to buy?
✗ What **have you** to buy?

* Auxiliary verbs are sometimes called helping verbs. *Do*, *be*, and modals are auxiliary verbs.

8 Look at each statement. Write a question about the underlined information.

1. He has to wear a suit <u>because he has a meeting</u>.   *Why does he have to wear a suit?*

2. Nasir has to leave <u>at 3:00</u>. _____

3. <u>Yes</u>, you have to ask your manager. _____

4. She has to go <u>to Hong Kong</u> next week. _____

5. <u>No</u>, I don't have to study tonight. _____

6. <u>Yes</u>, we have to bring our books to class. _____

7. We have to bring <u>our student IDs</u> to the exam. _____

8. I have to call <u>Professor Clark</u> after class. _____

9. <u>No</u>, Lily doesn't have to give her presentation today. _____

10. Rosa <u>has to give her presentation</u> tomorrow. _____

9 SPEAK. Work with a partner. Ask and answer questions about things you have to do. Ask two Yes/No questions and two Wh- questions.

Student A: *Do we have to do homework tonight?*
Student B: *No, we don't.*

Student A: *What do you have to do after class?*
Student B: *I have to go to the grocery store.*

PRACTICE

10 Complete the article with the correct forms of *can* and *have to*. Then listen and check your answers.

Wedding Customs around the World

Customs for marriage are different around the world. For example, in some countries, arranged marriages are common. In an arranged marriage, young people (1) ____can't____ choose their own husbands or wives. They (2) _____ marry the person their family chooses. In other societies, young people (3) _____ get their parents' approval before they marry. They (4) _____ make their own decisions. What is the custom in your country? (5) _____ you choose your husband or wife, or are arranged marriages common?

Wedding ceremonies are also different around the world. For example, in China, couples (6) _____ do research to decide on a lucky day for their wedding. A wedding (7) _____ begin on the half hour because the hands on the clock are moving up. The bride has a choice for the color of her dress; she (8) _____ wear red, but red is a lucky color for weddings. In some countries such as Panama, the groom (9) _____ give the bride 13 coins. In Sweden, the bride (10) _____ put a gold coin from her mother in one shoe and a silver coin from her father in the other shoe.

◀ A bride and groom pose for a wedding photo, Shanghai, China.

UNIT 13 LESSON 2 419

11 EDIT, WRITE & SPEAK.

A Find and correct five more errors with *can* and *have to*.

Dear Wedding Advisor,

    Can my bride make all the decisions about our wedding, or does she ~~has~~ *have* to think about my family's ideas, too? My fiancée, Sally, wants to get married on a beach in Hawaii. My mother is very unhappy about this. She says: "You can't to get married on a beach! The wedding can't be in Hawaii. You has to get married close to home. Sally haves to think about our family, too." Sally disagrees. She says: "A wedding can be anywhere. It hasn't to be indoors. It's my wedding, so I should to decide. My opinion should be the most important."

    Please help! Who is right, my fiancée or my mother?

Jeff

B Complete the chart with Jeff's mother's opinions and Sally's opinions from exercise **A**.

Jeff's Mother's Opinions	Sally's Opinions
A wedding can't be on a beach.	A wedding can be anywhere.

C Work with a partner. Discuss these questions.

1. What is your opinion?
2. What should Jeff do?

12 LISTEN & SPEAK.

A Listen to the information about Indian weddings. Match each word with the correct definition. Write the letter on the line.

1. mehndi _____
2. henna _____
3. sari _____
4. garlands _____

a. strings of flowers
b. an event where women put henna designs on their skin
c. traditional Indian clothing for women
d. dye that colors the skin

▲ A bride and groom eat traditional sweets at their wedding, Gujurat, India.

B Listen again. Then complete the sentences. Use *have to* or *don't have to* and words from the box.

| do | exchange | put | ~~wait~~ | walk | wear |

1. You can't wash henna off your skin. You _____have to wait_____ for it to wear off.

2. A new bride _____ housework until the henna wears off.

3. A bride _____ red, but most brides do wear red or red and white.

4. The bride and groom _____ garlands of flowers.

5. The groom _____ a red mark on the bride's forehead.

6. The bride and groom _____ around the fire.

13 APPLY.

A Work with a partner. What are wedding ceremonies like in your country? Complete these sentences and add two more sentences of your own.

In (*name of country*) _____, the bride (has to / doesn't have) to wear _____.

The groom (has to / doesn't have to) _____.

The wedding ceremony (has to be / doesn't have to be) _____.

_____.

_____.

B Ask and answer questions about wedding customs in your partner's country.

Does the bride have to wear a certain color?   *What does the groom have to wear?*

UNIT 13 LESSON 2 421

LESSON 3 Can/Could/Would: Polite Requests and Offers

EXPLORE

1 READ the conversation about customs. Notice the words in **bold**.

Disappearing Cultures

Olivia: Your lecture was very interesting. **Could I ask** you a question?

Dr. Park: Of course.

Olivia: Are cultural differences disappearing[1]? People are becoming more similar because of movies, the Internet, and travel, right?

Dr. Park: Yes, cultures are becoming more similar because of these things, but there are still areas that have little contact with the outside world.

Olivia: **Can you give** me an example? I'd like to learn more about this.

Dr. Park: Sure. One example is Vanuatu in the South Pacific. There are still traditional tribes in the very remote[2] areas of the mountains.

Olivia: That's interesting. I'd really like to go there. **Could you tell** me more about it?

Dr. Park: Well, sure. It's a very interesting place, but tourists aren't always good for places such as Vanuatu. When tourists go to see traditional cultures, life in the village changes. Traditions become tourist attractions.

Olivia: Interesting. I didn't think about that.

Dr. Park: Do you want to do some research on this topic?

Olivia: Definitely. **Could you recommend** some articles?

Dr. Park: **I'd be happy to. Would you like to meet** next week to talk about it?

Olivia: Sure. Thanks.

[1] **disappear:** to go away over time
[2] **remote:** far away and hard to reach

▶ Men perform a traditional dance with spears, Ekasup Village, Vanuatu.

▲ Men from a different part of Vanuatu perform a traditional dance in brightly colored costumes.

2 CHECK. Read the questions. Circle *Yes* or *No*.

1. Are cultural differences disappearing?	a. Yes.	b. No.
2. Are people and cultures becoming more similar because of movies, the Internet, and travel?	a. Yes.	b. No.
3. Is Vanuatu in Africa?	a. Yes.	b. No.
4. Does tourism change the culture of tribes?	a. Yes.	b. No.
5. Does Dr. Park want to do some research on this topic?	a. Yes.	b. No.

(1. a. Yes is circled)

3 DISCOVER. Complete the exercises to learn about the grammar in this lesson.

A Look at the questions from the conversation in exercise **1**. Notice the words in **bold**. Then circle **T** for *true* or **F** for *false* for each statement.

Could I ask you a question?   **Can you give** me an example?   **Could you recommend** some articles?

1. These words are polite.   T   F
2. These words show something is possible.   T   F
3. We use these words to request something.   T   F

B Discuss your answers from exercise **A** with your classmates and teacher.

UNIT 13   LESSON 3   **423**

13.6 Can You/Could You/Would You for Polite Requests

Can/Could/Would	Subject	Base Form of Verb	
Can	you	help	me?
Could			
Would			

Answers
Sure. No problem.
OK. Just a minute.
I'm sorry but I can't right now.

1. Use *can, could,* and *would* to make polite requests.	**Can you open** the door? **Could you open** the door? **Would you open** the door?
2. Use *can, could,* or *would* before the subject in polite requests.	**Can** you help me with my homework? **Could** you carry this for me? **Would** you close that window?
3. *Could* is more polite than *can*. To make a request more polite, use *please* after the subject (*you*) or at the end of the request.	**Could** you help me? **Can** you help me, please?
4. Use *can't* to refuse a request even when the request uses *could* or *would*.	A: **Could** you help me with this exercise? B: Sorry. I **can't** right now.
5. To refuse a request, we usually explain or apologize.	I'm sorry. I **can't** right now. I **can't** do it right now. I'm late for class.

REAL ENGLISH

Thanks anyway is often used as a response when someone refuses a request. It is usually used when the person wanted to help but couldn't.

A: *I'm having trouble with this exercise. Could you help me?*
B: *Sorry. I'm having trouble with it, too.*
A: *OK.* **Thanks anyway.**

4 Rewrite each imperative to make it a polite request.

1. Give me some ideas for my project. <u>Could you give me some ideas for my project?</u>

2. Explain the answer, please. _____

3. Tell me about the article. _____

4. Please repeat the question. _____

5. Show me that website. _____

6. Help me with the assignment. _____

7. Do some research for me. _____

8. Recommend some books about your country. _____

424 MODALS: PART 2

5 Work with a partner. Ask and answer the requests from exercise **4**. Accept the requests for items 1–4. Politely refuse the requests for items 5–8.

Student A: *Would you give me some ideas for my project?*

Student B: *Sure.*

Student A: *Thanks.*

13.7 *Can I/Could I/Would You Like* for Polite Offers

Can/Could/Would	Subject	Base Form of Verb	
Can	I	get	you some coffee?
Could	I	carry	your suitcase for you?
Would	you	like	some help?

Answers
Sure. Thanks.
Thanks, that would be great.
No thanks. I'm fine.

1. Use *can* or *could* to offer to do something for someone.	**Can** I help you with that? **Could** I get you some more coffee?
2. Use *would you like* to make an offer.	**Would you like** another piece of cake?
3. Respond to an offer with *thank you* or *thanks* to accept or with *no thanks* to refuse.	**Sure.** Thanks. **Thank you.** I'd like that. **No thanks.** I'm fine.

6 Complete each request. Use the verb in parentheses and *Can I* or *Would you*.

1. (help) A: _____Can I help_____ you? B: Yes. I'd like some information.

2. (make) A: _____ a suggestion? B: OK. What is it?

3. (like) A: _____ to look at a map? B: Oh, you have a map? Thanks.

4. (help) A: _____ you with your bags? B: Yes, thank you.

5. (like) A: _____ a free movie ticket? B: Sure! Thanks.

6. (get) A: _____ you anything? B: No, thanks. I'm fine.

7. (like) A: _____ a ride to the party? B: Thanks. I'd like that.

8. (give) A: _____ you a ride to the party? B: No, but thanks. I'm going later.

7 SPEAK. Work with a partner. Practice the conversations in exercise **6**.

Student A: *Can I help you?*   Student B: *Yes, I'd like some information.*

PRACTICE

8 Complete each conversation with a request or an offer from the box. Write the letter on the line.

> a. Can I get it for you?
> b. Can I help you with directions?
> c. Can I help you with it?
> d. Really? Can you send me the link, please?
> e. Could you get me a cup of coffee?
> f. Would you like me to close the window?
> g. Would you like me to introduce you?
> h. Would you wait five minutes? I'd like to go with you.

1. A: I'm lost.
   B: _b_

2. A: I found a good online travel site.
   B: ____

3. A: It's cold in here.
   B: ____

4. A: I'm ready to leave.
   B: ____

5. A: I can't reach that book on the shelf.
   B: ____

6. A: I don't know them.
   B: ____

7. A: I'm having trouble with this.
   B: ____

8. A: I'm going to the coffee shop.
   B: ____

9 **SPEAK.** Work with a partner. Practice the conversations in exercise **8**. Add an affirmative response to each conversation.

Student A: *I'm lost.*

Student B: *Can I help you with directions?*

Student A: *Sure.*

10 **WRITE, LISTEN & SPEAK.**

A Read the conversations. Underline any requests or offers that are not polite. Then rewrite them in your notebooks to make them polite.

Conversation 1

Jessie: You always tell me such interesting things about Panama. I'd like to go there sometime. <u>Give me some suggestions for places to see</u>.

    Could you give me some suggestions for places to see?

Felipe: Oh. What do you want? The names of my favorite places?

Jessie: Yes. Tell me the name of a hotel, too.

Felipe: Sure. Let me know if you have any other questions.

Jessie: Great. Thanks, Felipe!

Bora Bora, French Polynesia, in the South Pacific

Conversation 2

Agent: Hello. Adventure Travel Company. Do you want help?

Hans: Yes, I want some information about tours to the South Pacific.

Agent: Hold on for a minute.

Hans: OK.

Agent: Hello, I'm back. Now give me your name.

B Listen and check your answers from exercise **A**.

C Work with a partner. Practice the conversations from exercise **A**.

11 APPLY. Work with a partner. Read the situations. Then role-play a request and an offer in each situation.

1. You see a tourist (*your partner*) on the street. The tourist seems confused. Offer to help.

   Student A: *Would you like some help?*

   Student B: *Yes, thanks. I'm lost. Could you help me find the Martin Hotel?*

   Student A: *Sure. I can show you. / Oh, I'm sorry. I don't know that hotel.*

2. You are at the airport. You missed your plane. Your partner is the customer service agent for the airline.

3. You are interested in a trip to Japan. Your partner is a travel agent.

4. You are on a plane. You want to put your suitcase above your seat. It is very heavy. Your partner is another passenger on the plane.

5. You are at home. A friend comes to see you.

6. You're in class. You and your partner are both students. You forgot your book.

7. You are in a very crowded cafeteria. You are sitting by yourself at a table. Your partner is walking around and looking for a place to sit.

UNIT 13   LESSON 3   **427**

Review the Grammar UNIT 13

Charts 13.1, 13.3, 13.4, 13.6, 13.7

1 Complete the conversation below. Use words from the box. You can use some words more than once.

| can | can't | could | have to | should | would |

Driver: Excuse me. Are you lost? (1) __Would__ you like some help?

Tourist: Oh, hello! (2) _____ I ask you a question? We're trying to get to the waterfall, but I don't see a bus.

Driver: There aren't any buses today, so you (3) _____ go by taxi. I drive a taxi, so I (4) _____ take you there.

Tourist: Oh, really? That's great. (5) _____ you tell me the price?

Driver: Sure. Here's my card with the price. The waterfall is amazing. You (6) _____ definitely see it.

Tourist: Yes, I know! I've come all this way, so I (7) _____ leave without a visit to see it.

Driver: That's true. Here's my car. (8) _____ I help with your bags?

Tourist: Thanks!

Charts 13.1–13.4, 13.6, 13.7

2 EDIT. Read the e-mails. Find and correct six more errors with offers, requests, *should*, *can*, and *have to*.

Hi Patricia,

After you told me about your trip to Papua New Guinea, I decided to plan a trip there, too! Could you ~~to~~ give me some tips? Here are some questions.

- Have I to get a visa?
- Where I should stay?
- What about clothing? Can women wear shorts?

Thanks for any suggestions!

Best,
Donna

Hi Donna,

That's exciting! Papua New Guinea is amazing! Could you like to have lunch next week? I have a lot of information for you. Yes, you have to get a visa. I went with a tour group. I think you should to go with a tour group, too. On a tour, you haven't to worry about hotels or transportation. Also, would like you to borrow some guide books? I have a few really good ones. See you soon!

Patricia

428 MODALS: PART 2

Charts 13.1–13.5

3 LISTEN, WRITE & SPEAK.

A Read the statements. Then listen to the conversation about the Huli Wigmen in Papua New Guinea. Circle **T** for *true* or **F** for *false*.

1. The Huli women grow their hair long for wigs. T (F)
2. Visitors can learn about Huli traditions. T F
3. The Huli women don't have to work hard. T F
4. The Huli men and women live together. T F
5. The Huli people do dances for visitors. T F

B Listen again. Then complete each sentence about the Huli with *can/can't, should/shouldn't,* or *have to/don't have to*.

1. Huli women ____don't have to____ make wigs.
2. For strong hair, Huli men _____ eat special food.
3. When they are growing their hair, the boys _____ run or go near fires.
4. Visitors _____ give the Huli people money.
5. The men _____ wear wigs all the time.
6. There are special buildings for men. Women _____ go inside them.
7. Huli women _____ do most of the work.
8. Huli men _____ work.

▲ Huli boy, Papua New Guinea

C In your notebook, write *Yes/No* questions and *Wh-* questions about the Huli. Use *should, can, have,* and information from exercise **B**.

D Work with a partner. Ask and answer your questions from exercise **C**.

Student A: *Should visitors give the Huli some money?*
Student B: *Yes, they should.*

UNIT 13 REVIEW THE GRAMMAR 429

Connect the Grammar to Writing

1 READ AND NOTICE THE GRAMMAR.

A Read the e-mail. What does the writer want? Discuss with a partner.

Dear Ms. Glenn,

I have to take my daughter to her school, so I can't meet with you this morning. I'm very sorry. Could you meet with me after class tomorrow?

I'm having trouble with questions, especially questions with *who*. Can you help me with this? I'm also having trouble with the present progressive. Would you please show me some more examples?

Thank you.

Best,
Carlos Santos

> **GRAMMAR FOCUS**
>
> In the e-mail in exercise **A**, the writer uses *can, could,* and *would* to make polite requests.
> **Could you** meet with me after class?

B Read the e-mail in exercise **A** again. Underline the polite requests. Then work with a partner and compare answers.

C Complete the chart with information from the e-mail in exercise **A**. What requests does the writer make?

Requests
Could you meet with me after class tomorrow?

430 MODALS: PART 2

Write a Request

2 BEFORE YOU WRITE. Think of a situation when you need to write a request for information: for example, advice about a course, help with a computer problem, or permission to miss a class. What kind of information do you need? What do you want to do? Complete the chart with your requests. Use the chart from exercise **1C** as a model.

Requests

3 WRITE a request for information or permission. Use two or three polite requests. Use the information from your chart in exercise **2** and the e-mail in exercise **1A** to help you.

WRITING FOCUS — Using Polite Language to Make Requests

Writers use the modals *could* and *would* to make polite requests. Requests with *would* and *could* are more polite than requests with imperatives because they are less direct.

Imperatives:
  Meet with me after class.
  Help me with this.
  Show me some more examples.

Polite requests:
  Could you meet with me after class?
  Can you help me with this?
  Would you please show me some more examples?

4 SELF ASSESS. Read your request. Underline the polite requests. Then use the checklist to assess your work.

☐ I used *Could you* or *Would you* to make polite requests. [13.6]
☐ I used *may* or *can* to request permission. [13.6]
☐ I put *can*, *may*, *could*, and *would* before the subjects in my requests. [13.6, 13.7]
☐ I used polite language to make requests. [WRITING FOCUS]

UNIT 14 Education and Learning

The Future

◀ A child touches an image on a wall designed for people with seeing disabilities, Franklin D. Roosevelt Memorial, Washington, DC.

Lesson 1
page 434

Future with *Be Going To* and Present Progressive

Lesson 2
page 443

Future with *Will*; Possibility with *May/Might*

Lesson 3
page 452

If Clauses; Future Time Clauses

Review the Grammar
page 460

Connect the Grammar to Writing
page 462

433

LESSON 1   Future with *Be Going To* and Present Progressive

EXPLORE

1 READ the conversation about an unusual school. Notice the words in **bold**.

An Unusual College Experience

Professor Mills: OK, Hannah, here's your final exam. You did very well. **Are** you **going to take** another math course next semester?

Hannah: No, **I'm not**. **I'm not going to be** on campus next semester. **I'm spending** a semester at sea.

Professor Mills: At sea?... Do you mean on a boat? That sounds more like a vacation than a semester at college.

Hannah: No, really, it's not a vacation. **I'm going to take** two biology courses and courses on modern Southeast Asian history and Chinese art history, too.

Professor Mills: Where does the ship go?

Hannah: From Australia to Indonesia, Singapore, and then Malaysia. Then, **I'm going to do** community service[1] for a couple of weeks at the end.

Professor Mills: Where **are** you **going to do** that?

Hannah: In Indonesia. **I'm working** at a medical clinic[2] there.

Professor Mills: What's your major?[3] Are you planning to be a doctor?

Hannah: No. I'd like to get a job in a medical field, but **I'm not going to be** a doctor.

Professor Mills: Well, have a good semester.

Hannah: Thanks!

[1] **community service:** unpaid work to help people
[2] **clinic:** a small hospital
[3] **major:** the main subject that a student is studying

▲ Nowadays students can take courses on boats like this one.

434   THE FUTURE

▼ A family health clinic, Indonesia

2 CHECK. Look at the list of activities in the chart. Does Hannah plan to do these activities in the future? Check (✓) *Yes* or *No* for each activity.

Activity	Yes	No
1. Study on campus next semester		
2. Take a math course		
3. Take two biology courses		
4. Do community service		
5. Work at a medical clinic in Indonesia		
6. Be a doctor		

3 DISCOVER. Complete the exercises to learn about the grammar in this lesson.

A Find these statements and questions in the conversation in exercise **1**. Write the missing words.

1. _____ you _____ another math course next semester?

2. I _____ on campus next semester.

3. I _____ a semester at sea.

4. I _____ two biology courses and courses on modern South East Asian history and Chinese art history, too.

5. Then, I _____ community service for a couple of weeks at the end.

6. Where _____ you _____ that?

B Look at the sentences from exercise **A**. Choose the correct word to complete the statement. Then discuss your answer with your classmates and teacher.

The actions in exercise **A** are _____ .   a. past   b. present   c. future

14.1 Future with *Be Going To*: Statements

Affirmative

Subject	Be	Going To	Base Form of Verb
I	am / 'm	going to	move.
He / She / It	is / 's	going to	move.
We / You / They	are / 're	going to	move.

Negative

Subject	Be Not	Going To	Base Form of Verb
I	am not / 'm not	going to	move.
He / She / It	is not / 's not / isn't	going to	move.
We / You / They	are not / 're not / aren't	going to	move.

1. Use *be going to* + the base form of the verb to talk about:
   a. future plans;
   b. a prediction or something you feel certain about in the future

   a. I'm **going to study** in Japan next year.
   b. I think Ed**'s going to like** his new job.
   I listened to the weather report. It**'s going to rain** this afternoon.

2. Future time expressions can come at the beginning or end of a sentence.

   I'm **going to visit** my sister <u>this weekend</u>.
   It**'s going to snow** <u>tonight</u>.
   <u>Next semester</u> she**'s going to take** Chinese.

3. Do not use *the* in future time expressions with *next*.

   ✓ I'm going to study in Mexico <u>next year</u>.
   ✗ I'm going to study in Mexico <u>the</u> next year.

4 Complete each sentence with the correct form of *be going to* and the verb in parentheses.

1. (have) Hannah _____is going to have_____ an interesting experience next semester.
2. (be) It _____ a lot of fun.
3. (study) She _____ on a ship.
4. (take) The students _____ biology courses.
5. (travel) They _____ to different countries.
6. (do) I _____ community service for a couple of weeks.
7. (not be) She _____ on campus.
8. (graduate) We _____ May.

> **REAL ENGLISH**
>
> In conversation, *going to* is often pronounced *gonna*.
>
> I'm **gonna** graduate in June.
> (= I'm going to graduate in June.)
>
> Do not use *gonna* in writing.

5 SPEAK. Work with a partner. Discuss your study plans. Use *be going to*.

(take / not take) another English course   (study / not study) another language

I'm going to take another English course.

14.2 Future with *Be Going To*: Questions

Yes/No Questions

Be	Subject	Be Going to	Base Form of Verb	
Are	you	going to	leave	tonight?
Is	she			

Short Answers

Affirmative		Negative	
Yes,	I am.	No,	I'm not.
	she is.		she isn't.

Wh- Questions

Wh- Word	Be	Subject	Be Going To	Base Form of Verb	
When	is	she	going to	leave?	
How	is	he	going to	get	there?
What	are	you	going to	take	next?
Who	are	we	going to	meet	tomorrow?

Answers

In a couple of hours.
At 2:00.

By bus.
He's going to walk.

Biology and math.
I'm not sure yet.

Our new clients are from Los Angeles.

---

1. *Be* comes before the subject in *Yes/No* questions and in most information questions.

   Are you going to go to the library?
   When **are** you going to do your homework?

2. **Remember:** *Wh-* questions with *Who* or *What* can be about a subject or an object. The word order is different.

   Questions about a Subject:
   Who **is going to do** it?
   What **is going to happen** tomorrow?

   Questions about an Object:
   Who **are** you going to ask?
   What **are** they going to do tomorrow?

---

6 Look at each sentence on the right. Write a question about the underlined word or phrase.

1. They're going to <u>register for their courses</u>. *What are they going to do?*

2. <u>Yes</u>, I'm going to be on campus tomorrow. _____

3. She's going to study <u>math</u> next semester. _____

4. <u>No</u>, I'm not going to take French next semester. _____

5. I'm going to get there <u>by bus</u>. _____

6. <u>Yes</u>, our teacher's going to give us a test tomorrow. _____

7. This course is going to end <u>in two weeks</u>. _____

8. I'm going to <u>do my homework</u> tonight. _____

9. I'm going to go on vacation <u>in June</u>. _____

10. <u>No</u>, it's not going to rain tonight. _____

7 SPEAK. Work with a partner. Ask and answer questions 6–10 in exercise **6** on page 437. Use your own answers, not the answers in the book.

Student A: *Is our teacher going to give us a test tomorrow?*

Student B: *No, she isn't.*

14.3 Future with Present Progressive

Statements

Present Progressive	Future Time Expression
I'm leaving	tomorrow.
She isn't working	on Monday.
They're coming	next week.

Yes/No Questions

Present Progressive	Future Time Expression
Are you leaving	tomorrow?
Is she coming	tonight?

Short Answers

Affirmative		Negative	
Yes,	I am.	No,	I'm not.
	she is.		she isn't.

Wh- Questions

Present Progressive	Future Time Expression
What are you doing	tonight?
When is she leaving	tomorrow?
Where are they going	next week?

Answers

I'm working.
In the afternoon.
To Seoul.

1. Use the present progressive to talk about plans already made for the near future. The present progressive is commonly used with these verbs to talk about the future: *arrive, leave, fly, drive, meet, stay, visit, come, take,* and *get*.	They have their train tickets. They**'re arriving** on Monday. **I'm visiting** my parents this weekend.
2. Time expressions and context show present or future meaning.	**Time Expressions** **I'm taking** French <u>this semester</u>. (*present*) **I'm taking** French <u>next semester</u>. (*future*) **Context** Al's my friend. He**'s studying** art. (*present*) When **are** you **leaving**? (*future*)

REAL ENGLISH

With schedules, the simple present often has a future meaning.

*Class **ends** at 10:30 today.*
*The plane **leaves** at 9:00 tomorrow morning.*

8 Complete each statement with the present progressive for future. Underline the future time expressions.

1. Jeff ___isn't taking___ (not take) courses on campus <u>next semester</u>.

2. We _____ (start) classes next week.

438 THE FUTURE

3. My parents _____ (come) to visit in a couple of weeks.

4. My brother _____ (not start) college this year.

5. I _____ (study) in India next year.

6. The university _____ (not offer) that course next semester.

7. Suzy _____ (graduate) in June.

8. We _____ (not go) to the party tomorrow night.

9 Use the words in parentheses to complete each question with the present progressive for future.

1. _____ (you / take) a history course next semester?

2. _____ (When / Pedro / give) his presentation?

3. _____ (we / start) classes next week?

4. _____ (Who / teach) this class next semester?

5. _____ (Where / she / study) next year?

6. _____ (she / arrive) tomorrow?

7. _____ (Why / he / leave) tonight?

8. _____ (How / you / get) there?

10 SPEAK. Work with a partner. Make sentences about the future. Use the words from the box and the present progressive.

| After class I . . . | Tomorrow . . . | . . . tonight. |

After class I'm meeting my friends.

PRACTICE

11 LISTEN to each statement or question. Is it present or future? Check (✓) the correct column.

	Present	Future		Present	Future
1.	☐	✓	6.	☐	☐
2.	☐	☐	7.	☐	☐
3.	☐	☐	8.	☐	☐
4.	☐	☐	9.	☐	☐
5.	☐	☐	10.	☐	☐

12 **EDIT.** Read the announcement. Find and correct six more errors with *be going to* and the present progressive for future.

News from the Study Abroad Office

- **NEW PROGRAM**

    is going to have
Our college ~~having~~ a new program next fall. Five students are going to go to Scotland in September. They going to study at the University of Edinburgh. They stay in dormitories on campus. Everyone is very excited about this new program.

- **PROGRAM CANCELLATION**

We are not send students to study in Turkey this year. We only received one application for the program. However, we offer it again next year.

- **NEW OFFICES**

We moving to the new Student Union Building on August 1, so the office not going to be open from July 30 until August 1.

▼ A view of Edinburgh, Scotland

13 Complete the conversations with the correct form of *be going to* or the present progressive for future and the verbs in parentheses.

1. **Nate:** (1) _____ (you / take) Spanish again next semester?

    Ellen: No, (2) _____ (I / take) Italian instead.

    Nate: Really? Why (3) _____ (you / do) that?

    Ellen: (4) _____ (I / study) in Rome next year, so I want to learn some Italian.

    Nate: Wow! (5) _____ (you / love) Rome. It's an amazing city!

2. **Julie:** Look at these dark clouds. (6) _____ (It / rain).

    (7) _____ (I / go) inside to get some coffee. Would you like to join me?

    Dora: Oh, thanks, but I can't. (8) _____ (I / meet) my sister.

    (9) _____ (We / go) to a movie this afternoon.

    Julie: What (10) _____ (you / see)?

    Dora: I forget the name. It's a new foreign film. My sister really wants to see it.

14 SPEAK. Role-play a conversation with your partner. Choose one of the topics from the box or your own idea. Use *be going to*. Include at least two questions.

| the weather | plans for the weekend | plans for next semester |

Student A: *What are you going to do this weekend?*   Student B: *I'm going to visit my sister. . . .*

15 LISTEN, WRITE & SPEAK.

A Listen to the discussion about three students' plans after graduation. Look at the activities in the chart. Who is going to do each activity? Check (✓) the correct column.

Activities	Sonya	Trey	Mylo
1. Go to college next year		✓	
2. Do community service			
3. Get a job and save money			
4. Go to India			
5. Teach			

B Use the words to write Yes/No questions and Wh- questions with *be going to* about the students' plans from exercise **A**.

1. What / Trey / do / next year   *What is Trey going to do next year?*

2. When / they / graduate _____

3. Where / Trey / study _____

4. Sonya / go / to college next year _____

5. Who / work _____

6. Why / Mylo / visit India _____

▶ Mehrangharh Fort and Jaswant Thada mausoleum overlooking Jodhpur, Rajasthan, India

UNIT 14 LESSON 1 441

▲ Students at a school near Amboseli National Park, Rift Valley Province, Kenya

7. What / Sonya / teach in Kenya _____

8. What / Sonya / do in Nairobi _____

9. Where / Sonya / live in Kenya _____

10. Mylo and Sonya / go to college _____

C Work with a partner. Ask and answer the questions from exercise **B**.

16 APPLY.

A Work in a group. What do you think about these students' plans? Discuss these questions.

1. Who is going to have the most interesting experience? Why?

2. Which experiences are going to help students find a job in five or six years?

3. How about you? Do you know anyone who is going to do anything similar?

B In your notebook, write your answers to questions 1 and 2 in exercise **A**. Write at least two sentences for each item.

442   THE FUTURE

Future with *Will*; Possibility with *May/Might* — LESSON 2

EXPLORE

1 **READ** the article about the Internet and the future of education. Notice the words in **bold**.

The Internet and the Future of Education

How **will** the Internet **change** education in the future? First, it **will be** easier and less expensive to get an education. Already thousands of people are taking free online courses. According to experts, colleges **will offer** even more online and hybrid[1] courses in the future. This **will change** the student population: People from poor families **will have** better access[2] to education. More older people **will take** courses online.

Second, with more online courses in the future, the role[3] of the teacher **may change**. The teacher **may not be** the expert. Instead, the teacher **may direct** the learning experience with online assignments or courses. Then, in class he or she **may take** the role of tutor or discussion leader. Teachers **might not need** to teach basic[4] skills or concepts[5] in the future; instead, students **might learn** all of the basic concepts for the course online.

What do you think?

Will the Internet **make** education easier?

☐ Yes   ☐ No   ☐ I'm not sure

CLICK TO VOTE

Yes 73%
No 22%
I'm not sure 5%
Votes

Will the Internet **make** education better?

☐ Yes   ☐ No   ☐ I'm not sure

CLICK TO VOTE

Yes 64%
No 20%
I'm not sure 16%
Votes

[1] **hybrid:** a combination of two types of things
[2] **access:** a way to reach something
[3] **role:** a job
[4] **basic:** simple and necessary
[5] **concept:** idea

▲ A classroom from the early 1900s, Molson Schoolhouse Museum, Molson, Washington, USA

UNIT 14   LESSON 2   443

2 CHECK. Match each topic in Column A with the correct information in Column B. Write the letter on the line.

Column A

1. The Internet __d__
2. Education ____
3. People ____
4. Teachers ____
5. Colleges ____

Column B

a. take more free courses
b. be cheaper
c. assign online materials
d. make education easier and cheaper
e. offer more online and hybrid courses

3 DISCOVER. Complete the exercises to learn about the grammar in this lesson.

A Find these sentences in the article from exercise **1** on page 443. Write the missing words.

1. First, it _____ easier and less expensive to get an education.
2. Second, with more online courses in the future, the role of the teacher _____.
3. The teacher _____ the expert.
4. Teachers _____ to teach basic skills or concepts in the future; instead, students _____ all of the basic concepts for the course online.

B Look at the sentences in exercise **A**. Notice the verbs. Then look at the statements below and circle **T** for *true* and **F** for *false*. Discuss your answer with your classmates and teacher.

a. The sentence with *will* is about the present.   T   F
b. The base form of the verb comes after *will (not)*,   T   F
   may (not), and *might (not)*.

14.4 Future with *Will*: Statements

Affirmative

Subject	Will	Base Form of Verb	
I			
You			
He			
She	will	need	help.
It	'll		
We			
You			
They			

Negative

Subject	Will Not/ Won't	Base Form of Verb	
I			
You			
He			
She	will not	need	help.
It	won't		
We			
You			
They			

1. *Will* is a modal. Use the base form of the verb after *will*.	The test **will be** easy.

2. Use *will*:
 a. to make predictions
 b. to talk about things you are certain about in the future
 c. for promises and offers
 d. for decisions you make at the time of speaking
	a. In 2060, all classes **will be** online.
	 b. In five years, **I'll be** 30.
	 c. **I'll call** you tonight.
	     A: It's cold in here.
	     B: **I'll close** the window.
	 d. A: I'm going to the coffee shop.
	     B: **I'll go** with you.

3. Do not use *will* to talk about future plans. Use *be going to*.	✓ We're **going to visit** our grandparents this weekend. ✗ We <u>will visit</u> our grandparents this weekend.
4. *Won't* is the contraction of *will not*.	Sam **won't** be at the party. He's sick.
5. The contractions *'ll* and *won't* are used in conversation and informal writing.	**We'll** be at home at around eight o'clock tonight. Don't worry. You **won't** need your coat on the plane.

4 Complete each sentence with *will* or *won't* and the verb in parentheses.

1. In the future, many more people _____ (take) courses online.

2. This course _____ (be) online next semester.

3. They _____ (send) me information about the course soon.

4. Online courses _____ (make) education cheaper.

5. Professors _____ (not teach) courses in the future.

6. Professor Patel _____ (send) the assignment tomorrow.

> **REAL ENGLISH**
>
> *Probably* is often used with *will* to talk about something in the future that is not certain. *Probably* goes between *will* and the base form of the verb in the affirmative and before *won't* in the negative.
>
> It'll **probably** rain tomorrow.
> We **probably** won't get our tests back tomorrow.

7. I _____ (help) you with the assignment after class.

8. Don't ask Brett. He _____ (not know) the answer.

9. Professor Lee _____ (tell) us about the test tomorrow.

10. It's 11:00. The library _____ (not be) open.

11. Do you have Megan's number? I _____ (call) her now.

12. We _____ (get) our grades on Monday.

5 Complete the conversations with 'll or won't and the words in parentheses. Then listen and check your answers.

1. **Berta:** Bye! (1) _____I'll see_____ (I / see) you in class tomorrow.

   Jess: OK. It's raining, and I think (2) _____ (there / be) a lot of traffic on your way home, so be careful.

   Berta: OK, (3) _____ (I / drive) slowly.

2. **Tasha:** Your cold sounds terrible. Have some hot tea with lemon. (4) _____ (It / make) you feel better.

   Kim: Please don't worry about me. (5) _____ (I / be) fine.

   Tasha: OK, but get some sleep and feel better!

   Kim: OK. Thanks. (6) _____ (I / call) you tomorrow.

3. **Cory:** Why are you studying now for next week's vocabulary test? (7) _____ (You / not remember) all the words next week.

   Sid: There are a lot of words on the list. I'm studying a few each day. (8) _____ (It / help) me remember them.

   Cory: Well, I guess (9) _____ (I / do) the same thing, but I don't have a list of all of the words.

   Sid: (10) _____ (I / e-mail) you my list.

   Cory: OK. Thanks!

6 SPEAK. Work with a partner. Talk about things you are certain about in the future. Use *will*, *'ll*, *won't*, and the words listed.

On Sunday . . .

After class . . .

In ten years . . .

On Sunday we'll be happy because we don't have class.

446 THE FUTURE

14.5 Future with *Will*: Questions

Yes/No Questions

Will	Subject	Base Form of Verb
Will	it / they	help?

Short Answers

Affirmative			Negative		
Yes,	it / they	will.	No,	it / they	won't.

Wh- Questions

Wh- Word	Will	Subject	Base Form of Verb
Where	will	he	be?
When	will	we	meet?
How	will	they	know?
What	will	you	say?
Who	will	you	ask?
Why	will	she	laugh?

Answers

At home.
After class.
We'll tell them.
Nothing.
Sasha.
Because it's a funny story.

1. Do not use the contraction *'ll* in short answers.	✓ Yes, I will. ✗ Yes, I'll.
2. **Remember:** *Why* is often used with negative questions.	Why won't she like it?
3. **Remember:** *Wh-* questions with *Who* or *What* can be about a subject or an object.	Questions about a Subject: Who will be there? What will happen next? Questions about an Object: Who will you go with? What will they do?

7 Look at each sentence on the right. Write a question about the underlined word or phrase.

1. <u>No</u>, we won't be late for class. _____Will we be late?_____

2. <u>Yes</u>, the teacher will be there at 9:00. _____

3. We'll get our tests back <u>tomorrow</u>. _____

4. <u>No</u>, the test won't be difficult. _____

5. <u>Yes</u>, of course I'll help you. _____

6. They'll talk to <u>the professor</u>. _____

7. <u>Susan</u> will take notes. _____

8. The lecture will be <u>in Room 306</u>. _____

9. <u>No</u>, I won't be absent tomorrow. _____

10. <u>Yes</u>, there will be a final exam. _____

8 Work with a partner. Ask and answer questions 9–10 in exercise **7**. Use your own answers, not the answers in the book.

Student A: *Will you be absent tomorrow?*

Student B: *Yes, I will. I have a doctor's appointment.*

14.6 Possibility with *Might/May*

Affirmative Statements

Subject	Might/May	Base Form of Verb	
I / You / He / She / We / You / They	might may	have	a test tomorrow.

Negative Statements

Subject	Might Not/May Not	Base Form of Verb	
I / You / He / She / We / You / They	might not may not	have	a test tomorrow.

1. Use *might* or *may* to talk about possibility in the present or future.	Present Possibility: Sue isn't here. She **may** be sick. You **might** be right. Future Possibility: Sue isn't sure about tomorrow. She **may** come. I **might** go to the game tonight. I'm not sure yet.
2. Use *might* or *may* for actions or events that are possible in the future. Use *will* for actions or events that are certain in the future.	They **might** win. (= It's possible.) They **will** win. (= It's certain.)
3. *Might* and *may* are modals. Use the base form of the verb after *might* and *may*.	✓ It **might** rain. ✗ It might <u>rains</u>.
4. There is no negative contraction for *might* or *may*.	✓ He **might not** have time. ✗ He <u>mightn't</u> have time. ✓ We **may not** go. ✗ We mayn't go.
5. Do not use *may* and *might* for questions about possibility.	✓ Is it going to rain this afternoon? ✗ **May/might** it rain this afternoon?
6. **Be careful!** *Maybe* and *may be* are not the same. *Maybe* is an adverb. It comes before the subject and verb. *Maybe* is used in conversation and informal writing.	Bring a jacket. It **may be** very cold there. It's snowing. **Maybe** we won't have class tomorrow.

448 THE FUTURE

9 Complete each sentence with *may* or *might* and the verb in parentheses. Use *may* for 1–4. Use *might* for 5–8.

1. (study) I _____may study_____ at the library tonight.
2. (not come) She _____ to class tomorrow.
3. (have) We _____ a quiz tomorrow.
4. (rain) It _____ tonight.
5. (be) Your idea _____ better. Let's try it.
6. (not be) This _____ the best way to solve the problem.
7. (not go) I _____ to the party. I'm not sure yet.
8. (take) The homework _____ a long time.

10 Choose *may be* or *maybe* to complete each sentence.

1. There ____ a test next week.
    a. may be   b. maybe

2. ____ we'll be classmates again in another course.
    a. May be   b. Maybe

3. The new vocabulary words ____ on the quiz.
    a. may be   b. maybe

4. Trudy's not here. ____ she didn't know about the change in classrooms.
    a. May be   b. Maybe

5. Look at that traffic. We ____ late for class.
    a. may be   b. maybe

6. I'm not sure yet, but I ____ take an art class next semester.
    a. may   b. maybe

7. Are you feeling sick? ____ you should stay home.
    a. May be   b. Maybe

8. The weather forecast says it ____ sunny later.
    a. may be   b. maybe

11 SPEAK. Work with a partner. Talk about possibilities in the future. Use the words from the box.

| might | may | may be |
| might not | may not | maybe |

My parents might visit me next month.

UNIT 14 LESSON 2 **449**

PRACTICE

12 Complete the exercises.

A Circle the correct word(s) to complete the announcement.

> ### Announcement
>
> We are happy to announce some exciting changes at the college. Next year, all first-year courses (1) **will** / **might** be online. Many people want to know, "How (2) **this will** / **will this** change the college?"
>
> This change (3) **may be** / **will** help the college in many ways. First-year students (4) **aren't** / **won't** need to come to campus. This (5) **maybe** / **may** save them both time and money. The college will also (6) **saves** / **save** money because it (7) **won't** / **doesn't** spend as much money on classrooms and instructors. There (8) **maybe** / **may be** more students because of this plan. In two years, the college will (9) **reviews** / **review** the success of the online program. More courses (10) **may be** / **maybe** online in the future.

B Use the words to write Yes/No questions and Wh- questions with *will* or *won't*.

1. When / online classes / start ___When will online classes start?___
2. the change / help / the college _____
3. Who / not need / to come to campus _____
4. When / the college / review the online program _____
5. the college / spend less on classes _____
6. classes / be / more expensive _____
7. the college / need / more instructors _____
8. more students / take / online classes _____

C Work with a partner. Ask and answer the questions from exercise **B**. Use *will/won't*, *may*, and *maybe*. For your answers to 6–8, use your own ideas.

Student A: *When will online classes start?*   Student B: *They'll start next year.*

13 **EDIT.** Read the conversation. Find and correct seven more errors with *will*, *won't*, *may*, *maybe*, and *might*.

Kerry: Hey, did you hear the news? Next year a lot of our courses be online. *(will)*

Justin: Really? That's great! It'll be easier for me. I mightn't need to come to campus as often. Will many first-year courses be online?

Kerry: Yes, they'll. We won't has those huge lecture classes anymore, the ones with 600 students. Students will listening online. In a few years, all classes maybe online.

Justin: Online classes, that's interesting. Everyone might has more free time.

Kerry: That's true. May be I won't have any 8:30 classes!

450 THE FUTURE

▲ A professor prepares to record a lecture for an online course.

14 LISTEN & SPEAK.

A Listen to the conversation about online classes. Circle each correct answer.

1. Who is positive about online classes?   a. Keesha   b. Craig

2. What course are they talking about?   a. Math   b. Spanish

B Listen again. Complete the notes on Craig's opinions and ideas about online classes.

Craig's Opinions and Ideas
1. Students ____won't learn as much____ online.
2. The college _____ teachers.
3. Some teachers _____ their jobs.

C Work with a partner. Does Keesha agree or disagree with Craig's opinions and ideas? In your notebook, write her opinions and ideas about online classes.

15 APPLY. Answer these questions. Discuss your answers with a partner.

1. What is your opinion about online courses? Why?

2. What is your experience with online courses?

3. Do you think you might take an online course in the future? Why, or why not?

UNIT 14   LESSON 2   **451**

LESSON 3 *If* Clauses; Future Time Clauses

EXPLORE

1 READ the article about color and tests. Notice the words in **bold**.

Color and Test Scores

Mother: Good morning. I just made coffee. Would you like some breakfast?

Son: Thanks, Mom. I'll just have coffee. I'll be late **if I have breakfast.** I have my final exam today for math.

Mother: Oh, don't wear that red shirt **if you have an exam.** I read something about this last week. **When people see red before a test,** they get lower scores.

Son: Seriously?

Mother: Yes, really. They did some research about it. In the research study, everyone got the same test, but the test booklet[1] had three different covers. Some of the covers were red, some were green, and some were black. The people with the red covers got lower scores.

Son: Wow! I wonder why.

Mother: Think about it. We use red **when we want to show danger**, right? Teachers use it **when they grade papers.** Maybe red makes us nervous.

Son: Yeah, but I'm in a hurry. **If I change my shirt,** I'll miss my bus. Hmmm. Maybe this is a good idea. **When the other students see my red shirt,** maybe they'll get nervous. Then *they*'ll get lower scores, and *I'll* get the highest grade in the class.

Mother: I hope so. Good luck!

[1] **booklet:** a small book with a paper cover

452   THE FUTURE

2 CHECK. Read the statements. Circle **T** for *true* or **F** for *false*.

1. The son has time for breakfast.   T   F
2. He's wearing a red shirt.   T   F
3. His mother did research about the color red.   T   F
4. People get higher scores when they see red before a test.   T   F
5. The son has time to change his shirt.   T   F

3 DISCOVER. Complete the exercises to learn about the grammar in this lesson.

A Find these sentences in the conversation on page 452. Write the missing words.

1. I'll be late **if** I _____ breakfast.
2. **When** people _____ red before a test, they get lower scores.
3. **If** I _____ my shirt, I'll miss my bus.
4. **When** the other students _____ my red shirt, maybe they'll get nervous.

B Look at the sentences from exercise **A**. Choose the correct word(s) to complete each statement. Then discuss your answers with your classmates and teacher.

1. Each sentence has _____.
   a. one clause   b. two clauses
2. The verb after *if* is in the _____.
   a. present   b. future   c. present or future
3. The verb after *when* is in the _____.
   a. present   b. future   c. present or future

14.7 If Clauses

If I **have** time before class,	I usually **get** some coffee.	(habit or fact)
If Clause	Main Clause	
If I **don't understand**,	I'll **ask** the teacher.	(condition with future result)
If Clause	Main Clause	

1. Sometimes an activity or event depends on something else. This is a condition.	You'll get a good grade **if you study hard**. (Condition) **If it snows**, the buses are always late. (Condition)
2. An *if clause* shows a condition. The main clause shows a result.	**If you study hard**, you'll get a good grade. (Condition / Result) **If I don't feel better**, I'm going to stay home. (Condition / Result) **If you don't study**, you might fail the test. (Condition / Result)
3. For habits or facts, use the simple present in the *if* clause. Use the simple present in the main clause.	Habit: If I **have** time before class, I usually **go** to the coffee shop. Fact: **If I eat too many sweets**, I **feel** sick.
4. For future conditions, use the simple present in the *if* clause. Use the future in the main clause.	If I **go** to bed late, I'**ll be** tired tomorrow. If we **don't leave** now, we'**ll be** late. ✓ If we **miss** our plane, I'**ll call** you. ✗ If we **will miss** our plane, I'll call you.
5. When the *if* clause is at the beginning of the sentence, use a comma.	**If Professor Wang teaches the course,** I'll take it. I'll take the course if Professor Wang teaches it.

4 Underline the *if* clause in each sentence. Add a comma if necessary.

1. <u>If I have breakfast</u>, I'll be late for my exam.

2. Don't wear that red shirt if you have an exam.

3. If he has a test he studies hard.

4. If you study hard you'll get a good grade.

5. You can borrow a pencil if you don't have one.

6. If I don't understand the assignment I'll call you.

7. If they have questions they should ask the professor.

8. If the weather is nice we walk to class.

5 Complete each condition or result with the verb in parentheses.

1. If I ____don't have____ (not have) a test tomorrow, I'll go out with my friends.

2. If he _____ (finish) the assignment, he'll come with us.

454 THE FUTURE

3. If you _____ (not understand) the homework, you should ask the teacher.

4. If I _____ (get) good grades, I'll get into a good university.

5. If she _____ (study) engineering, she'll get a good job.

6. If I _____ (not take) notes in class, I don't remember anything.

7. If we _____ (be) late for class, our teacher gets angry.

8. If we _____ (not leave) soon, we'll be late for class.

6 SPEAK. Work with a partner. Use these sentence beginnings to talk about your plans.

If I have a lot of homework, . . .   If we don't have a lot of homework, . . .
If it rains on Saturday, . . .   If the weather is nice this weekend, . . .

If I have a lot of homework tonight, I'll stay up late.

14.8 Future Time Clauses with *Before*, *After*, and *When*

Before we leave, I'm going to call my sister.
  Future Time Clause — *Main Clause*

After I finish my homework, I'm going to go to the gym.
  Future Time Clause — *Main Clause*

When we graduate, we'll have a party.
  Future Time Clause — *Main Clause*

1. **Remember:** A time clause tells when an action or event will happen. It tells the order of events.	**After I watch the news**, I'm going to cook dinner.
2. Future time clauses often begin with *before*, *after*, or *when*. Use *after* and *when* for the first action or event. Use *before* for the second action or event.	**After** he eats dinner, he's going to watch TV. *First Event — Second Event* **When** he finds a job, he'll be very happy. *First Event — Second Event* **Before** I go to class, I'm going to eat lunch. *Second Event — First Event*
3. Use simple present in the future time clause, and future in the main clause.	When I **get** home, **I'll call** you. *Future Time Clause — Main Clause*
4. Time clauses with *when* are also used to talk about facts or habits.	Fact: **When a baby is hungry**, it cries. Habit: **When I get home**, I watch the news.
5. To talk about facts or habits, use the simple present in the time clause and the main clause.	Ken **listens** to music when he **exercises**. *Main Clause — Time Clause* When I **drink** coffee at night, **I can't sleep**. *Time Clause — Main Clause*
6. Use a comma after the time clause when it comes at the beginning of the sentence.	Before he goes, he'll call you. After I send this e-mail, I'm going to call Lisa. When I have a cold, I drink tea with honey.

7 Read each sentence. Which *event* or *action* will happen first? Circle **a** or **b**. Add a comma if necessary.

1. When everyone gets here we'll begin.
   (a)   b

2. The teacher grades homework after class ends.
   　　　　a　　　　　　　　　　b

3. When I graduate my parents will be very happy.
   　　a　　　　　　b

4. I might take a trip after I finish this course.
   　　a　　　　　　　b

5. Let's have a party after we finish our exams.
   　　a　　　　　　　b

6. Before we leave I'll call you.
   　　a　　　　b

7. She'll tell you her plans when you talk to her.
   　　a　　　　　　　b

8. When she gets home she takes her dog for a walk.
   　　a　　　　　　　b

8 Look at Lara's "To Do List." Then complete the sentences with *when, after,* or *before.*

1. _____When_____ Lara calls Tomoko, she's going to ask her for her lecture notes.

2. _____ she calls Tomoko, she's going to go to the library.

3. _____ she goes to the library, she'll start the research for a psychology paper.

4. She'll go to the library _____ she meets Polly and Brittany for dinner.

5. She plans to go to the college bookstore _____ she has dinner.

6. _____ she's at the bookstore, she'll buy more paper.

7. She plans to study _____ she goes to the bookstore.

8. She's going to do her math homework _____ she studies vocabulary.

> **TO DO LIST**
> A.M. - Call Tomoko & ask for lecture notes
> 11-3: Go to library to start research for psychology paper
> 6:30 - Meet Polly & Brittany for dinner
> After dinner:
>   college bookstore: buy more paper
>   finish math homework
>   study vocabulary

9 SPEAK. Work with a partner. Talk about your plans. Use the words from the box.

Before I go home today, . . .　　After I get home, . . .　　After I have lunch tomorrow, . . .
When I get home tonight, . . .　When I get up tomorrow, . . .

Before I go home today, I'm going to go to the library.

PRACTICE

10 Match each result on the right with the correct condition on the left.

1. If I have a lot of homework tonight, I __h__.
2. If I don't have a lot of homework at night, I _____.
3. If you miss a lot of classes, you _____.
4. If I feel sick, I _____.
5. If the teacher is sick, we _____.
6. If you're tired, _____.
7. If you have any trouble, I _____.
8. If you don't finish this now, you _____.

a. 'll help you
b. can do it tonight for homework
c. won't go to class
d. drink some coffee
e. usually watch a movie
f. might not have class
g. won't do well in the course
h. won't go out with my friends

11 Complete the exercises.

A Circle the correct verb to complete each sentence.

Rewards for Good Grades

How important are rewards in learning? Will children get better grades if they (1) **receive** / **will receive** something special for them? (2) **Will they study** / **Are they studying** harder if they (3) **get** / **will get** rewards?

Consider this example: Greta is taking a test tomorrow. Her father says to her, "Greta, if you (4) **will get** / **get** an A on your next test, I (5) **give** / **will give** you $20." Greta answers, "OK, Dad. If you are going to give me $20, (6) **I'll get** / **I get** an A."

There are several problems with this situation. After Greta (7) **is getting** / **gets** a few rewards, she'll probably expect them. If she (8) **gets** / **will get** a lot of rewards, she won't learn to do things on her own. Last, if she (9) **doesn't get** / **will get** rewards, she might not try to get good grades anymore.

Experts have advice for parents:

- Explain why good grades are important. Say, "If you (10) **will get** / **get** good grades, you (11) **are getting** / **are going to get** a good job in the future.
- Focus on effort, not grades. When your child (12) **works** / **will work** hard, say, "You worked hard. I'm proud of you."

Think carefully before you give your child a reward for good grades!

B Use the information from exercise **A** on page 457 and your own ideas to complete the sentences. Add commas if necessary.

1. Good grades are important. If children get good grades, _they'll get into good colleges._
2. Some parents give their children rewards when _____.
3. If children get rewards _____.
4. Parents should think about some experts' advice before _____.
5. Children may not work hard on their own after _____.
6. If children understand why good grades are important _____.
7. If children work hard in school _____.
8. When I have children, I _____ if they get good grades.

C Work with a partner. Discuss this question.

What do you think? Should parents give their children rewards for good grades? Why, or why not?

12 LISTEN & SPEAK.

A Read each statement. Then listen to the conversation. Choose the correct words to complete each sentence.

1. David is going to ____ soon.
   a. take a course   b. go to college
2. Martha is going to ____.
   a. study business   b. decide later about her future

B Listen again and complete the sentences from the conversation in exercise **A**. Add commas if necessary.

1. Why are you taking the course before _you need it?_
2. Then, I'm going to take another course before _____ the exam.
3. _____ a good score on the entrance exam, I won't get into a good university, and then _____ a good job.
4. If you're smart, _____ on the test. If _____ you won't.
5. If _____ you can do a lot better.
6. When _____ I'll figure it out.
7. _____ I'm going to work in my family's store.
8. If _____ for my father, everyone will be upset.

458 THE FUTURE

C Work in a group. Discuss these questions.

1. Do test prep courses help students get better scores? Why, or why not?
2. When should students take test prep courses?

13 APPLY.

A Work with a group. You are members of a committee to recommend changes in your education system, school, or program. Complete the chart with the changes you recommend and your reasons.

Changes	Reasons
1. We should make classes cheaper.	1. If classes are cheaper, students will take more classes. They'll learn more.

B Share your ideas with your classmates. Then discuss. Which ideas do you like? Which ideas will never happen? Why?

I like Group A's first idea. If we make classes cheaper, students will take more classes and learn more.

Review the Grammar UNIT 14

Charts 14.1, 14.4, 14.6–14.8

1 Circle the correct verb to complete each sentence in the advertisement. Then listen and check your answers.

The Outdoor English Experience

Outdoor English is a great new way to study English! At Outdoor English, you (1) **are learning** / **will learn** English and hike and camp in the mountains. When you (2) **arrive** / **will arrive** at Outdoor English, you (3) **are having** / **will have** two days of English lessons. You (4) **will also learn** / **are also learning** camping skills before you (5) **start** / **will start** your adventure. For example, (6) you **are learning** / **will learn** how to set up a tent, cook over a campfire, and stay safe in the mountains.

Then, you and your team members (7) **will hike and camp** / **are hiking and camping** in the mountains for a week with an experienced mountain guide. Your guide (8) **will be** / **maybe** your English teacher, too! After you (9) **will spend** / **spend** a week in the mountains, you (10) **return** / **will return** to share stories of your adventures with the other teams. This is an experience that you (11) **are never forgetting** / **are never going to forget**, and it is a great way to learn English!

Charts 14.1–14.8

2 EDIT. Read the conversation. Find and correct five more errors with *will/won't, be going to,* and the future with present progressive.

Hal: Hi, Adam. What are you doing?

Adam: Hey, Hal. I'm ~~make~~ making a packing list.

Hal: Where you are going?

Adam: I going to the Andes Mountains next month.

Hal: Wow. Are you going there for vacation?

Adam: No, I'm going to study Spanish.

Hal: Really? Are you going stay with a family?

Adam: No. I'm go with this unusual language program I found online. It combines hiking and camping trips with Spanish classes. After I will get there, I'll meet the other students in the program and the guides. Then, we're going to go on a two-week camping trip. The guides are Spanish teachers, too.

Hal: That sounds amazing! I'm sure you going to have a great time and learn a lot!

460 THE FUTURE

Charts
14.1–14.8

3 LISTEN, WRITE & SPEAK.

A Look at Ali's plans in the chart. Then listen to the conversation. Which plans is he sure about? Which plans is he unsure about? Check (✓) the correct column.

Plans	Sure	Not Sure
1. Take more English courses		
2. Study English for eight more months		
3. Take the English test in May		
4. Go to university next September		
5. Get married		

B Listen again. Complete the flow chart for Ali's plans.

Long-Term Goal: Be a _____

Take more English classes → Take English test → Get a good score
- Yes → _____ a vacation
- No → Study English in the summer

Apply to universities → Get accepted
- Yes → _____ in September
- No → _____ to Saudi Arabia

Get married after _____

Get a job before _____

C In your notebook, write about Ali. Use the words given and the facts in exercise **B**.

1. When / Ali / finish / his English course
   When Ali finishes his English course, he'll take a test.

2. If / he / not get / high score
3. If / he / get / high score
4. If / he / get accepted
5. If / he / not get accepted / to a university
6. After / he / finish university
7. Before / he / get married

Charts
14.1–14.8

4 SPEAK.

A Make a chart with your plans for the future. Use the chart in exercise **3B** as a model.

B Work with a partner. Share your charts from exercise **A**. Ask each other questions about your plans for the future. Then share the information about your partner with the class.

Martin is going to go back to France. After he graduates, he's going to look for a job in marketing . . .

UNIT 14 REVIEW THE GRAMMAR 461

Connect the Grammar to Writing

1 READ AND NOTICE THE GRAMMAR.

A Read Binh's personal statement. What are some of her plans for the future? Discuss with a partner.

My Plans for the Future

Right now, I'm a student at a community college. I'm going to be a nurse. Next semester, I'm starting a nursing program. When I finish it, I'm going to take a test to get my nursing license. If I pass, I'll apply for a job in a hospital. If I don't pass the test, I'll take a test preparation course and take the test again.

After I work for a couple of years, I might take more nursing courses and get a four-year degree. If I do that, I'll be able to get better nursing jobs. I think this is a good career plan because there will always be jobs for nurses.

GRAMMAR FOCUS

In her personal statement in exercise **A**, the writer uses different verb forms and modals to talk about her future plans.

I'm going to be a nurse.
Next semester, *I'm starting* a nursing program.

B Read the personal statement in exercise **A** again. Underline the verb forms and modals that the writer uses to talk about her future plans. Then work with a partner and compare answers.

C Complete the chart with information about the writer's personal statement.

Binh's long-term goal: Be a nurse

Reasons for goal: _____

Plans:

1. start a nursing program
2. _____
3. _____
4. _____
5. _____

462 THE FUTURE

Write a Personal Statement

2 **BEFORE YOU WRITE.** Complete the chart with ideas and information about your long-term goal and future plans. Use the chart from exercise **1C** as a model.

> My long-term goal: _____
> Reasons for goal: _____
> Plans: _____
> _____
> _____
> _____
> _____

3 **WRITE** a personal statement. Use the information from your chart in exercise **2** and the personal statement in exercise **1A** to help you.

> **WRITING FOCUS**   Using *If* Clauses and Time Clauses
>
> Writers use *if* clauses to show a condition. They use time clauses with *when*, *before*, and *after* to show the order of events.
>
> **Remember:** Use a comma when the *if* clause or time clause is at the beginning of the sentence.
>
> **If I pass,** I'll apply for a job as a nurse in a hospital.
> **When I finish it,** I'm going to take a test to get my nursing license.

4 **SELF ASSESS.** Read your personal statement. Underline the verb forms and modals that talk about the future. Then use the checklist to assess your work.

☐   I used *be going to* or present progressive to talk about future plans. [14.1, 14.3]
☐   I used *will* or *won't* for predictions and things I am certain about in the future. [14.4]
☐   I used *may* or *might* to express possibility in the future. [14.6]
☐   I used *if* clauses to talk about conditions in the future. [14.7, 14.8]
☐   I used future time clauses with *before*, *after*, and *when* to talk about the order of actions and events in the future. [WRITING FOCUS]

APPENDICES

1 Spelling Rules for Regular Plural Nouns

Rule	Examples
1. Add -s to most nouns.	student-student**s** teacher-teacher**s** pen-pen**s**
2. Add -es to nouns that end in -ch, -s, -sh, and -x.	watch-watch**es** class-class**es** dish-dish**es** box-box**es**
3. Add -s to nouns that end in a vowel + -y.	boy-boy**s** day-day**s**
4. Change the -y to -i and add -es to nouns that end in a consonant + -y.	city-cit**ies** country-countr**ies**
5. Add -s to nouns that end in a vowel + -o.	video-video**s** radio-radio**s**
6. Add -es to nouns that end in a consonant + -o. 　　Exceptions: photo → photo**s** 　　　　　　　 piano → piano**s**	potato-potato**es** tornado-tornado**es**

2 Common Irregular Noun Plurals

Singular	Plural	Explanation
man woman tooth foot goose	men women teeth feet geese	Vowel change
sheep fish deer	sheep fish deer	No change
child person mouse	children people mice	Different word forms
No singular form	belongings clothes groceries glasses jeans pajamas pants scissors shorts	

3 Simple Present Spelling Rules: -s and -es Endings

1. Add -s to most verbs.	like-like**s** sit-sit**s**
2. Add -es to verbs that end in -ch, -s, -sh, -x, or -z.	catch-catch**es** miss-miss**es** wash-wash**es** mix-mix**es** buzz-buzz**es**
3. Change the -y to -i and add -es when the base form of the verb ends in a consonant + -y.	cry-cr**ies** carry-carr**ies**
4. Do not change the -y to -i when the base form ends in a vowel + -y.	pay-pay**s** stay-stay**s**
5. Some verbs are irregular in the third-person singular form of the simple present.	be-**is** go-go**es** do-do**es** have-ha**s**

4 Spelling Rules for the -ing Form of Verbs

1. Add -ing to the base form of most verbs.	eat-eat**ing** do-do**ing** speak-speak**ing** carry-carry**ing**
2. Verbs that end in a consonant and silent -e: Drop the -e and add -ing.	ride-rid**ing** write-writ**ing**
3. One-syllable verbs that end in CVC*: Double the final consonant and add -ing. Do not double the final consonant for verbs that end in -w, -x, or -y.	stop-stop**ping** sit-sit**ting** show-show**ing** fix-fix**ing** stay-stay**ing**
4. Two-syllable verbs that end in CVC and have the stress on the first syllable: Add -ing, but do not double the final consonant.	listen-listen**ing** travel-travel**ing**
5. Two-syllable verbs that end in CVC: Double the final consonant only if the last syllable is stressed, and add -ing.	begin-begin**ning** refer-refer**ring**

*consonant + vowel + consonant

5 Spelling Rules for the -ed Form of Verbs

Rule	Examples
1. Add -ed to the base form of most verbs that end in a consonant.	start-start**ed** talk-talk**ed**
2. Add -d if the base form of the verb ends in -e.	dance-dance**d** live-live**d**
3. One-syllable verbs that end in CVC*: Double the final consonant and add -ed. Do not double the final consonant of verbs that end in -w, -x, or -y.	stop-stop**ped** rob-rob**bed** follow-follow**ed** fix-fix**ed** play-play**ed**
4. Change the -y to -i and add -ed when the base form ends in a consonant + -y. Do not change the -y when the verb ends in a vowel + -y.	cry-cr**ied** worry-worr**ied** stay-stay**ed**
5. Two-syllable verbs that end in CVC and have the stress on the first syllable: Add -ed, but do not double the final consonant.	travel-travel**ed** visit-visit**ed** order-order**ed**
6. Two-syllable verbs that end in CVC: Double the final consonant when the second syllable is stressed, and add -ed.	prefer-prefer**red** refer-refer**red**

*consonant + vowel + consonant

6 Spelling Rules for Adverbs Ending in -ly

Rule	Adjective	Adverb
1. Add -ly to the end of most adjectives.	careful quiet serious	careful**ly** quiet**ly** serious**ly**
2. Change the -y to -i and add -ly to adjectives that end in a consonant + -y.	easy happy lucky	eas**ily** happ**ily** luck**ily**
3. For many adjectives that end in -e: Keep the -e and add -ly.	nice free	nice**ly** free**ly**
4. For adjectives that end with a consonant followed by -le: Drop the final e and add -y.	simple comfortable	sim**ply** comforta**bly**
5. For most adjectives that end in -ic: Add -ally.	basic enthusiastic	basic**ally** enthusiastic**ally**

7 Spelling Rules for Comparative and Superlative Forms

	Adjective	Comparative	Superlative
1. One-syllable adjectives and adverbs: Add -er to form the comparative. Add -est to form the superlative.	tall fast	taller faster	the tallest the fastest
2. Adjectives that end in -e: Add -r to form the comparative, and -st to form the superlative.	nice	nicer	the nicest
3. Two-syllable adjectives and adverbs that end in -y: Change the -y to -i before adding -er or -est.	easy happy	easier happier	the easiest the happiest
4. One-syllable adjectives and adverbs that end in CVC*: Double the final consonant before adding -er or -est.	big	bigger	the biggest
5. Some adjectives have irregular comparative and superlative forms.	good bad	better worse	the best the worst

*consonant + vowel + consonant

8 Guide to Pronunciation Symbols

Vowels		
Symbol	Key Word	Pronunciation
/a/	hot far	/hat/ /far/
/æ/	cat	/kæt/
/aɪ/	fine	/faɪn/
/aʊ/	house	/haʊs/
/ɛ/	bed	/bɛd/
/eɪ/	name	/neɪm/
/i/	need	/nid/
/ɪ/	sit	/sɪt/
/oʊ/	go	/goʊ/
/ʊ/	book	/bʊk/
/u/	boot	/but/
/ɔ/	dog four	/dɔg/ /fɔr/
/ɔɪ/	toy	/tɔɪ/
/ʌ/	cup	/kʌp/
/ɛr/	bird	/bɛrd/
/ə/	about after	/əˈbaʊt/ /ˈæftər/

Consonants		
Symbol	Key Word	Pronunciation
/b/	boy	/bɔɪ/
/d/	day	/deɪ/
/dʒ/	just	/dʒʌst/
/f/	face	/feɪs/
/g/	get	/gɛt/
/h/	hat	/hæt/
/k/	car	/kar/
/l/	light	/laɪt/
/m/	my	/maɪ/
/n/	nine	/naɪn/
/ŋ/	sing	/sɪŋ/
/p/	pen	/pɛn/
/r/	right	/raɪt/
/s/	see	/si/
/t/	tea	/ti/
/tʃ/	cheap	/tʃip/
/v/	vote	/voʊt/
/w/	west	/wɛst/
/y/	yes	/yɛs/
/z/	zoo	/zu/
/ð/	they	/ðeɪ/
/θ/	think	/θɪŋk/
/ʃ/	shoe	/ʃu/
/ʒ/	vision	/ˈvɪʒən/

Source: The *Newbury House Dictionary plus Grammar Reference, Fifth Edition*, National Geographic Learning/Cengage Learning, 2014

9 Common Irregular Verbs

Base Form of Verb	Simple Past
be	was, were
become	became
begin	began
bend	bent
bite	bit
blow	blew
break	broke
bring	brought
build	built
buy	bought
catch	caught
choose	chose
come	came
cost	cost
cut	cut
dive	dived/dove
do	did
draw	drew
drink	drank
drive	drove
eat	ate
fall	fell
feed	fed
feel	felt
fight	fought
find	found
fly	flew
forget	forgot

Base Form of Verb	Simple Past
get	got
give	gave
go	went
grow	grew
hang	hung
have	had
hear	heard
hide	hid
hit	hit
hold	held
keep	kept
know	knew
lead	led
leave	left
lend	lent
let	let
lose	lost
make	made
meet	met
pay	paid
put	put
quit	quit
read	read
ride	rode
ring	rang
rise	rose
run	ran

Base Form of Verb	Simple Past
say	said
see	saw
sell	sold
send	sent
set	set
shake	shook
shut	shut
sing	sang
sink	sank
sit	sat
sleep	slept
speak	spoke
spend	spent
stand	stood
steal	stole
swim	swam
take	took
teach	taught
tear	tore
tell	told
think	thought
throw	threw
understand	understood
wake	woke/waked
wear	wore
win	won
write	wrote

Unit 10, Review the Grammar, Exercise 4, Page 337

Partner B

Mexican Gray Wolf

Mexican gray wolves are small wolves with long thick fur. They are very rare. In the past, they lived in parts of Mexico and the United States. Now they only live in the United States. These wolves are not dangerous to people, but they eat farm animals when they don't have enough food. Because of this, farmers and hunters killed many of the Mexican gray wolves. Now these wolves are very rare.

Unit 12, Lesson 2, Exercise 11B, Page 389

B Use your chart to answer Partner A's questions. Then ask Partner A questions to complete the chart.

Partner A: *What is the biggest art museum in the world?*

Partner B: *What do you think?*

Partner A: *I think it's the Louvre.*

Partner B: *No, the Metropolitan Museum is the biggest. It's in New York.*

Geography Trivia

small/ ocean?	The longest river in the world is the Nile.	big/ desert?
The highest waterfall in the world is Angel Falls (in Venezuela).	The biggest art museum in the world is the Metropolitan Museum of Art (New York).	The smallest country in the world is the Vatican.
large/ country?	The driest place in the world is the Atacama Desert in Chile.	large/ islands?

APPENDICES **A6**

GLOSSARY OF GRAMMAR TERMS

action verb: a verb that shows an action.
- He **drives** every day.
- They **left** yesterday morning.

adjective: a word that describes or modifies a noun or pronoun.
- She is **friendly**.
- Brazil is a **huge** country.

adverb: a word that describes or modifies a verb, an adjective, or another adverb.
- He eats **quickly**.
- She drives **carefully**.

adverb of manner: an adverb that describes the action of the verb. Many adverbs of manner are formed by adding *-ly* to the adjective.
- You sing **beautifully**.
- He speaks **slowly**.

affirmative statement: a statement that does not have a verb in the negative form.
- My uncle lives in Portland.

article: a word that is used before a noun: *a, an, the*.
- I looked up at **the** moon.
- Lucy had **a** sandwich and **an** apple for lunch.

auxiliary verb: (also called *helping verb*) a verb used with the main verb. *Be, do, have,* and *will* are common auxiliary verbs when they are followed by another verb. Modals are also auxiliary verbs.
- I **am** working.
- He **won't** be in class tomorrow.
- She **can** speak Korean.

base form of the verb: the form of the verb without *to* or any endings, such as *-ing, -s,* or *-ed*.
- eat, sleep, go, walk

capital letter: an uppercase letter.
- **N**ew **Y**ork, **M**r. **F**ranklin, **J**apan

clause: a group of words with a subject and a verb. See *dependent clause* and *main clause*.
- We watched the game. (one clause)
- We watched the game after we ate dinner. (two clauses)

comma: a punctuation mark that separates parts of a sentence.
- After he left work**,** he went to the gym.
- I can't speak Russian**,** but my sister can.

common noun: a noun that does not name a specific person, place, or thing.
- man, country, book, help

comparative adjective: the form of an adjective used to talk about the difference between two people, places, or things.
- I'm **taller** than my mother.
- Canada is **larger** than Mexico.

comparison: a statement of the similarities or differences between things, ideas, or people.
- Mexico City is more crowded than Buenos Aires.

conditional: a structure used to talk about an activity or event that depends on something else.
- **If the weather is nice on Sunday**, we'll go to the beach.

conjunction: a word used to connect information or ideas. *And, but, or,* and *because* are conjunctions.
- He put cheese **and** onions on his sandwich.
- I wanted to go, **but** I had too much homework.

consonant: the following letters are consonants: *b, c, d, f, g, h, j, k, l, m, n, p, q, r, s, t, v, w, x, y, z*.

contraction: two words combined into a shorter form.
- did not → **didn't**
- I am → **I'm**
- she is → **she's**
- we will → **we'll**

count noun: a noun that names something you can count. They are singular or plural.
- I ate an **egg** for breakfast.
- I have **six apples** in my bag.

definite article: *the*; it is used before a specific person, place, or thing.
- I found it on **the** Internet.
- **The** children are sleeping.

dependent clause: a clause that cannot stand alone as a sentence. It must be used with a main clause.
- I went for a walk **before I ate breakfast**.

direct object: a noun or pronoun that receives the action of the verb.
- Aldo asked a **question**.
- Karen helped **me**.

exclamation point: a punctuation mark that shows emotion (anger, surprise, excitement, etc.) or emphasis.
- We won the game**!**
- Look**!** It's snowing!

formal: language used in academic writing or speaking, or in polite or official situations rather than in everyday conversation or writing.
- *Please do not take photographs inside the museum.*
- *May I leave early today?*

frequency adverb: an adverb that tells how often something happens. Some common adverbs of frequency are *never, rarely, sometimes, often, usually,* and *always*.
- *I **always** drink coffee in the morning.*
- *He **usually** leaves work at six o'clock.*

frequency expression: an expression that tells how often something happens.
- *We go to the grocery store **every Saturday**.*
- *He plays tennis **twice a week**.*

future: a verb form that expresses an action or situation that has not happened yet. *Will, be going to,* the present progressive, and the simple present are used to express the future.
- *I **will call** you later.*
- *We're **going** to the movies tomorrow.*
- *I'm **taking** French next semester.*

helping verb: see *auxiliary verb*.

if clause: a clause that begins with *if* and expresses a condition.
- *If you drive too fast, you will get a ticket.*

imperative: a verb form that gives an instruction or command. Use the base form of the verb to form the imperative.
- ***Turn** left at the light.*
- ***Don't use** the elevator.*

indefinite article: *a* and *an*; they are used before singular count nouns that are not specific.
- *We have **a** test today.*
- *She's **an** engineer.*

indefinite pronoun: a pronoun that refers to people or things that are not specific or not known. *Someone, something, everyone, everything, no one, nothing,* and *nowhere* are common indefinite pronouns.
- ***Everyone** is here today.*
- ***No one** is absent.*
- *Would you like **something** to eat?*

independent clause: see *main clause*.

infinitive: an infinitive is *to* + the base form of a verb.
- *He wants **to see** the new movie.*

informal: language that is used in everyday conversation and writing.
- *Who are you talking to?*
- *We'll be there at eight.*

information question: see *Wh- question*.

irregular adjective: an adjective that does not change form in the usual way.
- *good → better*
- *bad → worse*

irregular adverb: an adverb that does not change form in the usual way.
- *well → better*
- *badly → worse*

irregular verb: a verb form that does not follow the rules for regular verbs.
- *swim → swam*
- *have → had*

main clause: (also called *independent clause*) a clause that can stand alone as a sentence. It has a subject and a verb.
- *I **heard the news** when I was driving home.*

measurement word: a word used to talk about a specific quantity of something.
- *We need to buy a **box** of pasta and a **gallon** of milk.*

modal: an auxiliary verb that adds additional meaning to a verb, such as ability or possibility. *May, might, can, could, will, would,* and *should* are common modals.
- *Julie **can** speak three languages.*
- *He **may** be at the office. Call him.*

negative statement: a statement that has a verb in the negative form.
- *I **don't have** any sisters.*
- *She **doesn't drink** coffee.*

non-action verb: a verb that does not describe an action. Non-action verbs indicate states, senses, feelings, or ownership. They are not common in the progressive.
- *I **love** my grandparents.*
- *They **have** a new car.*

non-count noun: a noun that names something that cannot be counted.
- *Carlos drinks a lot of **coffee**.*
- *I need some **salt** for the recipe.*

noun: a word that names a person, a place, or a thing.
- *They're **students**.*
- *It's an excellent **hospital**.*

GLOSSARY OF GRAMMAR TERMS G2

object: a noun or pronoun that receives the action of the verb.
➢ Mechanics fix **cars**.

object pronoun: a word that takes the place of a noun as the object of the sentence: *me, you, him, her, it, us, them*.
➢ Rita is my neighbor. I see **her** every day.
➢ Can you help **us**?

past progressive: a verb form used to talk about an action that was in progress at a specific time in the past.
➢ He **was watching** TV when the phone rang.

period: a punctuation mark that is used at the end of a statement. It is also called "a full stop."
➢ She lives in Moscow**.**

phrase: a group of words that does not have a subject or a verb.
➢ He lives **near the train station**.

plural noun: a noun that names more than one person, place, or thing.
➢ He put three **boxes** on the table.
➢ Argentina and Mexico are **countries**.

possessive adjective: an adjective that shows ownership or relationship (*my, your, his, her, its, our, their*). It is used with a noun.
➢ **My** car is green.
➢ **Your** keys are on the table.

possessive noun: a noun that shows ownership or a relationship.
➢ **Leo's** apartment is large.
➢ The **girls'** books are on the table.

possessive pronoun: a pronoun that shows ownership or relationship: *mine, yours, his, hers, its, ours, theirs*. Possessive pronouns are used in place of a possessive adjective + noun.
➢ My sister's eyes are blue. **Mine** are brown. What color are **yours**?

preposition: a word that describes the relationships between nouns. Prepositions describe space, time, direction, cause, and effect.
➢ I live **on** Center Street.
➢ We left **at** noon.

pronoun: a word that takes the place of a noun or refers to a noun.
➢ The teacher is sick today. **He** has a cold.

proper noun: a noun that names a specific person, place, or thing.
➢ **Maggie** lives in a town near **Dallas**.

punctuation: the use of specific marks to make ideas within writing clear, such as commas (,), periods (.), exclamation points (!), and question marks (?).
➢ John plays soccer**,** but I don't**.**
➢ She's from Japan**.**
➢ That's amazing**!**
➢ Where are you from**?**

quantifier: a word that describes the quantity of a noun.
➢ We need **some** potatoes for the recipe.
➢ I usually put **a little** milk in my coffee.

question: a sentence that asks for an answer.
➢ Is she a teacher?

question mark: a punctuation mark (?) that is used at the end of a question.
➢ Are you a student**?**

regular: a noun, verb, adjective, or adverb that changes form according to standard rules.
➢ apple → apples
➢ talk → talked, talking
➢ small → smaller
➢ slow → slowly

sentence: a thought that is expressed in words, usually with a subject and verb. It begins with a capital letter and ends with a period, exclamation point, or question mark.
➢ Karen called last night.
➢ Don't eat that!

short answer: an answer to a *Yes/No* question.
➢ A: Did you do the homework?
➢ B: **Yes, I did./ No, I didn't**.

simple past: a verb form used to talk about completed actions.
➢ Last night we **ate** dinner at home.
➢ I **visited** my parents last weekend.

simple present: a verb form used to talk about habits or routines, schedules, and facts.
➢ He **likes** apples and oranges.
➢ Toronto **gets** a lot of snow in the winter.

singular noun: a noun that names only one person, place, or thing.
➢ They have a **son** and a **daughter**.

statement: a sentence that gives information.
➢ My house has five rooms.
➢ He doesn't have a car.

stress: we use stress to say a syllable or a word with more volume or emphasis.

subject: the noun or pronoun that is the topic of the sentence.
- *Patricia is a doctor.*
- *They are from Iceland.*

subject pronoun: a pronoun that is the subject of sentence: *I, you, he, she, it,* and *they.*
- *I have one brother. **He** lives in Miami.*

superlative: the form of an adjective or adverb used to compare three or more people, places, or things.
- *Mount Everest is **the highest** mountain in the world.*
- *Evgeny is **the youngest** student in our class.*

syllable: a part of a word that contains a single vowel sound and is pronounced as a unit.
- *The word pen has one syllable. The word pencil has two syllables (pen-cil).*

tense: the form of the verb that shows the time of the action.
- *He **sells** apples.* (simple present)
- *They **sold** their car.* (simple past)

time clause: a clause that tells when an action or event happened or will happen. Time clauses are introduced by conjunctions, such as *when, after, before,* and *while.*
- *I'm going to call my parents **after I eat dinner**.*
- *I called my parents **when I got home**.*

time expression: a phrase that tells when something happened or will happen. Time expressions usually go at the end or beginning of a sentence.
- ***Last week** I went hiking.*
- *She's moving **next month**.*

verb: a word that shows action, gives a state, or shows possession.
- *Tori **called** me last night.*
- *She **is** my classmate.*
- *She **has** three daughters.*

vowel: the following letters (and some combinations of the letters) are vowels: *a, e, i, o, u,* and sometimes *y.*

Wh- question: (also called *information question*) a question that asks for specific information, not an answer with "*Yes*" or "*No.*" (See also *Wh-* word.)
- ***Where** do they live?*
- ***What** do you usually do on weekends?*

Wh- word: a word such as *Who, What, When, Where, Why,* or *How* that is used to begin a *Wh-* question (information question).
- ***Why** are you crying?*
- ***When** did they leave?*

Yes/No question: a question that can be answered by "*Yes*" or "*No.*"
- A: **Do you live in Dublin?** B: *Yes, I do. / No, I don't.*
- A: **Can you ski?** B: *Yes, I can. / No, I can't.*

INDEX

Note: All page references in blue are in Split Edition B.

A

A/an
- before adjectives, 23, 312
- consonants and use of, 13, 149, 174, 312
- before count nouns, 149, 150, 174
- before nouns used as adjectives, 316
- before singular nouns, 13, 312
- *the* vs., 150
- use of, 13

About, 91
Above, 52
Action verbs
- explanation of, G1
- verbs as both linking and, 323

Addresses, *at* in, 52
Adjectives
- to add interest, 339
- *and* to connect, 23
- comparative forms of, 376–378, 402, A4, G1
- to describe weather, 63
- descriptive, 23
- *enough* with, 332
- explanation of, 23, 322, G1
- *how* and *what* questions with, 314
- irregular comparative forms of, 376
- linking verbs with, 323
- to modify nouns, 312, 338
- nouns used as, 316
- possessive, 30, 393, G3
- with same form as adverbs, 324
- superlative forms of, 385–387, 402, A4
- *too/very* with, 331

Adverbs
- to add interest, 339
- comparative, A4
- *enough* with, 332
- explanation of, G1
- frequency, 127–128, 142, G2
- *-ly* ending for, 324, A3
- of manner, 322, G1
- to modify verbs, 338
- with same form as adjectives, 324
- superlative, G4
- *too/very* with, 331

Advice, 408, 409
A few, 166
Affirmative imperatives, 106, G2
Affirmative statements
- *be able to* in, 354
- *be going to* in, 436, 445
- *be* in, 6–7
- *can* in, 345, 415
- explanation of, G1

- *have to* in, 417
- indefinite pronouns in, 195, 197
- *know how to* in, 346
- *me too* in, 128
- *might/may* in, 448
- in past progressive, 299
- in present progressive, 210
- *probably* in, 445
- *should* in, 408
- in simple past, 244, 258–259, 274
- in simple present, 82
- *some* in, 157
- *there is/there are* in, 180
- *will* in, 445

After, in time clauses, 290, 307, 455
Ago, 245
Agreement, subject-verb, 143
A little, 166
Almost, 127
Almost never, 127
A lot of, 165
Also, 159
Always, 127, G2
Am, 6. See also *Be*
And
- to connect independent clauses, 361, 371
- to connect two adjectives, 23
- to connect verbs in present progressive, 239
- when to use, 6, 14, G1

Answers. See also Short answers
- *be* in, 45
- *can/could* in, 346
- *can/may* in, 415
- *do/does* in, 418
- to polite requests, 424
- about possession, 394
- to questions with comparative adjectives, 378
- *well* to begin, 135
- to *Wh-* questions, 133, 137, 222, 447
- to *Yes/No* questions, 121, 181, 182, 409

Any, 157
Anyone/anybody, 197
Anything, 195
Apostrophes
- with contractions, 7, 16, G1
- with possessive nouns, 31

Are, 14. See also *Be*
Around, 91
Articles
- definite, 150, G1
- explanation of, G1
- indefinite, 150, G2

At
- in addresses, 52
- in clock times, 61, 91
- in general location, 53

Auxiliary verbs
- explanation of, G1

B

Be
- adjectives with, 312
- affirmative statements with, 6–7
- contractions with, 7
- descriptive adjectives with, 23
- forms of, 6
- frequency adverbs with, 127
- guidelines for use of, 38
- negative statements with, 16
- plural noun with, 14, 16
- in present, 6–7, 16, 44, 45
- in present progressive, 210, 212
- questions with, 44, 45, 133, 378
- short answers with, 45
- in simple past, 244, 251–252
- in simple present, 82
- singular noun with, 13
- before *there* in *Yes/No* questions, 181
- *where* with, 54

Be able to, 354, 370
Because, 282
Before, in time clauses, 290, 307, 455
Be going to, affirmative and negative statements in, 436, 445
Behind, 52
Below, 52
Between, 52
Both, 27
But, 361, 362

C

Can/can't, 334, 335, 346, 415
Can/may, 415
Can you, 424
Capital letters, 275, G1
Clauses
- dependent, G1
- explanation of, 290, 361, G1
- *if,* 454, 463, G2
- independent or main, 361–362, 371, G2
- time, 290, 292, 306, 307, 455, 463, G4

Commas (,)
- explanation of, G1
- with *if* clauses, 454, 463
- with time clauses, 292, 455, 463

Common noun, G1

I1 INDEX

Comparative adjectives
    explanation of, 376, 377, G1
    irregular forms of, 376
    more with, 377
    questions with, 378
    spelling rules for, A4
    use of, 402
Comparative adverb spelling rules, A4
Comparison
    comparative adjectives to make, 376–378, 402, G4
    explanation of, G1
    possessive pronouns to make, 393
    superlative adverbs to make, 385–387, 402, G4
Conditional, 454, 463, G1
Conjunctions
    explanation of, G1
    use of, 6, 14, 23, 159, 239, 361, 362
Consonants
    a before, 13, 149, 174, 312
    adjectives ending in consonants + *-y*, 377, 386
    -ed ending and, 259, A3
    explanation of, 13, G1
    plural of nouns ending in consonant plus *-y*, 14, A1
    with superlative adjective ending, 385, 386
Contractions
    for *be*, 7
    explanation of, 7, G1
    for *is* and *are*, 16
    negative (of *be*), 45, 220
    in present progressive, 210, 212, 220
Conversations
    answers to *why* questions in, 282
    can't and *couldn't* in, 344
    contractions *'ll* and *won't* in, 445
    incomplete sentences in, 361
    maybe in, 448
    pronunciation of *going to* in, 436
    questions in present progressive in, 222
    really in, 49, 269
    slow in, 324
Could/couldn't, 334, 346, 370, 415
Could you, 424, 430
Count nouns
    a/an with, 149, 150, 174
    explanation of, 148, G1
    a few with, 166
    how many with, 166
    many/a lot of with, 165
    measurement words with, 156
    some and *any* with, 157
    there is/there are with, 180
    the with, 150

D
Definite article, 150, G1
Dependent clauses, G1
Descriptive adjectives, 23
Did
    with *not* in simple past negative statements, 267
    in simple past *Wh-* questions, 282
    in *Yes/No* questions and affirmative short answers, 280
Didn't
    in simple past negative short answers, 280
    in simple past negative statements, 267
Direct object, G1
Do/does
    know how to with, 346
    in *simple present Wh-* questions, 133
    in *Yes/No* questions, 120
Do not, for emphasis in negative imperatives, 107
Don't/doesn't
    in simple present negative short answers, 121
    in simple present negative statements, 90

E
-ed ending
    pronunciation of, 260
    spelling forms with, 259
    for verbs, 259, A3
Enough, 190, 332
-er ending, 376, 377
-es/-s ending. See *-s/-es* ending
-est ending, 385
Everyone/everybody, 197
Everything, 195
Exclamation point (!), 275, G1, G3
Explanations, transition words for, 175

F
Formal language, G2
Frequency adverbs, 127–128, 142, G2
Frequency expressions, 128, G2
Future
    be going to in, 436–437
    explanation of, G2
    if clauses in, 454, 463
    might/may in, 448
    modals to talk about plans in, 462
    with present progressive, 438
    with time clauses, 455, 463
    verb forms and modals to talk about, 462
    will in, 445, 447

G
Go. See Irregular verbs
Going to. See *Be going to*
Good/well, 322
Greetings, 4

H
Hardly ever, 127
Have. See Irregular verbs
Have to, 417, 418
Helping verbs. See Auxiliary verbs
How
    adjectives with, 314
    be going to with, 437
    questions with, 133, 314
    to talk about weather, 63
How about, 95
How far, 346
How many, 166
How many . . . are there?, 182
How much, 166
How much . . . is there?, 182
How often, 133

I
If clauses, 454, 463, G2
I'm, 16
Imperatives, 106, G2
In
    terms for place with, 52
    terms for time with, 61, 91
In back of, 52
Indefinite articles, 150, G2
Indefinite pronouns
    in affirmative statements, 195, 197
    explanation of, G2
    in negative statements, 195, 197
    in *Yes/No* questions, 195, 197
Indentation, paragraph, 115
Independent clauses, 361, 362, 371, G2
Infinitives
    explanation of, 92
    following superlative adjectives, 386
Informal speech, 165
Information questions. See *Wh-* questions
In front of, 52
-ing ending
    for nouns used as adjectives, 316
    for verbs in present progressive, 213, A2
In my opinion, 205
Introductions, 10, 68
Introductory phrases, 205
Irregular noun plurals, 14, A1

Irregular verbs
- *do, go, have,* 84
- list of common, A5
- in simple past, 261, 267–268

It
- to talk about time, 60
- to talk about weather, 63

K
Know how to, 346

L
Last, 245
Learn how to, 356
Let's + verb, 151
Like
- with infinitive, 92
- in questions about weather, 63

Linking verbs, 323
Location, 52
Lots of, 165
-ly ending
- adjectives with, 324
- adverbs of manner with, 322, A3

M
Main clauses, 361, 362, 371, G2
Many, 165
Maybe vs. *may be,* 448
Measurement words, 156, G2
Me too/me neither, 128
Might/may, 448
Modals. *See also* Verbs
- *can/could* as, 344–346, 370
- *can/may* as, 415
- explanation of, 344, G2
- *might/may* as, 448
- *should/shouldn't* as, 408, 409
- to talk about future plans, 462
- *will* as, 445

More, 377
Much, 165
Must, 417

N
Near, 52
Necessity, 417, 418
Need, with infinitive, 92
Negative imperatives, 106
Negative statements
- *any* in, 157
- *be going to* in, 436
- *be* in, 16
- *can't/cannot* in, 345, 415
- *don't/doesn't* in, 90
- explanation of, G2
- *have to* in, 417
- indefinite pronouns in, 195, 197
- *know how to* in, 346

me neither in, 128
might/may in, 448
- in past progressive, 299
- in present progressive, 212, 438
- *probably* in, 445
- *shouldn't* in, 408
- in simple past, 244, 267
- in simple present, 90–91
- *there is/there are* in, 180
- *will* in, 445

Never, 127
Next, 436
Next to, 52
Non-action verbs, 231, G2
Non-count nouns
- *a little* with, 166
- explanation of, 148, G2
- *how much* with, 166
- list of common, 148
- *much/a lot of* with, 165
- *some* and *any* with, 157
- *there are* with, 180
- *the* with, 150, 174

No one/nobody, 197
Not, with *be,* 16
No thank you/no thanks, 425
Nothing, 195
Nouns
- adjectives to modify, 23, 312, 338
- common, G1
- count, 148–150, 156, 157, 165, 166, 174, G1
- explanation of, 6, G2
- with frequency expressing, 128
- irregular, 14, A1
- non-count, 148, 150, 157, 165, 166, 174, 180, G2
- object, 100
- plural, 14–16, 31, A1, G3
- possessive, 31, G3
- proper, 7, 13, G3
- as sentence subject, 275
- singular, 13, G3
- used as adjectives, 316

O
Object nouns, 100
Object pronouns, 100, G2
Objects
- direct, G1
- explanation of, 99, G3
- questions about, 223, 246, 284, 394, 437, 447

Offers
- *can/could/would* in, 425
- *some* in, 157

Often, 127, 142

On
- in dates and days of week, 61, 91
- terms for location with, 52

One, 376
One of, 385
On weekends, 94
Opinion, 205
Or, 159
Or something, 200
Over, 52

P
Paragraphs
- format for, 77
- indentation of, 115

Past, simple. *See* Simple past
Past progressive
- affirmative statements in, 299
- explanation of, 299, G3
- negative statements in, 299
- simple past vs., 300

Past time clauses
- *before* and *after* in, 290
- *when* in, 292
- when to use, 290, 306

Period (.), 44, 275, G3
Permission, *can/may* for, 415
Phrase, G3
Place, prepositions of, 52–53, 76
Please, 106
Plural, 14
Plural nouns
- *be* with, 14
- common irregular forms of, A1
- explanation of, 14, G3
- possessive form of, 31
- pronunciation of, 15
- spelling rules for regular, A1
- use of, 14

Polite offers
- answers to, 424
- *can you/could you/would you* as, 424, 430

Polite requests
- answers to, 153, 425
- *can I/could I,* 425, 430
- *would you like,* 153, 425, 430

Possession
- pronouns and adjectives that show, 393
- *whose* plus noun to ask about, 394

Possessive adjectives
- explanation of, 30, G3
- use of, 393

Possessive nouns, 31, G3
Possessive pronouns, 393, G3

Prepositions
    explanation of, G3
    of place, 52–53, 76
    of time, 61, 76, 91, 290
Present progressive
    affirmative statements in, 210, 438
    and to join verbs in, 239
    to describe activities in present time, 238
    future with, 438
    -ing for verbs in, 213
    negative statements in, 212
    non-action verbs in, 231
    short answers in, 220
    simple present vs., 230
    Wh- questions in, 222, 223
    when to use, 210, 230, 238
    Yes/No questions in, 220
Present simple. *See* Simple present
Probably, 445
Progressive. *See* Past progressive; Present progressive
Pronouns
    adjectives to modify, 23, 338
    explanation of, G3
    indefinite, 195, G2
    object, 100, G3
    possessive, 393, G3
    as sentence subject, 275
    subject, 6, 30, G4
    use of, 403
Pronunciation
    of *can/can't*, 345
    of *going to*, 436
    of past *-d/-ed* endings, 260
    of plural nouns, *-s* and *-es* endings, 15
    of *-s* and *-es* ending in simple present, 85
    symbols for, A4
Proper nouns, 7, 13, G3
Punctuation
    commas as, 292, 454, 455, 463, G1, G3
    exclamation points as, 275, G1
    explanation of, G3
    periods as, 44, 275, G3
    question marks as, 44, G3

Q
Quantifiers, G3
Question mark (?), 44, G3
Questions. *See also Wh-* questions; *Yes/No* questions
    be going to in, 437
    be in, 44, 45, 54,133, 378
    can/could in, 346
    explanation of, G3
    have to in, 418

how in, 63
indefinite pronouns in, 195, 197
much, many, and *a lot of* in, 165, 166
about an object, 223, 246, 284, 394, 437, 447
in present progressive, 220, 222, 223, 328
should in, 409
in simple past, 251
in simple present, 120–121
some and *any* in, 157
about a subject, 134, 233, 246, 284, 378, 387, 394, 437, 447
subject and verb order in, 44, 54, 60, 61, 120, 220, 223, 251, 281, 282, 284, 346, 378, 387, 394, 409, 415, 418, 424, 437
superlative adjectives in, 387
this, that, these, those in, 69
about time, 60
about weather, 63
what and *who* in, 223, 284
when in, 61
with *where + be*, 54
with *whose*, 394
will in, 447

R
Rarely, 127
Read, 268
Really, 49, 269
Regular, G3
Regular verbs, 258
Requests, 424

S
Schedules, simple present in, 438
-'s ending, 31
Sentences. *See also* Affirmative statements; Negative statements; Imperatives; Questions
    explanation of, G3
-s/-es ending
    pronunciation of, 85
    for regular plural nouns, 14, A1
    for verbs in simple present, 82, 83, A2
Short answers. *See also* Answers
    be able to in, 354
    be in, 45
    can/could in, 346
    can/may in, 415
    do/does in, 418
    explanation of, G3
    know how to in, 356
    in present progressive, 220, 438
    to questions with comparative adjectives, 378
    should/shouldn't in, 409

in simple past, 251, 280
in simple present,
    to *Yes/No* questions, 121, 181, 182, 220, 251, 437
Should/shouldn't, 408, 409
Simple past
    affirmative statements in, 244, 258–259, 274
    be in, 244, 251–252
    explanation of, G3
    irregular verbs in, 261, 267–268, A5
    negative statements in, 244, 267
    past progressive vs., 300
    past time clauses with *before* and *after* in, 290
    pronunciation of *-ed* ending in, 260
    regular verbs in, 258
    short answers in, 251, 280
    time expressions in, 245
    Wh- questions in, 252, 282, 284
    Yes/No questions in, 251, 280
Simple present
    affirmative short answers in, 121
    affirmative statements in, 82
    be in, 6–7, 16, 44, 45
    explanation of, G3
    frequency adverbs in, 127
    frequency expressions in, 128
    imperatives in, 106
    irregular verbs in, 84, 268
    negative short answers in, 121
    negative statements in, 90–91
    prepositions of time in, 91
    present progressive vs., 230
    pronunciation of *-s* and *-es* in, 85
    for schedules, 438
    spelling rules for, 83, A2
    to talk about habits or routines, 114
    verbs plus infinitives in, 92
    verbs plus objects in, 99
    when to use, 82, 230
    Wh- questions in, 133–134, 137
    Yes/No questions in, 120–121
Singular, 13
Singular nouns, 13, G3
Slow/slowly, 324
So, 361, 371
Some and *any*, 157
Someone else, 199
Someone/somebody, 197
Something, 195
Sometimes, 127
Spelling rules
    for adverbs ending in *-ly*, 324, A3
    for comparative forms, 376, 377, A4
    for *-ed* form of verbs, 259, A3
    for *-ing* form of verbs, 213, A2

INDEX 14

for *maybe/may be,* 448
for regular plural nouns, 14, A1
for simple present, 83, A2
for superlative forms, 385, 386, A4
for *there, they're, their,* 186
Statements, G3. *See also* Affirmative statements; Negative statements
Stress, G4
Subject. *See also* Affirmative sentences; Negative sentences; Questions
 explanation of, G4
 questions about, 134, 233, 246, 284, 378, 387, 394, 437, 447
Subject pronouns, 6, 30, G4
Subject-verb agreement. *See* Affirmative statements; Negative statements; Questions
Suggestions
 how about to make, 95
 let's + verb to make, 151
Superlative adjectives
 explanation of, 385, 386, G4
 irregular forms of, 385
 questions with, 387
 spelling rules for, A4
 use of, 402
Syllable, G4

T
Take, different uses of, 261
Tense, G4. *See also specific tenses*
Than, 376, 377
Thanks anyway, 424
Thank you/thanks, 425
That, 68, 69
The
 a/an vs., 150
 before superlative adjectives, 385, 386
 use of, G1
The most, 386
There is/there are
 in affirmative statements, 180
 in negative statements, 180
 in *Yes/No* questions, 181, 182
There's one, 182
There vs. *they're* and *their,* 186
These
 general uses for, 68
 questions and answers with, 69
 use of, 68
This, 68
This is, to introduce people, 10
Those, 68, 69
Time
 prepositions of, 61, 76, 91, 290
 questions about, 60

Time clauses
 before, after, and *when* in, 307, 455
 commas with, 292, 455, 463
 explanation of, 290, 292, 455, G4
 future, 455
 when to use, 290, 306
Time expressions
 explanation of, G4
 present or future meaning in, 438
 in simple past, 245
Too much/too many, 189
Too/very plus adjective or adverb, 331
To + verb, 386
Transition words, 175

U
Under, 52
Unfortunately, 205
Until, 91
Usually, 127, G2

V
Verbs. *See also* Modals
 action, 323, G1
 adverbs to modify, 338
 auxiliary, 418, G1
 base form of, A5, G1
 -ed ending for, 259, A3
 explanation of, G4
 followed by infinitives, 92
 followed by objects, 99
 in future, 462
 as imperatives, 106, 107
 irregular, 84, 261, 267–268, A5
 linking, 323
 non-action, 231, G2
 regular, 258
 in simple past, 258, 261, 267–268, A5
 in simple present, 92, 99
Very
 to make an adjective stronger, 312, 331
 to make an adverb stronger, 312
Vowels, 13, G4

W
Want
 with infinitive, 92
 vs. *would like,* 153
Was/were, 244, 251, 252, 258, 299
Weather, 63
Well, 135
Well/good, 322
Wh- questions. *See also* How; What; When; Where; Who; Whose
 answers to, 133, 137, 222, 327, 447
 be going to in, 437
 can/can't in, 415
 can/could in, 346

comparative adjectives in, 378
do/does in, 418
explanation of, G4
in present progressive, 222, 223, 438
should in, 409
in simple past, 252, 284
in simple present, 133–134
superlative adjectives in, 387
will in, 447
Wh- words, G4. *See also* How; Wh- questions; When; Where; Who; Why
What, 60, 63, 69, 387
What for, 282
What kind of, 314
When,
 be going to with, 437
 past time clauses with, 292
 questions with, 61, 133
 in time clauses, 307, 455
Where, 54, 133
Which, 378
Who, 133, 134, 222, 223, 284, 378, 387, 437
Whose, 394,
Who's vs. *whose,* 394
Why, 133, 222, 252, 447
will
 affirmative and negative statements with, 445
 use of, 448
Will not/won't, 445
Would like vs. *want,* 153
Would you, 424
Would you like, 153, 425

Y
Yes/No questions. *See also* Questions
 be able to in, 354
 be going to in, 437
 be in, 44, 45
 can/could in, 346
 can/may in, 415
 comparative adjectives in, 378
 explanation of, G4
 have to in, 418
 indefinite pronouns in, 195, 197
 in present progressive, 220, 438
 short answers to, 121, 181, 182, 220
 should in, 409
 in simple past, 251, 280
 in simple present, 120–121
 superlative adjectives in, 387
 there is/there are in, 181, 182
 this, that, these, those in, 69
 will in, 447
Yesterday, 245
 -y to *-ies,* 14, 83, 377, 386, A1, A2, A3
You, 7, 30

CREDITS

Text and Listening

263: Exercise 11: "The Inca Road." Source: http://www.nationalgeographicexpeditions.com/experts/karin-muller/detail, **270:** "Harriet Chalmers Adams." Source: http://www.squidoo.com/harrietchalmersadams. **301:** Exercise 7: "The Paralympic Games." Source: http://pri.org/stories/2012-09-06/paralympics-focus-elite-competition. **310:** "Fennec Foxes." Source: http://animals.nationalgeographic.com/animals/mammals/fennec-fox/. **318:** Exercise 13: Listen & Write. Source: http://video.nationalgeographic.com/video/photography/photographers/ocean-soul-dangerous-shark/. **320:** Source: http://news.nationalgeographic.com/news/travelnews/2011/12/111228-mountaingorillas-king-grooming-uganda-tourist-animals/. **329:** Source: http://newswatch.nationalgeographic.com/2009/09/18/iberian_lynx_conservation/. **336:** Exercise 1: "A Dangerous Situation." Sources: http://video.nationalgeographic.com/video/photography/behind-the-shot/king-cobra-klum/; http://photography.nationalgeographic.com/photography/photographers/photographermattias-klum/. **352:** "Winter the Dolphin." Source: http://www.hanger.com/prosthetics/experience/patientprofiles/winterthedolphin/Pages/WintertheDolphin.aspx. **358:** Exercise 12: Listen & Speak. Source: http://www.pbs.org/wgbh/nova/physics/sophie-germain.html. **359:** Sources: http://www.paralympic.org/news/london-2012-numbers; http://www.paralympic.org/TheIPC/HWA/HistoryoftheMovement. **365:** Exercise 12: Edit. "Aimee Mullins." Sources: http://www.paralympic.org/TheIPC/HWA/HistoryoftheMovement; http://www.ted.com/talks/aimee_mullins_the_opportunity_of_adversity.html. **381:** Exercise 14: Listen & Speak. Source: http://www.phuketland.com/phuket_links/index.htm. **382:** "Geography Trivia" Source: http://www.worldatlas.com/geoquiz/thelist.htm. **422:** Source: http://news.nationalgeographic.com/news/2003/04/0418_030418_tvmareki.html. **A7:** "Geography Trivia." Source: http://www.worldatlas.com/geoquiz/thelist.htm. **Definitions for glossed words:** Sources: *The Newbury House Dictionary plus Grammar Reference*, Fifth Edition, National Geographic Learning/Cengage Learning, 2014; *Collins Cobuild Illustrated Basic Dictionary of American English*, Cengage Learning 2010, Collins Cobuild/Harper Collins Publishers, First Edition, 2010; *Collins Cobuild School Dictionary of American English*, Cengage Learning 2009, Collins Cobuild/Harper Collins Publishers, 2008; Collins Cobuild Advanced Learner's Dictionary, 5th Edition, Harper Collins Publishers, 2006.

Photo

240–241: ©Phil Schermeister/National Geographic Creative; **242–243:** ©Doug Pearson/Getty Images; **246 :** ©Martin Engelmann/age fotostock; **249:** ©Johnathan Ampersand Esper/Getty Images; **250:** ©Doin Oakenhelm/Shutterstock; **255:** ©Annie Griffiths Belt/National Geographic Creative; **256–257:** ©Andrew Evans/National Geographic Creative, **256 inset:** Brian Gratwicke/Andrew Evans/National Geographic Creative; **260:** ©Florian Kopp/imagebro/age fotostock; **263 top:** ©Karin Muller/National Geographic Creative, **263 bottom:** ©Hiram Bingham/National Geographic Creative; **265:** ©Keith Ducatel/AFP/Getty Images/Newscom; **266:** ©Pete Mcbride/Getty Images; **271:** ©UIG via Getty Images; **272:** ©DEA/G. DAGLI ORTI/Getty Images; **274:** ©Danita Delimont/Getty Images; **276–277:** ©Cory Richards/National Geographic Creative; **278:** ©Nic Bothma/EPA/Landov; **279:** ©The Green Belt Movement; **283:** ©NASA; **288:** © Royal Geographical Society (with IBG); **293:** ©AF archive/Alamy; **294:** ©Luis Marden/National Geographic Creative; **295:** ©Martin Strmiska/Alamy; **297:** © Royal Geographical Society (with IBG); **298:** © Royal Geographical Society (with IBG); **302:** ©GL Archive/Alamy; **303:** Classic Image/Alamy; **304:** ©Hulton Archive/Getty Images; **306:** ©Hulton Archive/Getty Images; **308–309:** ©Brian J. Skerry/National Geographic Creative; **310:** ©INTERFOTO/Alamy; **311:** © Brahim MNII/Alamy; **312:** ©Laszlo Halasi/Shutterstock; **313:** ©Robin Moore/National Geographic Creative; **315:** ©AnetaPics/Shutterstock; **317:** ©Rex Features via AP Images; **318:** ©Brian J. Skerry/National Geographic Creative; **319:** ©Brian J. Skerry/National Geographic Creative; **320:** Courtesy of Jonathan Rossouw & John J King II; **320 background:** ©winnieapple/Shutterstock; **321:** ©Guenter Guni/Getty Images; **325:** ©Michael Nichols/National Geographic Creative; **327:** ©Courtesy of Wildlife Conservation Trust; **328:** ©Roel Hoeve/Foto Natura/Getty Images; **329:** ©Marcelo del Pozo/REUTERS; **330:** Pete Oxford/Getty Images; **334:** ©Paul Sutherland/National Geographic Creative; **335:** ©Konrad Wothe/Getty Images; **336 top:** ©Rebecca Hale/National Geographic Creative, **middle:** © Indiapicture/Alamy, **bottom:** ©David Courtenay/Getty Images; **337:** ©Hung Chung Chih/Shutterstock; **338:** ©Joel Sartore/National Geographic Creative; **340–341:** ©Dustin Ghizzoni and John Jurko II; **342–343:** ©Unimedia Europe/Unimediaimages Inc/Unimedia Europe/Newscom; **345:** ©Cameron Lawson/National Geographic Creative; **348:** ©Dave Hill Mirrorpix/Newscom; **349:** ©Axel Seidemann/AP Images; **350 top:** ©UNIMEDIA/SIPA/Newscom, **middle:** ©AFP/Getty Images, **bottom:** ©CB2/ZOB/WENN.com/Newscom; **352-353:** ©Clearwater Marine Aquarium; **359:** ©Matthew Lloyd/Getty Images; **360:** ©AFP/Getty Images; **365:** ©Phil Cole/Getty Images; **366:** ©Bruce Hall; **367:** ©Alison Wright/National Geographic Creative; **368:** ©Brian A. Witkin/Shutterstock; **370:** © Pankaj & Insy Shah/Getty Images; **372–373:** ©Frans Lanting/National Geographic Creative; **374–375:** ©Tommy Heinrich/National Geographic Creative; **381 top:** ©Adisa/Shutterstock, **bottom:** ©Taylor Kennedy-Sitka Productions/National Geographic Creative; **383:** ©Kenneth Garrett/National Geographic Creative; **384:** ©De Agostini/Getty Images; **386:** ©EschCollection/Getty Images; **388:** ©Paul Kennedy/Getty Images; **389:** ©Prisma Bildagentur AG/Alamy; **391:** ©Maremagnum/Getty Images; **392:** © Robert Harding World Imagery/Alamy; **397 top right:** ©VIEW Pictures Ltd/Alamy, **top left:** ©Novarc Images/Alamy, **bottom:** ©Richard Nowitz/National Geographic Creative; **399:** ©Nickolay Vinokurov/Shutterstock; **400:** ©Ira Block/National Geographic Creative; **402:** ©Liysa/Getty Images; **404–405:** ©chattakan kosol. www.facebook.com/yodapix; **406:** ©vladimir zakharov/Getty Images; **407:** ©XPACIFICA/National Geographic Creative; **410:** ©Sean Pavone/Shutterstock; **412:** © David Grossman/Alamy; **413:** ©O Furrer/age fotostock; **414:** ©Jorge Royan/Alamy; **419:** ©XPACIFICA/National Geographic Creative; **421:** ©Scotty Robson Photography/Getty Images; **422:** ©Danita Delimont/Alamy; **423:** ©Thierry Falise/Getty Images; **427:** ©AchimHB/Thinkstock; **429:** ©Timothy Allen/Getty Images; **430:** ©David Gilder/Shutterstock; **432–433:** ©Joe Geinert/National Geographic Creative; **434:** ©Greg Pease/Getty Images; **435:** ©Peter Charlesworth/Getty Images; **440:** ©Kyle Smith Photography/Getty Images; **441:** ©Boris Stroujko/Shutterstock; **442:** ©Cultura Travel/Philip Lee Harvey/Getty Images; **443:** ©Pete Ryan/National Geographic Creative; **444:** © Aurora Photos/Alamy; **451:** ©Matt Slocum/AP Images; **452:** © keith morris/Alamy; **453:** ©Roy Mehta/Getty Images; **457:** ©Evgeniya Porechenskaya/Shutterstock; **459:** ©Tetra Images–Erik Isakson/Getty Images; **460:** ©Heeb Christian/Prisma/SuperStock; **462:** © sturti/iStockphoto; **A7:** © Nagel Photography/Shutterstock

(continued on page C2)

CREDITS (cont'd)

MAP

242, 249, 256, 289, 320, 329, 374, 383, 406, 422, 428: National Geographic Maps

ILLUSTRATION

246, 305, 326, 390, 443, 456, 461: Cenveo Publisher Services